Managerial Accountant's Compass

T0383956

This is the first detailed view of the managerial accountant's role and responsibilities in organization setting. Its aim is to foster role development: the opportunity to work at an advanced level of practice. Accounting studies develop technical skills associated with topics and responding to defined scenarios, but they provide very little guidance on how to recognize and approach the broad problems or challenges under conditions of uncertainty.

It is a double-first because it provides the managerial accountant's compass as a general purpose analytical framework for managerial accounting, independent of any selected theory and method. The metaphor of a compass creates a mental schema for its four points named (1) goals and principles, (2) boundaries and constraints, (3) methods and models, and (4) collegial relationships. Dynastic Chinese and some other Central Asian cultures view the center as a fifth principal direction, giving a total of five points. The center represents a high-standard ethical conduct and self-care, or moral compass.

The managerial accountant's compass offers an integrated and systematic guide to approaching situations that are constantly changing. It gives a protective starting pattern that produces new meanings and awareness of the ambiguity and uncertainty for each situation. Ultimately the managerial accountant's compass can help you make more effective sense of yourself, your expertise and your practice in the organization where you work, which should open career opportunities.

Dr. Gary R. Oliver, B A Anthrop. & Philosophy (Macq), M Com Acctg & Info Sys (UNSW), Grad Dip Soc Sc (UNE), B. Sc. (Psych). Hons (USQ), Grad Cert Higher Ed (Usyd), M Ed Higher Ed (USyd), PhD Economics (USyd), FCMA, FCPA, is Senior Lecturer in Accounting in the Business School at The University of Sydney, Sydney, Australia.

Routledge Studies in Accounting

For a full list of titles in this series, please visit www.routledge.com/
Routledge-Studies-in-Accounting/book-series/SE0715

Managerial Accountant's Compass
Research Genesis and Development

Gary R. Oliver

Routledge
Taylor & Francis Group
NEW YORK AND LONDON

First published 2019
by Routledge
605 Third Avenue, New York, NY 10017

and by Routledge
2 Park Square, Milton Park, Abingdon, Oxon, OX14 4RN

First issued in paperback 2020

Routledge is an imprint of the Taylor & Francis Group, an informa business

Library of Congress Cataloging-in-Publication Data
A catalog record for this book has been requested

ISBN 13: 978-0-367-73316-2 (pbk)
ISBN 13: 978-1-138-09454-3 (hbk)

Typeset in Sabon
by Apex CoVantage, LLC

This book is dedicated to the memory of my Managerial Accountant father who strongly believed that practicing managerial accounting contributed high value to society and who died unexpectedly on May 30, 2012, while the initial draft was being completed.

Contents

Figures

Tables

Acknowledgments

The IMA Statement of Ethical Professional Practice is published with its permission, copyright IMA (Institute of Management Accountants), imanet.org.

Preface

Having been a managerial accountant in industry, government and the education sector for over 30 years, I found they all had one thing in common. The everyday expectations that my manager had of me were always different from what I was told when I was hired. (The expectations of non-accountant managers were also different to what my hiring manager had outlined.) This was not an error in specifying my role and responsibilities. Nor was it an error in distinguishing between different levels of managerial accountant duties, although this frequently played a part. The symptoms of the problem were being asked for information well beyond the terms of reference I had been given for a task or project, being asked ad hoc questions on totally unrelated matters in cost and managerial accounting, and being assigned to fix problems left unresolved after earlier attempts by other managers. Sitting in meetings with other managerial accountants, I found the same was true for them.

In the tradition of self-help, I started tentatively assembling my own answer to this problem, always expecting to find a book or article that described the problems I had witnessed and setting out a systematic solution. I began with the history of the profession but found little of use. Outside it, there were some promising lines of enquiry. Systems and cybernetics asked for interrelationships to be considered (e.g., Checkland, 1999). Neurolinguistic programming used language and other types of communication to enable a person to recode brain responses to stimuli (Bandler & Grinder, 1989). Social complexity theory emphasized starting points, emergent phenomena, and chaos (Waldrop, 1992). At the same time, I was asking others what criteria they used, and that become the first generation of the managerial accountant's compass.

Eventually, when I began teaching managerial accounting to postgraduate students in 2009 using case studies, I revised the original analytical framework then called the managerial accounting compass. The third generation is described in this book based on classroom experience and feedback from colleagues. Its emphasis changed from accounting to accountants to orient new managerial accountants to their role and responsibilities so they can make use of their skills and abilities. Contact the author for supplementary materials at: managerialaccountantscompass.mail.com.

The managerial accountant's compass combines immediate concerns and the context for planning the future to guide thinking. Thinking spans a range: critical or evaluative thinking, creative thinking, problem solving, and decision making. The managerial accountant's compass can help new and old managerial accountant's make sense of their role and responsibilities to their employer and the wider society. The author welcomes constructive feedback. Contact address: foundry@email.com.

Many thanks to the staff at Routledge associated with this book for their wholehearted support. David Varley enthusiastically accepted the manuscript and guided its revision. Megan Smith handled the paperwork very ably. Mary Del Plato was patient while the argument was refined. Chris Mathews ensured excellence in the production. The structure and content of the entire book has benefited from the comments of the anonymous reviewers.

Extended Abstract

The first holistic view of the managerial accountant's potential contribution to the organization is examined in detail from a normative, post positivist and realist position using the metaphor of the compass to operationalize the role and responsibilities of the managerial accountant. Its aim is to give the managerial accountant (particularly the new managerial accountant) a systematic framework to select, apply and defend their work. The contribution of the managerial accountant's compass is role development. 'Role development' is the opportunity to work at an advanced level of practice. The managerial accountant's compass is constructed around the role, responsibilities, skills, and abilities of the managerial accountant. It is supported with a wide range of references and examples to show it is capable of broad application.

The managerial accountant's compass answers a long-standing need for an integrated approach to the increasingly complex role and responsibilities of the managerial accountant (Chapter 1). These complexities arise from the managerial accountant straddling issues of operations and strategy in heterogeneous organizations, and, having to contend with the fact that an essential component of management knowledge is managerial accounting knowledge. Despite these developments, the managerial accountant lacks a model to frame their role and responsibilities and confidently apply their skills and abilities.

The managerial accountant's compass is pan-theoretical (Chapter 2). Since the managerial accountant's focus is inwards, ten theories inform managerial accounting in the 21st century. In alphabetical order they are: Contingency theory, Disruptive Innovation Process theory, Institutional theory, Price-Change, Principal-agent theory, Resource-Based View of the Firm, Stakeholder theory, Transaction-Cost approach, and, Wealth Creation. Each has a particular focus but there is overlap and interrelationships between them. Together they provide multiple perspectives. A pan-theoretical approach avoids theoretical 'blind spots' from the source discipline or theory limitations. So, no single theory is privileged over the others.

Discourse is integral to the managerial accountant (Chapter 3). Many tasks involve identifying objects and measuring them, then giving a rationale for the resulting calculations or estimates. One result is that the numbers and calculations that accounting uses can become reified and removed from the contextual specificity. Another is that their use tends to be framed in narrative with rhetoric. The managerial accountant's compass recognizes that by viewing accounting concepts and classifications as discourse highlights the constructive nature of accounting. Discourse draws attention to the ambiguity of concepts and classifications, the skill required to use them, and, the ways in which they can be used to justify or defend judgements and decisions. That is, they are used to represent and understand the world and this is a reciprocal relationship. They can also be contested in terms of power, knowledge, and as rules or practices. Viewing the concepts and classifications as discourse allows the managerial account to be aware that there are vested interests including their own.

Information is central to the work of the managerial accountant (Chapter 4). Information has value, but that value must be anticipated because the recipient judges whether it is useful. Information also has many-dimensions. The basic is whether it is financial and non-financial but different definitions may apply depending upon whether it is labelled by an accountant or non-financial manager. Others are: quantitative versus qualitative, external versus internal, primary versus secondary, time-horizon (past, present, future), operational versus strategic, and, evaluation versus prediction. Information is produced through sourcing/searching, filtering, integration, aggregation and, interpretation. This is assisted by considering its qualitative characteristics or attributes and judging its quality. The managerial accountant's compass draws attention to the time required to select and present useful information and the likelihood that the full cost of the process is understated.

The role, responsibilities, skills and abilities of the managerial accountant are examined in three stages. The first is to specify them at three levels: entry, intermediate and senior (Chapter 5). This suggests that different descriptions and recommendations are likely from different levels of managerial accountant even when the managerial accountant's compass is used. It implies that the managerial accountant changes and develops over time. The second is to pair each level with critical success factors (Chapter 6). This allows the managerial accountant to consider how their performance is likely to be judged. It suggests that this can occur by task or by overall function. Third and finally, the important yet overlooked aspects of making recommendations, decisions, and judgements are explored (Chapter 7). This is taken as a process which may entail problem solving, creativity and analysis as they are allied to completing tasks and functions which have constraints. These suggest the managerial accountant's compass guides applying knowledge, skills and abilities but judgements are also made by both participants and third parties on success independent of the process and findings.

Based on the foregoing, a visual representation of the managerial accountant's compass is introduced, and its context is outlined (Chapter 8). Four contextual factors are identified as influential. First, geographical factors influence the socio-economic climate, and the industry in which the organization operates. Second, industry sector characteristics affect its profitability or capability (for non-profit organizations). A notable example is including technology adoption. Third, organization characteristics affect its survival. Examples include stage, size, culture, innovation and creativity, operations, its systems and processes, and, perceived vulnerability to decisions made outside the organization. Finally trends and particular events may impact the geographical situation, industry, and organization. These four contextual factors can affect the understanding sought by the managerial accountant and their approach. They also interact with the cardinal points of the managerial accountant's compass.

The first four of five cardinal points of managerial accountant's compass are then discussed (Chapter 9). The four traditional cardinal points consist of: (1) goals and principles, (2) methods and models, (3) boundaries and constraints, and, (4) the collegiate relationship of the managerial accountant with other managers. These comprise a set of reference points that analysis should not overlook, or, inadequately address.

The fifth compass point which is the center is ethics and self-care because it is sufficiently important to receive individual attention (Chapter 10). The managerial accountant is expected by the both public and institutions to display a high standard ethical conduct. Ethical conduct refers to awareness, understanding and observing the ethical code for the high standard of ethical decision making that is expected of the managerial accountant. Information should be prepared, and recommendations made, by ethical management accountants based on ethical accounting practices. Self-care is treated as accompanying ethical conduct. It is important because organizations are inclined to blame the individual for deficiencies in its systems and failures to communicate but stress, anxiety and exhaustive can reduce effectiveness. It is also important because managerial accountants are not taught how to assess their own wellbeing. Taken together, awareness of ethical conduct and the need for self-care reduce vulnerability, and this is an alias for the center cardinal point.

The managerial accountant's compass consists of an outer perimeter and inner cardinal points. The starting point can be either the context or one of the cardinal points. Also, none of the five cardinal points of the managerial accountant's compass are privileged. In other words, the starting point can be any compass point, and, then they can be taken any order. The cardinal points can also be considered in paired horizontal groups (goals and principles; relationships with others) and vertical groups (boundaries and constraints; methods and models). The immediacy and simplicity of a visual representation of the managerial accountant's compass provides an avenue to ensure its detail is not overlooked.

Finally, there is an evaluation of the managerial accountant's compass (Chapter 11). The chapter opens by outlining some answers to the scenarios from chapter 1 by applying the managerial accountant's compass. Then both limitations are acknowledged, and some criticisms are anticipated. Its benefits as an orienting schema and implications for use are identified. This leads to considering its scope which includes operations and strategy, short and long-term, projects, fads and the formulation and evaluation of public policy. For the researcher some directions for its future development are suggested. The chapter closes with a summary and the suggestion that the managerial accountant's compass offers the discipline of accounting an analytical framework which can explore its potential.

Key words: Accountant, Costs, Decision making, Discourse, Ethics, Grounded theory, Managerial accounting compass, Role, Responsibilities, Strategy

Part I

Genesis of the Managerial Accountant's Compass

1 Establishing the Need for the Managerial Accountant's Compass

This chapter establishes the need for a systematic analytical framework to be available for managerial accountants. It is motivated by five imperatives. Although organizations in society are heterogeneous, a systematic approach is possible. Students of accounting and junior managerial accountants lack a single integrated framework to help them marshal and use the plethora of managerial accounting concepts, methods[1] and processes.[2] The importance of an integrated framework becomes apparent when the career of management accountants is considered. It is a progressive trajectory with at least three broad levels (entry, intermediate and senior) most probably across many organizations in different industries. There are also opportunities for the managerial accountant to move into non-accounting managerial positions that utilize their accounting knowledge. The expression non-accounting manager is used to emphasize that most of the relationships that the managerial accountant has are with employees outside their organizational unit, and this requires a thoughtful approach. In the rapidly changing socioeconomic environment with changes in work–life balance, the potential benefit of an integrated and systematic framework for planning and decision making has both short-term and long-term payback through becoming a more effective individual and team member. The remainder of this chapter explores these imperatives and outlines the structure of the book.

1.1 Organizations and Societies Are Heterogeneous

In any given year, there are approximately 200,000 newly qualified accountants worldwide. Despite advances in transaction processing technology, the employment trend is upwards with "heightened demand for newly qualified accountants" (Robert Walters, 2015: 13). International and country statistics suggest accountants form a very large occupation group who have wide employment opportunities not only in capital cities, but also suburbs and regional towns. Accountants have retained full-time job hours at a time of growing part-time, casualization and job-sharing. So far, outsourcing and off-shoring trends have had little impact on accountants. The most common level of educational attainment for accountants is bachelor's degree. It is possible for accountants to seek employment with just their degree, or complete membership studies to join one of the professional accounting bodies.

However, during their studies accountants have very little guidance on what to expect.[3] The managerial accountant's compass is designed as a guide to help uncover and make sense of the myriad of unfamiliar and complex managerial accounting issues that new accountants face. Students and new employees already have to cope with unfamiliar operational, organizational and people practices, and foibles. Concerted effort is required to master concepts, processes and skills, but also in overcoming unfamiliarity in putting knowledge and skills into practice. The managerial accountant's compass is a knowledge organizer and guides effort.

When managerial accountants encounter difficulties, it is difficult to learn from them. Newspapers and journals frequently describe organizational difficulties and career changes, but the failure is either unclear or undisclosed. Students also lack familiarity with failure in their ordinary degree studies with attention to very few cases where the existence of the organization as a going concern is jeopardized. The vignettes below illustrate the potential for failure that managerial accountant may navigate. Where the reader is likely to be unfamiliar with an organization, some additional commentary is provided. Each vignette consists of a short, impressionistic scene designed to give insight into ideas in a setting (Alexander & Becker, 1978).

- Automation enables manufacturing efficiencies by standardizing routine operation, but Mercedes Benz will abandon automation of its production line for its S-class flagship passenger vehicle at their largest plant in Sindelfingen, Germany. It wants to increase the scope for customers to personalize their order. "The Mercedes-Benz S-Class is too complex for robots to assemble. Robots can't deal with the degree of individualization and the many variants that we have today", said Markus Schaefer, the head of production at Mercedes-Benz (Behrmann & Rauwald, 2016).
- Growth is always sought but can be problematic. Deutsche Bank expanded beyond its core business of financing the foreign expansion of German organizations. In the United States, it sold toxic mortgage securities before the 2008 global financial crisis and subsequently was accused of failure of oversight and internal control of its FX traders who buy/sell currencies for its own accounts and for customers. The demand from US Department of Justice and Commodity Futures Trading Commission exceeded USD 7 billion. Deutsche publicly apologized and reviewed its operations and strategy.

- Performance incentive schemes may be dysfunctional or gamed. Austrade, the Australian federal government business development agency, allowed staff to earn bonuses of AUD12M between 2007 and 2014. It promoted a controversial company that later collapsed. It allowed bonuses to be paid without checking the bona fides of the organization used to earn those bonuses. One organization was the collapsed Indian pyramid scheme associated with Pearls Group India. (Klan & Bearup, 2016)
- The behavior of cartels in charge of procurement or sales is unpredictable. The Organization of the Petroleum Exporting Countries (OPEC) acts as a volume seller for its oil-producing nations who reduce supply-side production based on estimated non-OPEC output and OPEC stockpile, and expected world oil demand. In mid-2016, OPEC decided to maintain high production levels, and thus low prices to eliminate higher-cost producers and regain market share. It uses short-term quotas to regulate supply to manipulate prices and avoid fluctuations that might affect the economy of OPEC members.
- Rent-seeking behavior is opportunistic. Australia Post is the Australian government solely owned postal service. In 2017, its profit after tax increased 162.1% despite an 11.8% decline in addressed letter volume and 5.6% growth in domestic parcels. In the previous year, its then CEO Ahmed Fahour claimed its letter service will "never ever make money again" and sought a government subsidy (Durkin & Lynch, 2016). Letters are a steadily declining product as a result of digital communications, but Australia Post is obligated to provide a frequent, reliable service at a fair price.
- Often employees are retrenched using the justification of cost reduction. Optus is a major telco in Australia. It reframed the retrenchments of employees from the company's customer service and network roles as a strategic initiative to win customers. Optus intends to use savings from shedding 10%of its workforce to support its ambitions to buy rights to broadcast sport and pay for the cost of hiring sports stars to promote it in the media. (Burke, 2016)

In the background of these vignettes is the managerial accountant providing cost, performance, control, and strategic information and recommendations to non-accounting managers. Without a criterion framework like the managerial accounting compass, the managerial accountant cannot be expected to go beyond their knowledge of how to apply methods and processes to assist organization and anticipate consequences during and after implementation. Given their limited knowledge of the organization, and time constraints, it is unlikely that she or he should do so without further guidance and insights into possible pitfalls. There is a need for a systematic framework, which allows the managerial accountant to take into account goals, principles boundaries, and relationships and organizational context.

1.2   No Single Integrated Framework Exists

Despite the discussion in textbooks of methods and processes in different organizations, no single integrated framework is provided. This occurs against a background where the target entity is given different names. In the discussion that follows, the term 'organization' is preferred to 'business', 'company', 'corporation' 'entity' or 'enterprise'. It is an umbrella term because it refers to for profit and not-for-profit, listed corporations and privately held organizations. An organization is a social unit with a purpose, a structure of management and rules of conduct. Some are discipline-specific. For example, strategic management prefers the term 'firm'. Another expression, 'enterprise', is used to emphasize the commercial aspects of organization. The managerial accountant is employed by or contracted to any of these organizations. All these forms of organization require the managerial accountant to contribute to decision making, and all make a range of decisions and require the managerial accountant to apply the knowledge and skills he or she acquired in formal education. However, managerial accountants have become prisoner to simple definitions of accounting for their role and responsibilities.

The standard definition of accounting emphasizes reckon. A common textbook definition is process of identifying, measuring, analyzing, interpreting and communicating information for the pursuit of an organization's goals. This definition is responsible for managerial accounting being identified with cost accounting[4] and the financial reporting of production (manufacturing, construction, mining and agriculture), or sales (merchandising). Early definitions recognized the financial and managerial sides of an organization and its concern with economic and social phenomena (Duncan, 1909). A broader view of managerial accounting is that it is concerned with information outputs. It provides managers and employees with information used for organizational decisions as well as monitoring progress against goals. Like financial accounting, it has processes for identifying, measuring, accumulating, analyzing, interpreting and communicating information in a timely and reliable manner. However, the primary role of the managerial accountant is to provide the non-accounting managers and employees of an organization with the accounting viewpoint in planning, control, and making decisions and judgments. The information, advice and assistance given by the managerial accountant concerns the costs[5] in the organization (Boyns & Edwards, 2013), its use of tangible and intangible resources (Barney,

Wright & Ketchen, 2001), improving its profitability[6] (Drury & Tayles, 1995), the effectiveness of its processes and productivity (Banker, Datar & Kaplan, 1987), and the impact of potential threats and opportunities from either competitors or changes in the external environment of the organization (Bromwich, 1990). Any of these may involve organization change (Burns & Scapens, 2000). The managerial accountant therefore has a wide remit and should revisit their earlier analysis if significant new information becomes available or the passage of time affects their assumptions and estimates.

Most frameworks are specific to a given analysis task and there are very few generic frameworks apart from decision making. Most textbooks have a preferred decision-making framework. Generally, it consists of three stages: define the problem, assemble relevant information and evaluate the consequences of options. The limitations of these frameworks are twofold. First, they assume there is a clear decision awaiting determination. A desirable framework should also require reflection. Second, it ignores the pitfalls of decision making, particularly insufficient attention, and the impact of heuristics and biases. Most decision frameworks place undue emphasis on its finalization rather than its consequences or difficulties of implementation. The framework also overlooks the pernicious effect of particular cognitive biases that overplay the need for the decision or the obviousness of what is perceived as the preferred option. Explicit frameworks are thus specific to a task and provide little substantive substructure to avoid overlooking what may later be considered relevant factors by the managerial accountant, their manager or other non-accounting managers. They also assume the framework covers matters valued by society such as ethics and health. A systematic framework therefore needs to be generally applicable as well as directly articulate wider values often described as 'doing the right thing'. Therefore, the framework should be broadly useful across the function of management accounting.

1.3   Career Trajectories Within Management Accounting

The managerial accountant in an organization is appointed at different levels (entry, intermediate and senior). These are discussed in Chapter 5, which details differences for each of these three levels. While the focus is on the role and responsibilities of the managerial accountant, these are incomplete without considering what makes a managerial accountant successful. This is a matter of performance and is viewed through the literature on critical success factors. Those for a managerial accountant are specified in Chapter 6. Of course, they are subject to any specific performance objectives that are defined in an organization-wide evaluation scheme, or form part of an employment contract.

The career of some managerial accountants has been foreshortened by insufficient effort to practice ethical behavior. Public attention to ethics in accounting occurs frequently. The failures of Enron and WorldCom focused attention on the unacceptable ethical behavior of the accounting profession (Salter, 2008). The managerial accountant should be aware of Enron since it is likely that early actions by its accountants were legal but unethical and then illegal. This is often an event history (Baucus & Near, 1991). Enron also suggests the difficulty in coping with ethical challenges from peers, supervisors and external parties. The code of the Institute of Management Accountants (2017, originally issued 2005) which is found in many textbooks (e.g., Horngren,[7] Datar, Foster, Rajan & Ittner, 2015; Hilton & Platt, 2014) and discussed in Chapter 10 is unique among professional codes for its two-level hierarchy. Textbooks include ethical dimensions to many problems, but these are artificial. Students can either deduce the appropriate answer from the scenario or use a template to give the correct answer. They lack any direct and indirect financial and peer pressure. Textbooks also suffer from hindsight when discussing examples of unethical behavior that has become public. An integrated framework should anticipate the subtle pressures on a managerial accountant and the reality of loss of income. Textbooks also overlook the attendant career consequences (e.g., loss of current accounting job, and/or potential for continued future unemployability in many other jobs) of becoming a whistleblower. Since ethics disrupts career ambitions, the managerial accountant's compass places ethics at its center.

Another career disruption can occur with unfamiliar work. A hallmark of the managerial accountant is skill in applying the managerial accounting methods and processes competently to new situations. The managerial accountant should aim at building a portfolio of skills covering:

- Creating models using existing guidelines and processes in various topics of managerial accounting
- Identifying and applying accounting guidelines that have general business acceptance (e.g., the managerial accounting principle that benefits exceed costs)
- Developing criteria that go beyond measuring accounting return or payback and extends to improvements in value generation before recommending a preferred option or beginning evaluation
- Using a decision-making framework that recognizes cognitive biases, human or behavioral factors, and demand effects to please supervisors in considering information and making decisions
- Recognizing that a decision is preceded by developing a range of acceptable and reasonable options
- Balancing operational or short-term targets with long-term strategic goals
- Successfully communicating difficult or unpleasant accounting information to non-accountants

However, the managerial accountant does not have a framework for integrating these separate accomplishments. The managerial accountant's compass brings these together. The other side of the career trajectory is obtaining a position outside accounting where managerial accounting knowledge is valued.

1.4   Managerial Accounting Knowledge Is Commonplace Outside Accounting

The managerial accountant quickly develops inside knowledge about the organization and its environment. Although some of this knowledge is particular to the organization, much of it can be applied to functions outside managerial accounting (in the same or a different organization). That is, accounting knowledge has value to non-accounting managers. The knowledge and skills of interest include determining costs, evaluating performance, devising and monitoring controls, assessing risk and reformulating strategy. This knowledge has many practical uses including

- Understanding the nuances in meaning of accounting concepts and classifications and the measurement of profit
- Being able to classify and interpret the cost structures of the organization
- Evaluating a cost reduction program to ensure it directly and quickly improves the 'bottom line'
- Being able to assemble separately available information
- Develop collegiate relationships to both provide and receive feedback on the use of accounting information
- Seeking and working with richer and more extensive information than is found in financial reports and statements
- Comparing this information and understanding with details from other organizations, including other potential employers

In addition to knowledge, the skills of the managerial accountant include

- The ability to balance different types of information (e.g., financial and non-financial; quantitative and qualitative)
- Persuasion in negotiation and making recommendations (prepared for challenges but capable of defending a point of view)
- Setting goals and devising criteria
- Understanding an organization from the 'inside' (no longer thinking like a consumer/customer who deals with the organization from the outside)
- Successfully developing solutions to new and unfamiliar problems and opportunities (questions) that are re-usable
- Showing leadership in methods, processes and work groups

Accounting knowledge opens a career opportunity as a manager in many organizational functions in any organization size. The knowledge that managerial accounting pioneered (and continues to pioneer) is now formalized in the routine calendar of organizations. Two major events in most organization calendars are budgeting (for revenues and expenses) and making investments (capital budgeting) at both the organization aggregate level, as well as for its individual organizational units.[8] In addition, there are the monthly routines of evaluating organization unit performance through considering variances and reporting on projects (whether or not they have capital budgeting implications). Throughout the year, it is also necessary to set and review selling prices for new and existing products (or services), manage inventory (and inventory turnover), determine break-even and quote for jobs, projects or tenders. These activities in which the managerial accountant develops expertise are also tasks carried out by non-accounting managers for their organizational or functional unit. The managerial accountant is therefore not only able to assist non-accounting managers but could perform much of their role outside managerial accounting. The managerial accounting compass therefore can also be used outside accounting in these areas where it has already been proven.

An alternate career opportunity outside accounting is that of owner or entrepreneur. An owner needs to be able to find avenues for improvement, particularly once they have established routines (e.g., for production and sales). The owner/entrepreneur can remove or reduce unproductive costs using the concepts of non-value adding (wasting effort or time) and value engineering (to improve the function or reduce the cost). An owner/entrepreneur needs to ensure adequate cash flow by being able to use capital wisely, understand administrative expenses and use general ledger accounts to track trends. The owner/entrepreneur with a managerial accounting background is likely to make decisions informed by balancing quantitative and qualitative criteria. Irrespective whether it is a non-accounting organization function or as owner/entrepreneur, the managerial accountant needs a framework like the managerial accountant's compass to guide their application of accounting knowledge and skills. The use of the managerial accountant's compass also involves planning and negotiating recommendations.

1.5   Central Place of Plans and Recommendations in Organizations

Where managers are concerned with planning the framework needs to accommodate the process leading up to decisions.[9] Planning is the process of setting goals, determining resource requirements, and devising a means of achieving goals. Decision making involves formulating options, evaluating them and choosing between them (Baron, 2008). It is distinguished from problem solving tasks of fixing agendas, setting goals, and designing actions (Simon et al., 1987). Planning relies on information being structured and analyzed. Managerial accountants use methods and processes to give non-accounting managers recommendations on how to use accounting information to help them plan and manage organizational resources. Recommendations are suggestions or proposals as to the best course of action together with supporting evidence. So, there is close connection between plans, recommendations and decisions, and the managerial accountant is involved in all three.

Planning is a process that generates plans. The characteristic of a plan is that it is executed in a series of steps and is then evaluated against its goals. However, even reputable textbooks collapse plans into budgets (e.g., Horngren et al., 2015; Hilton & Platt, 2014) and their outputs. Budgets are important to the goal-setting function of an organization because they express the wishes and objectives of management in specific, tangible and quantitative terms. While it is true budgets are commonly prepared for the entire organization as a whole, as well as for organizational units, a budget is not the only plan an organization needs. For example, the organization needs contingency plans to anticipate disruption to supplies (e.g., raw materials, inventory) or shutdowns to production or sales (e.g., owing to lack of energy). Even planning for changes to government regulation (e.g., taxation and depreciation rates) is amenable to a goals framework that is informed by information and thus requires the managerial accountant to ask two layers of questions before providing accounting information. The goals framework should suggest broad questions (Drucker, 1954, 1974), such as

- What are we trying to achieve?
- What does the information (e.g., numbers) assume?

before going on to ask typical accounting questions such as

- What does the information include and exclude?
- What is the average dollar cost per unit of resources (organization-wide and within specific organizational units)?
- How many dollars in sales revenue do indirect costs (including marketing) attract or return?
- Where are the greatest expenditures (by activity, product and organizational unit)?
- What (activity, product and organizational unit) earns the greatest profits?
- What can the organization do to maximize profit and minimize expenditure?
- What is the required rate of return to make a new project worthwhile?
- What is the change in total costs if I don't do this?

These and similar questions can be prompted by the interplay between them to see where they lead. The managerial accountant does not usually ask such specific questions, although non-accounting managers with related responsibilities (e.g., sales, production) may ask them. As will be shown later in discussing the managerial accountant's compass, even comparing tactical and strategic matters such as pricing (products or services), product preference (emphasize or de-emphasize) and resourcing (e.g., investing in equipment) can surface information that can be useful when trying to determine options from which to make a recommendation for decision makers.

The managerial accountant is involved with two broad types of recommendation and decision (Demski, Gerald & Feltham, 1976). The first is decision facilitation. Here the role is to ensure that managers and employees are fully informed so they can competently choose among options.[10] So, it is a direct input intended to reduce the uncertainty of the decision maker and change their beliefs (Baiman, 1982) before they make any decision and increase the likelihood of making a better decision with respect to the desired objectives. For example, when choosing among the make versus buy alternative, it is helpful to have a comprehensive analysis of all product or service costs. The second is decision influencing. It is concerned with the behavior, motivation and performance of managers and employees particularly in relation to incentives or rewards. For example, many organizations compare budget with actual performance, as represented by reporting variances, to motivate a line manager. However, the failure to investigate why there have been discrepancies outside those due to changes in budgeted output is commonplace. In both these circumstances, the managerial accountant responsibility can end when the non-accounting manager is provided with the circumspect information and thus opportunities to improve organizational performance are lost. This opportunity may be prompted using the managerial accountant's compass requirement to consider goals and boundaries.

The psychology of decision making suggests that the process and structure used by managers is often incomplete. An extended decision process that is consistent with the managerial accountant's compass is provided in Chapter 7, which draws on both traditional decision theory (Simon, 1979) and problem solving (Robertson, 2017). Where non-accounting managers use an intuitive view of decision making, the managerial accountant can highlight commonly overlooked aspects of the model (e.g., specifying in advance the evaluation criteria). Modeling thus is one of the cardinal points in the managerial accountant's compass. The managerial accountant can also emphasize the importance of identifying the resources to be used together with their costs/benefits. Since accounting is the language of business, there is value in uncovering any ambiguities in the non-accounting manager's understanding of accounting terminology. This is elaborated in Chapter 3. This can have a direct improvement in productivity by avoiding misunderstandings with its consequent value destruction, and perhaps unintended behavioral consequences. Taking the earlier points together makes a strong case for the managerial accountant's compass.

1.6 Confirming the Need for a Systematic and Integrated Framework for the Managerial Accountant

Starting with the observation that there is no general framework available to students or practitioners, a case was made that a framework that worked for managerial accountants would be useful for non-accountants dealing with the same issues that confront managerial accountants. Although organizations and society are heterogenous, the managerial accountant's compass can handle this diversity. Its underlying nature—that is its planning features—makes it viable. This chapter has introduced the issues covered in more detail in later chapters to justify the managerial accountant's compass.

The remainder of the book is structured in parts and chapters that construct the managerial accountant's compass. Part II identifies the resources associated with the managerial compass. It begins with the theories that apply to managerial accounting (Chapter 2), discusses the discourse of managerial accounting showing that concepts and classifications represent the world in the managerial accounting compass (Chapter 3) and highlights the importance of information to the managerial accountant's compass (Chapter 4). Part III examines the role, responsibilities, performance and decisions of the managerial accountant. It identifies the role and responsibilities, abilities and skills of the managerial accountant (Chapter 5). These are then converted into critical success factors to suggest performance standards for the managerial accountant at three levels (Chapter 6). The recommendations, decisions and judgments made by the managerial accountant are examined both as a process and a checkpoint (Chapter 7). Part IV presents the managerial accountant's compass. The model of the managerial compass is introduced, and the context or perimeter is discussed (Chapter 8). Then the first four of five cardinal points are detailed (Chapter 9). This continues with the fifth cardinal point on ethical conduct and self-care (Chapter 10). The final Part V provides an evaluation, summarizes conclusions on using it and considers directions for further development (Chapter 11).

The next part contains three chapters: theory (Chapter 2), discourse (Chapter 3) and information (Chapter 4). Chapter 2 introduces the prevailing theories that guide the managerial accountant in analysis and discussing their recommendations with non-accounting managers. An advantage of a pan-theoretical approach is that more than one theory can guide understanding and application of the managerial accountant's compass.

Notes

1. Method is used in the chapters to refer to a usually established, systematic, ordered or arranged set of techniques for accomplishing a task with accuracy and efficiency. It may be manual, use a tool, or require prerequisite skills and knowledge.
2. Process is used in the chapters to refer to the transformation of input data into outputs or a series of work tasks that organize resources to satisfy a goal or outcome.
3. Some books over-promise, claiming solutions to virtually any managerial accounting problem. For example, Shim (2008) uses the solved problems approach and examples to illustrate the concepts and methods. Their apparent authoritative and comprehensive nature masks their focus on giving a result and not what it means, treating organization characteristics that influence the selection of a preferred option from a range of options as subordinate to technical accomplishments.
4. Sometimes managerial accounting is used synonymously with cost accounting. However, cost accounting is focused on the methods and processes for recording, analyzing and reporting measurements of manufacturing products, trading and performing services both in aggregate and in detail. In this sense, it refers to methods and thus could be retitled the cost method of accounting. Managerial accounting is concerned with the provision of financial and non-financial information to managers within the organization and their use of it in decisions. The managerial accountant analyses, interprets and communicates information relevant to an organization's goals. Managerial accounting thus embraces the disciplines of accounting, finance, management and statistics. Thus, the use of both terms is appropriate depending upon the context and emphasis.
5. Costs are a sacrifice made for a purpose, measured using resources.
6. In not-for-profit organizations, profitability equates to obtaining sufficient revenue (in the form of income and grants) for the level of its expenditure.
7. Charles (Chuck) Horngren (1926–2011) is credited with changing the emphasis from accumulation and calculation of product costs for use in financial statements to exploring the use of costs for different purposes. The first managerial accounting textbook, self-described as a 'preliminary edition', preceded Horngren by over ten years (Vatter, 1950). Horngren authored *Cost Accounting: A Managerial Emphasis* in 1962. It continued a tradition begun by McKinsey (1920) who founded the firm that bears his name that became focused on efficiency (Flesher & Flesher, 1996). In later years, after stepping away from his textbook, Horngren was concerned with accounting as a primary decision-making tool and warning that greed was destructive to wise decision making.
8. 'Organizational unit' is a convenient way to refer to different levels below the entire organization. For example, an organization unit may be any of corporate head office, a subsidiary, a division, a territory (e.g., mid-west), a branch office (e.g., New York), a department (e.g., accounting), or sub-department (e.g., accounts receivable), a business function (e.g., R & D), or a reporting segment that is artificially created to avoid revealing competitor sensitive information.
9. 'Managerial accounting decisions' includes formulating managerial accounting recommendations.
10. Accounting information is only one part of the information base that managers have at their disposal (Rowe, Birnberg & Shields, 2008). So, prerequisites for success are the manager has the information, it is sufficiently condensed to be comprehensible, and the manager or employee has faith in it to rely on it. So, the value of accounting information to a manager or employee is relative. Other sources of information include direct observation of processes, gossip and intuition.

Part II

Resources Contributing to the Managerial Accountant's Compass

2 Pan-theoretical Approach to the Managerial Accountant's Compass

The aim of establishing a pan-theoretical basis for ten commonly utilized theories in managerial accounting is to highlight their compatibility with the managerial accountant's compass. The description pan-theoretical is adopted from the health discipline and its allied fields, where it takes four related but alternative forms: (1) identifying common themes or principles that apply to multiple theories (e.g., Basseches & Mascolo, 2009; Morris, Fitzpatrick & Renaud, 2016;); (2) blending all or selected elements from different theories together (e.g., Rich, 2011), (3) encompassing all the targeted theoretical approaches in a generic theory (e.g., Horvath & Luborsky, 1993) or (4) subordinating the other theories in a meta-theory (e.g., Bordin, 1976; Shea, 2016). The approach taken here is the first of the four: to examine the candidate theories. This approach is taken because the theories themselves are so different they cannot be encompassed, blended or subordinated. The objective is not to produce a generic theory, but identify the insights and limitations, which would allow the managerial accountant to discover more patterns and relationships than are revealed by a single theory, and thus become more informed about the issue or challenge they are examining.

A theory both explains phenomena by identifying its elements and their relationship and provides a guide to its application so it produces useful insights. While there are many economic, management and sociological theories, the ten examined are selected on the basis of their inclusion in managerial accounting textbooks as relevant to operations or strategy. The reference or originating disciplines are economics (Price Change; Transaction Cost; Wealth), strategy (Resources; Resource Conversion), organization (Contingency; Institutional; Stakeholder), politics (Principal-Agent), and business (Disruptive Innovation). Other theories were examined including impression management (Goffman, 1959); legitimacy (Dowling & Pfeffer, 1975); litigation risk (Skinner, 1994; Francis, Philbrick & Schippe, 1994); management forecast credibility (Rogers & Stocken, 2005) and proprietary costs (Verrecchia, 1983), but they were rejected because they have a financial, international, legal or interpersonal focus that reduces their insights for managerial accounting. The theories are grouped according to their perspective. Two are concerned with approaches to economics that are common to all aspects of managerial accounting: Price Change (or Price Mechanism) theory and Wealth theory. Five theorize governance: Contingency theory, Institutional theory, the Principal–Agent (Agency) theory, Stakeholder theory and Transaction Cost theory. Three theorize value: Disruptive Innovation Process theory, the Resource-Based View (RBV), the Resource Conversion Into Capabilities and Competencies theory. Each theory is discussed separately to consider what are its themes for the managerial accountant. Within each theory the characteristics of the theory are identified together with any variants. No theory is perfect, so its major limitations are also discussed. Then its applications in managerial accounting are identified. Finally, the chapter concludes by considering the consequences for the managerial accountant's compass.

To take a pan-theoretical approach and apply the theories to an issue or challenge that requires attention, it is recommended that the managerial accountant follow three steps. First identify all the theory that most closely addresses the issue or challenge. That is, situate the problem in the most immediately relevant of the available theories. Column 2 (Issue) of Table 2–4 in the chapter summary can assist this process. Second, identify the related theories for the problem. That is, move from narrow to broad or more-embracing theories. Column 4 (Closely Related Theory) of Table 2–4 in the chapter summary can assist this process. Third take a different perspective. That is, select a theory from a different perspective and apply it identifying the new dimensions and relationships that it adds to understanding the issue or challenge. Read across from the chosen theory to Column 5 (Alternative Perspective) of Table 2–4 in the chapter summary to identify an alternate perspective. These steps can be repeated until they no longer provide further insights. The directly economic approaches open the list of theories as they provide a macro and micro introduction to the products and services that bring in customers, which is the concern of most organizations (Drucker, 1954).

2.1   Common Economic Approaches

While there are many economic approaches to wealth creation, value, prices and growth, Robbins (1935, 1938) highlights the importance of scarcity to economic theories. Scarcity arises from having seemingly unlimited human wants and needs in a world where there are insufficient productive resources to satisfy those wants and needs. This view is a useful guide to the managerial accountant because it is a reminder to

- Focus on human behavior which establishes a relationship between ends and scarce means which have many possible uses
- Use scarcity to account for wealth[1] creation

- Investigate the economic problems using data and deduction and resist the temptation to turn a social problem into economic opportunity or make policy

In trying to understand economically driven behavior, the managerial accountant can select from at least four broad classes of economic theory. Classical economics, which asserts the power of the market system, regulates demand and supply, the allocation of production, and social organization[2] and thus results in flexibility of prices and wages (Smith, 1976; Ricardo, 2005). Wealth Creation theory originates with this approach. Neoclassical (or neoliberal) economic theories emphasize marginal utility (and individual utility maximization) instead of cost of production, as determinants of exchange value (Marshall, 1890). The Price Change (or Price Mechanism) theory originates with this theory. Marxist and neo-Marxist views expect conflict to occur between forces of production, organization of production, relations of production, and societal thinking and ideology (Marx, 1990). New classical economics (Lucas, 1972) believes people make choices based on their rational outlook, available information and past experiences, so current expectations are the future state of the economy. Thus, the theories clearly differ on their explanation of economic phenomena. When they become embodied in government economic policies that affect organizations and individuals, their antecedent economic approach can be unclear.[3] Classical wealth creation theory, which depends on production and not accumulation, is considered next.

Wealth Creation Theory

Wealth Creation theory suggests that the ability to efficiently transform resources (factor inputs) into desired products and services is the source of wealth (Smith, 1976). This rejects the accumulation of commodities as well as the accumulation of a specific commodity (e.g., gold). Nor does wealth reside in the resource reserves that a nation may be endowed with (whether or not it knows this). In this view, wealth exists in the productive knowledge of its people of a nation. Knowledge is required for production into an output with value greater than the sum of the individual parts. Production is the conversion of inputs, the factors of production, into desired output. Additionally, knowledge is required to correctly assess the demand for the output in terms of satisfying needs and wants.

Wealth creation is concerned with aggregate production relationships with three characteristics:

- It uses factors of production to describe the components of price. They are land including any natural resource, labor effort that people contribute to the production of goods and services, capital stock including machinery, tools and buildings, and entrepreneurship which combines the other factors of production.

- The law of diminishing marginal productivity acknowledges that output is constrained when some factors of production are fixed in quantity. If other factors of production are held constant (capital and/or materials), then increasing quantities of a single input results in less additional output. So, there are limits to substitution.
- Constant-returns-to-scale describes the relationship between output and all available inputs. Thus, a production process may be replicated.
- People engage in profit-maximizing behavior. That is, people attempt to maximize the difference between the revenue earned from a sale of a particular product or service and the costs of producing it.

According to this view, wealth-creating activities include farming, mining, tourism, international education and manufacturing, while health services, lawyers, police, banks, insurers, financiers and government absorb wealth.

The limitations of wealth creation theory lie in its economic origins. There are some difficulties in defining exactly what constitutes wealth, and equating it with money or property only serves to confuse. The solution of using a dual-perspective privileges the criterion of societal conditions (value in exchange, market) and downplays popular or individual judgment of utility (value in use). Organizations that confuse the latter with the former and pursue economic wealth can ultimately fail to satisfy their stakeholders or destroy value.

The managerial accountant familiar with Wealth Creation theory will master some general goals that guide their analysis and recommendations. One is the purpose of all production is to produce something that is useful. This is an antidote to the popular emphasis on consumption or consultant's advocacy of marketing (Drucker, 1954). Another is the institutional framework required for competitive markets to function. This reminds the managerial accountant that some sources of wealth (e.g., foreign exchange trading, commodity investment, property rent) are dependent upon government policy as well as trading sentiment so governments can be expected to discourage private cartels, oligopolies and monopolies, although they are frequently outwitted. Danelian (1939) describes the bureaucratic monopoly of A. T. & T. It operates as a 'state within a state'. In contrast, Herling (1962) and Sultan (1974) describe conspiratorial price fixing among the major manufacturers of electrical equipment, apparently ignored by directors of the participating organizations. It also opens opportunities for the state to provide products, services or incentives if private producers fail to supply them, so efficiencies and market failures should always be considered. Wealth Creation theory gives a macro rationale for the organization. It also suggests that costs determine prices and demand determines quantities, but this is examined separately.

Price Change Theory (Price Mechanism)

Price Change Theory or the Price Mechanism uses economic profit maximization. It assumes that there is a demand and revenue curve for quantity sold, a cost curve for quantity produced, and a relationship between sales and production (Marshall, 1890). So, there are only the determinants of the price[4] of products[5] or services are (1) supply, and (2) demand and prices are not static over time. Supply refers to those factors that determine how difficult a product is to make or a service is to perform. Demand is how much people are willing to spend to get a product or service. The more money, and hence the more alternative products or services which a buyer is willing to give up to buy a particular product or service, the higher is the demand. Supply and demand can be graphed as shown in Figure 2–1.

Straight lines are an over-simplification, so curved lines are shown. The intersection of the curves is equilibrium or market clearing. At a price above the equilibrium, the price is expected to fall. At a price below the equilibrium, there is a tendency for the price to rise. Disequilibrium occurs when the amount demanded does not equal the amount supplied. A surplus is the amount by which the quantity supplied exceeds the quantity demanded at the current price. A shortage is the amount by which the quantity demanded exceeds the quantity supplied at the current price. There are some unambiguous movements: (1) an increase in demand shifts the demand curve to the right; (2) while a decrease in demand shifts the demand curve to the left; (3) an increase in the supply shifts the supply curve to the right; (4) while a decrease in supply shifts the supply curve to the left. However, changes in equilibrium price and equilibrium quantity resulting from two different events need to be considered separately.

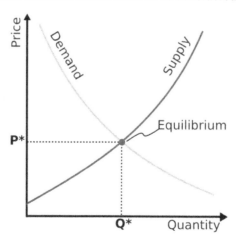

Figure 2–1 Twin determinants of price (Demand and Supply), where P* is the particular market price, and Q* is the particular market quantity at the point of equilibrium where there is no pressure for the price either to increase or decrease.

The major insights from the demand or supply curve come from determining movements and shifts. A movement is a change in either the demand or supply curve. A shift (displacement) moves the demand and/or the supply curve, which results in a new market equilibrium. A shift can occur in two directions, upwards (right) and downwards (left). Shifts can result from a variety of events. They include increases in the consumers' level of income as well as many types of changes (e.g., in the price of competitors' products or the availability of substitute or complementary goods, different taste preferences, buyer expectations, number of buyers, season and weather). Supply curve shifts also result from a variety of events. They include changes to input prices, technological progress, expectations and the number of sellers. The joint interaction of demand and supply thus captures the market.

Price changes[6] provide both price signal information and incentives to market participants. A price signal (to participants) is how much others consider a product or service is worth, suggests how difficult it is to produce, and rewards producers who are efficient and produce it for less. A high price signals that a product or service is relatively valuable to those buying it, and it encourages suppliers to enter the market offering a lower price. The demand–supply curve suggests that those who provide the product or service at low cost should be rewarded by high profits. On the demand side, a high price encourages consumers to consider different products or services, as well as economize on usage. The signal of a low price is that there is no need to conserve or use frugally a product or service. Nagle and Müller (2018) advocate using price to manage customer perceptions and thus prices are no longer static changing only with consumer price index or interest rate changes.

Many more factors can be identified as Figure 2–2 suggests. The figure distinguishes internal from external factors. Internal factors that include objectives, costing, pricing approach, customer and channels for distribution all affect short- and long-term pricing.

There are limitations to Price Change theory. Although one of the few things economists agree on is the framework of supply and demand for determining prices, inadequate information may reduce its applicability. For example, unchanging consumer preferences and income, and unchanged prices of substitute products are assumed. Consumers may offset their uncertainty about getting a better future price with the cost of searching further. Thus, determining the price of a product or service needs to be established in a particular transaction at a particular place and at a given time, and this is relevant to the managerial accountant.

An important concern of the managerial accountant is prospective price changes and their effects. As shown in Figure 2–2, many factors can affect price, but the timing of price changes is up to the organization. Changes in the cost of inputs which may be outside the control of the organization may be so significant that the either the price of the product or service, or the product or service itself, must be changed. For example, reducing the size or weight of a confectionary bar to avoid increasing its price requires changes to production. Competitors, including competitors overseas, with

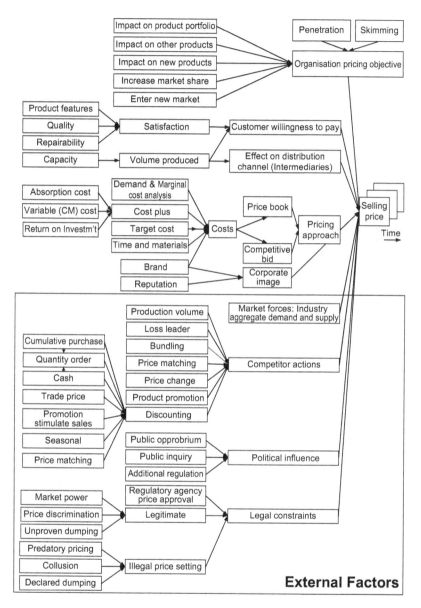

Figure 2–2 Comprehensive set of price factors grouped by internal decisions and external factors.

lower costs of production thus can immediately reduce their price, while still offering a product of the same quality. Where a price is set within a price range the organization should make important strategic and operational decisions where demand changes. For example, will a reduced size confectionary bar move it from the medium to small category? In addition, costs imposed by governments (e.g., directly via taxes) or indirectly via regulation (often described as red tape[7] and green tape[8]) may need to be recouped. Often some costs are temporarily absorbed by the organization. The timing when they are passed on then becomes important. Periodic price list revisions (e.g., building materials) may enable catch-up on costs born since the last price change. More frequent price changes may be necessary in times of inflation or surcharges (e.g., aviation fuel premium on airplane tickets) may be introduced. Price Change theory reminds the managerial accountant that looking at supply and demand gives insights into pricing. This is discussed in Chapter 7 as part of the role and responsibilities of the managerial accountant. The managerial accountant will be more aware of the need for price changes if costs are kept visible. The next group of theories focus on governance.

2.2   Governance Theories

Governance comprises the language, norms, culture, policies, codes, rules, social relationships, systems, and disclosure by those in formal control. Five governance theories are discussed: Contingency theory, Institutional theory, the Principal–Agent (Agency) theory, Stakeholder theory and Transaction Cost theory. Governance is both the process and exercise of authority and control in organizations, so the theories encompass both structure and social relationships.

Contingency (or Structural-Contingency) Theory

Contingency theory is an organization theory that combines leadership with structure and control. It avoids explanations based on the behavior or personality traits of those in control. Unlike scientific management (Taylor, 1911), it claims that there is no single best way to structure an organization, lead an organization, or make short or long-term decisions. The optimal course of action depends upon many internal and external factors that need to be investigated. Contingency theory and Situation (Leadership) theory are similar in that both focus on the behavior of leaders considering subordinates, but Situation theory treats only leader capability as contingent not the other variables. There are many approaches to using contingency theory. Fiedler's Contingency Model (1964), later Contingency Management theory, accepts that the preferred style of a leader is difficult to change, and achieves desired outcomes by adapting situational elements (the contextual factors of group atmosphere, task structure and the power position of the leader). The leadership style and favorableness of the situation are then calculated. Other views emphasize that organization structure interacts with uncertainties in the environment (e.g., resources, regulation) and various aspects of performance (Pennings,

1964). These 'fit' approaches attempted to match the organization with its environment (e.g., Managerial Grid model, Blake & Mouton, 1964, Situational Leadership model, Hersey & Blanchard, 1969). Reddin (1970) added effectiveness to the task and working relationship making it a 3D framework although he also espoused compassion. They also formalized earlier findings that recognized the place of task dimensions, working relationships and readiness to act (introducing decision making). Decision making also used Contingency theory known as Decision Participation Contingency theory, also known as Normative Contingency theory (Vroom & Yetton, 1973). All these theories encourage an examination of what works in the circumstances.

A major limitation with Contingency theory is empirically testing the variables that can influence organization structure and performance. This requires time and even assiduous effort and may produce findings that lack any predictive value. Since Contingency theories were developed from the functionalist theories of organization structure in organizational studies and sociology, they lack the dynamics to handle adapting to a changed situation.

Contingency theory in accounting has two main thrusts (Otley, 2016). First the design of accounting information systems should be flexible (Tiessen & Waterhouse, 1983). This will enable them to respond to the organizational structure and the environment. Their focus is task and technology. Second the performance of internal subunits can be improved despite their interdependencies and external factors (Otley, 2016). This is a control issue. Both these thrusts use assessment of the 'fit' between strategy or operations and the managerial accounting information systems but appear to encounter difficulties because multiple contingencies then impact on organizational design. Contingency theory on organization design is further explored with Institutional theory.

Institutional Theory

Institutional theory examines the normative and resilient aspects of social structure. Three forms of institutional theory can be identified with the first examined in greater detail. Sociological institutionalism focuses on cultural and ideational causes (DiMaggio & Powell, 1983; Meyer & Rowan, 1977). Historical institutionalists focus on macro-level political or economic determinants (Pierson & Skocpol, 2002). Historical institutionalism uses institutions to explain phenomena (Armenta, 2005). The common feature of these forms of institutional theories is that either a higher level is invoked to explain lower-level outcomes, or exogenous factors are attributed to have unpredictable effects. That is, institutional analyses do not examine aggregations or patterns of individual action.

In the sociological form, structures are defined broadly. For example, Hall and Taylor (1996) include formal and informal procedures, schemes, rules, norms, conventions, routines, cognitive scripts, moral guides and symbol systems. Institutions may influence, superimpose conditions, or constrain to either facilitate or limit action. The organizational structures constitute hypothesized infrastructures through which normative, cognitive and dependency agencies exert their influence. So, the institutions are the codified cultural constructions, not the organizations that mirror them and use a cultural framework.

The major limitation of Institutional theory is its apparent emphasis on conformity to the norms, rules or requirements and the consequences of constraints. This may inhibit agility and diversity. It is always possible that seeking institutional legitimacy may encourage homogeneity of organizational structures, thus stifling innovation. For example, an atypical institutional response to environmental factors may be judged as lacking isomorphism among organizations with the same focus, thus undermining its legitimacy or support.

Accounting distinguishes two streams of institutional theory labeled old and new (Rutherford, 1994; Ribeiro & Scapens, 2006). The 'old' focuses established aspects of the social system and the impact of the environment on the organization, while responding to the environment or its networks as a whole. Thus, it rejects neoclassical economics and considers how managerial accounting practices are taken for granted but shape rules and routines to become institutionalized in an organization (Burns & Scapens, 2000). New institutional theory examines the conditions leading to transformation, the means of change and whether change actually occurs (Burns & Baldvinsdottir, 2005). This may also involve considering power of institutions (Hardy, 1996). The distinction leads to omissions. So, Ribeiro and Scapens (2006) recommend that both old and new institutionality are studied together. Institutional theory reminds the managerial accountant to expect both some adherence and non-observance of organizational routines, norms, conventions and rules. The managerial accountant should not rely on controls being observed just because they are in place and apparently understood by all. Institutional theory is silent on principal–agent behavior apart from Mitnick's institutional theory of agency where the principal is able to shape an institution through rational choice (Mitnick, 1974). As they have common settings Institutional theory can be used in conjunction with Principal–Agent theory.

Principal–Agent (Agency) Theory

Principal–Agent theory also known as the Principal–Agent Problem, or Agency Dilemma or Agency theory (Eisenhardt, 1989; Fama & Jensen, 1983; Jensen & Meckling, 1976; Mitnick, 1975; Ross, 1973) concerns the difficulties in motivating one party (the agent, for example, an office holder or a manager) to act on behalf of another (the principal who is the owner or owner's representative). An agent is unlikely to act in the best interests of the principal, particularly when it is costly for the principal to observe the activities of the agent, when the activities are costly to the agent, or when the agent is uncertain about the wishes of the principal. For example, if a store owner employs someone to serve on the counter when they are absent, then it is costly to ensure that the employee zealously attends to customers, and declares all the day's takings. The owner therefore has to determine what incentives to offer and controls to exercise, to align the interests of the agent with those of the principal. This becomes even more problematic when there are many agents. For example, a senior agent may act out of self-serving motives to retain mediocre or even incompetent employees, build an administrative empire to create a set of subservient acolytes, or wastefully compensate agents for achieving minimal performance conditions to bolster their own salary. There is also the issue of asymmetric information. The agent has more information than the principal owing to their daily attention to, and involvement in operations.

The major limitation of Principal–Agent theory is its simplification of both organizational conflict and its solution. The most common solution is offering monetary incentives including piece rates/commissions, profit sharing, efficiency wages, performance measurement, the agent posting a bond, or punitive action (e.g., charge-backs). These generally require advanced mathematics, which can make understanding difficult. Occasionally, there are job security threats or outright termination. Early motivational studies pointing out the value of intrinsic motivators (e.g., Herzberg, 1964) have yet to be adequately explored with the use of non-economic and non-contractual arrangements (e.g., cultural, social, psychological and political).

In accounting, many principal–agent issues are specific to the organization and industry (Baiman, 1990). The managerial accountant will bear in mind that Principle and Agent theory requires them to clarify organizational goals and provide adequate information. For example, in centralized capital budgeting, the submitting divisional manager may possess and use private information to obtain corporate agreement for the investment (Harris, Kriebel & Raviv, 1982). This may lead to further consideration of the motivating compensation and incentives as well as monitoring and evaluating performance systems for weaknesses or exploitation. Principal–Agent theory does highlight that people can successfully manage the organization, and this connects it to Stakeholder theory, which identifies groups and therefore personalities interested in influencing the direction of the organization.

Stakeholder Theory

Stakeholder theory combines the internal operations with market perceptions then superimposes values. It considers who should be identified as stakeholders, how they should be treated and how management can satisfy their interests. Stakeholder theory originated independently with Mitroff

(1983) and Freeman and Reed (1983). Mitroff (1983) was concerned with the collective thinking of managers in the organization and its consequences for managing, organizing and decision making. Freeman and Reed (1983) proposed that the groups or parties who have the capacity to affect an organization should be identified and their interests recognized. More recently, Post, Lee, Preston, and Sachs (2002) suggested stakeholders are not equal partly due to their differing potential benefit (wealth) and risk.

One means of grouping the array of individuals and organizations involved is to define groups of stakeholders. There is some flexibility on stakeholder groupings. The accounting approach is to consider the information needs of primary users (International Accounting Standards Board, 2018). Under this definition, primary stakeholders are existing and potential providers of resources to the organization. They require information because they make decisions about providing resources and may have claims on the resources of the entity. Table 2–1 outlines the framework for primary users.

Table 2–1 Primary and other users of general purpose financial reports under the conceptual framework.

Primary Users (Existing and Prospective)			Other Users
Criteria	• Resource providers • Make decisions about providing resources (and may have claims on the resources of the entity)		Financial information needs vary widely about main types of activities: • Financing (Borrowing money and selling shares) • Investing (Purchase resources) • Operating (Ordinary activities) Usually obtain their information from other sources and under different conditions
Equity investors	Shareholders buy, sell, retain/hold shares. Holders of ownership interests	Whether to invest based on future profitability, return or capital growth	• Regulatory agencies (whether entity is operating/complying within prescribed rules) • Government (e.g., taxation agency, corporation regulator) • Suppliers • Customers (honor warranties and support product lines) • Employees and Trade Unions (whether to pay increased wages, benefits and offer job security) • Members of public
Lenders	Holders of traded debt instruments	Whether to loan resources to receive return as interest	
Other creditors	May include (1) suppliers (if grant credit) and customers (if prepay goods and services); (2) employees (if provide services)	Whether to grant credit based on risks and ability to repay debts	

Examples include equity investors (stockholders, holders of ownership interests and other equity owners), lenders providing loans or other forms of credit (e.g., banks, holders of traded debt instruments) and other creditors in in their capacity of provisioning resources to the entity or providing goods or services on credit (e.g., customers, suppliers and employees). The primary users may also be subdivided into current and prospective. Of course, there are many other users that are separately identified in other groupings.

Another grouping uses stakeholders to perform three functions: descriptive (maps the stakeholders of a specific organization); instrumental (dependencies between investors and other stakeholders) and normative (rights of the various stakeholders on the basis of some moral argument). It is an amalgamation of work from Donaldson and Preston (1995) and Freeman (1984). Table 2–2 broadly follows Donaldson and Preston (1995) who identifies a narrow set of stakeholders. Consistent with the primary users defined above, it separates creditors and the owner from

Table 2–2 Nine stakeholder groups (based on narrow grouping).

Stakeholder	Possible Concerns
Community	Continuing employment, local economy, investment, participation and support in community activities, environmental protection, waste management, share-holding and open communication
Creditors including financiers who provide loans and advances of funds	Credit worthiness of organization, contractual compliance (e.g., covenants), profitability, liquidity and solvency
Customers	Fair trading practices, value-for-money product or service, quality product or service, customer after sales support, safe products and services
Employees	Compensation, benefits and incentives, job security, occupational health, safety, respect, open communication, appreciation and superannuation entitlements
Government	Taxation, value-added tax (goods and services tax), legislation, employment, financial reporting, legalities and externalities
Investors	Investment cost/price, return on investment and income stream
Owner	Profitability, longevity, market share, organization and brand reputation, succession planning, capital raising, growth and social responsibility
Suppliers (vendors) of products and supporting services	Quality of raw materials or components, payment capability and power of owner to negotiate terms
Trade unions for particular trades or industry types	Future employment prospects, quality of work, worker health, safe working conditions and worker protection

investors and omits political groups to identify a total of nine groups. It uses a narrow grouping. It excludes competitors and political groups, does not subdivide government into government legislative bodies (e.g., parliament), government regulatory agencies (e.g., property planning), government tax-collecting agencies (e.g., for income tax, value-added tax also known as goods and services tax, customs and excise), neighbors and future generations.

The narrow view accepts that there are secondary stakeholders affected by the organization or can affect its scope of action but does not aim to be exhaustive. Examples include the general public, communities, activist groups, social media groups, business associations and the media. This is not an exhaustive set of stakeholders. There are also the excluded stakeholders who are not part of the above groups or are not active in them. Examples include people (e.g., children) and the environment. Various attempts have been made to define stakeholders formally.

Stakeholder theory highlighted there were more groups interested in the outcomes from an organization than either the governing board (e.g., directors or trustees) or the investors (e.g., stockholders or shareholders). It encouraged senior management of an organization to engage with stakeholders to understand what each expects, their attitude toward the organization and its activities (e.g., neutral, supportive or opposed), and judge which stakeholders can significantly affect its operations. An alternative to stakeholder is constituencies (Shiller, 2003). Constituencies do not group in the same way as stakeholders since they may form around different kinds of interests, including some of the excluded interests discussed above.

The managerial accountant can use stakeholder theory for two purposes. One is to assess whether organizational actions, objectives or policies are likely to gain the favorable or unfavorable attention of any stakeholder. Conflict of interest is to be expected, and stakeholders may genuinely feel aggrieved. Blattberg (2004) suggests that trade-off between different positions is inevitable, which can result in either compromise or reconciliation. The other is to determine the level of attention stakeholders should be accorded. This can be represented using the stakeholder grid. It can suggest where the managerial accountant should improve their collegiate relationships. Stakeholder theory is one form of corporate governance. It can also be viewed economically through the Transaction Cost theorem.

Transaction Cost Approach Theorem (Transaction Theory)

Transaction Cost Approach theorem[9] also known as Transaction theory states that indirect costs (i.e. non-production costs) are incurred in performing an activity. The indirect costs include

- Search and information costs (e.g., finding a suitable external party)
- Negotiation and acceptance costs (e.g., specifying the requirements, negotiating price, finalizing an agreement)

- Monitoring and enforcement costs (e.g., coordinating delivery, assuring quality of the ordered product or service, and obtaining after sales support)
- The degree to which senior management or consultants are obliged to advise or oversee any of the above

Transaction costs were identified by Coase (1937, 1960) as the cost incurred in making an economic exchange in a market (that is, with an external party) with prices compared to the control exercised when dealing within the organization in a hierarchical relationship of control. Williamson (1975, 1981) replaced the external/internal with boundary and technology factors but with similar results. (The boundary of the firm is where the marginal costs of the firm or market are equivalent.) Essentially, there are two forms of organizing and coordinating economic transactions: institution (also known as hierarchy or firm) and markets. The decision rule between them depends upon costs. If external transaction costs are higher than the internal bureaucratic costs, the organization will grow because it can perform the activities cheaper; otherwise it will downsize. Transaction costs are not entirely avoided dealing with an internal party (e.g., between organizational units or organizational subunits), but they should be less (Cheung, 1987). There is a connection between Institutional theory and Transaction Cost theorem in that arrangements for organizational structure[10] may be influenced by apparent efficiencies.

The impact of transaction costs depends upon three factors (Williamson, 1975). There is the frequency with which transactions recur. Second, their uncertainty in terms of length of relationship, closeness of relationship and trust. Third the extent to which a specific and durable commitment is established between the parties. Williamson (1981) also points out that transaction theory highlights a tension in the behavior of managers. On one hand, there is bounded rationality. Humans have limited capacity to understand business situations, so they only consider a manageable number of factors. On the other hand, there is opportunism. A manager may pursue their own interests particularly if the penalties are low there. The other party may discern the opportunism, and this can create mistrust.

There are limitations to transaction costs concerning its assumptions, theory and empirical evidence. Its assumption of bounded rationality makes economics the basis for action. However, extrinsic rewards are not the sole basis for action. Some actions occur because people genuinely believe in the greater good; they are altruistic. Thus, opportunistic behavior does not have to be countered, and systems to address it are a wasted expense. Its view of the economy uses uncertainty and trust and posits only two types of governance structures (institution and market), which leave open how change occurs and how an organization adapts to change. For example, an organization with a long-term preferred supplier arrangement is effectively locked in. Also, its theory on behavior and governance believe organizations vary, but not individuals (Douglas, 1990). Individuals' actions are incorrectly presumed to be mainly driven by the cost of transactions. Individuals may also differ on willingness to take risks. Context is a serious omission because some processes contribute to the development and learning of individuals. Finally, the definitions used in it, make the actual costs opaque and the tests of the theory unclear (Macher & Richman, 2008). Consequently, more than one explanation may be possible with the data. Working with Transaction Cost theory therefore requires considerable calculative effort.

The managerial accountant has a choice between working with Principal–Agent theory, which focuses on the individual agent, and Transaction Cost theory, which focuses on the individual transaction. Where the managerial accountant considers directors and managers may act in their own best interests, pursuing salary and status, then Principal–Agent theory will be helpful. Where the managerial accountant considers that directors or managers may arrange transactions in an opportunistic way, then Transaction Cost theory will be helpful. Both deal with corporate governance in different ways. Principal–Agent theory is concerned with the protection of ownership rights of shareholders. Transaction Cost theory is concerned with the effective and efficient accomplishment of transactions by organizations. One risk from avoiding coordination costs is not performing the function. Another is transferring monitoring costs to the supplier.[11] Specifically, the Transaction-Cost Approach theory reminds the managerial accountant that any outsourcing decision should consider financial (cost-benefit) and non-financial (qualitative) factors. Transaction Cost theory does highlight that humans (managers, employees) are the most important resource of the organization and thus potentially bring value to it.

2.3   Value Theories

Value theories have three aspects. First, there is the creation or generation of a surplus (gain) from trade, other transactions, investments or relationships between activities. Second, there is value capture, that is, retaining a proportion of the value created in a transaction (Germany & Muralidharan, 2001). Finally, there is also value appropriation or who gains in a multiple stakeholder bargaining process (Coff, 1999). Although there are many specific theories, only one theory pinpoints creation, and that is Porter's five forces model (1998). It synthesizes the practical implications of economic research on industrial organizations and demonstrates that an organization, its suppliers, its customers, its rivals and new entrants, and purveyors of substitutes are all implicated in creating value. It also connects creation with capturing value through understanding the market. In a new market, value attracts early adopters and turns them into reference customers. In an existing market, value depends upon maximizing the market share captured from competitors. However, beyond the extreme short-term, there is no limit to creating new customer value because organizations are disproportionately rewarded when they create new value for customers and grow the entire market. So, theories that identify opportunities to compete on value from operations and customers and offer product or service leadership potentially offer a strong defense against competitors. Three theories provide insight into value. Disruptive Innovation Process theory addresses new products and services and differentiates between a disruptive and a sustaining innovation. The Resource-Based View of the Firm theory offers a holistic assessment of the latent value of the entire organization. A synthesized theory called Resource Conversion Into Capabilities and Competences produces value that can distinguish an organization's products or services from its competitors as well as reduce its costs. It synthesizes the significant extensions to Resource-Based View of the Firm that identify capabilities and competencies. Discussion begins with Disruptive Innovation Process theory as its focus is markets.

Disruptive Innovation Process Theory

Disruptive Innovation Process theory explains the empirical conditions to create a new market and value network, which eventually displaces the established market leading organizations, products and alliances. Bower and Christensen (1995) and later Christensen (1997) find that disruptive innovations tend to be produced by outsiders and entrepreneurs, rather than the existing market leaders.

They suggest disruptive innovation occurs for two reasons. First, competitors allocate their scarce resources to sustain existing products and are reluctant to deploy them to develop a new product or service. Second, the innovation is not profitable initially so existing competitors retreat to their higher margin products. The disruptive product or service can be in an existing or new market. In an existing market, it needs to be overlooked by competitors, and this can occur also for two reasons. First the incumbent may be preoccupied with its most demanding customers because they are usually highly profitable. Second, the product or service exceeds the needs of some of its segments and overlooks the needs of others. This may result from the new lower-priced product or service initially offering inferior performance, which appeals to a subset of competitor customers. One option for a disruptive innovator is to seek out new markets where there are non-consumers. That is, prospective customers who cannot afford the product or service at the price set by an existing incumbent. An innovator who can quickly offer attributes that the customers of competitors do value will find the innovation penetrate an established or new market. This suggests that there is a trajectory for disruptive innovations, but it is difficult to predict.

The major limitation of this theory is misidentification of innovation. Christensen, Raynor and McDonald (2015) distinguish a disruptive innovation from a sustaining innovation. A sustaining innovation changes competition in an industry after a new entrant builds a position in the established market and then appeals to overlooked segments. Christensen et al. (2015) give as examples Tesla (Moran, 2018) and Uber ("New Uber COO"). Both took an acceptable product and made it better to appeal to the existing customers of the incumbent's products and services (conventional internal combustion engine motors for vehicles, and taxis, respectively). Thus, a sustaining innovation is incremental because it enables or sustains an existing product.

On this basis, it is clear that many so-called disruptive elements to accounting (e.g., connectivity, easier data entry and online bookkeeping, machine learning and artificial intelligence) are sustaining and affect all professional organizations (Anon, 2015). The research on disruptive innovation in accounting is scarce, but by differentiating sustaining from disruptive innovation, the managerial accountant can understand the changes possible by considering the market addressed, the processes involved and the business model. Looking at the organization, the managerial accountant needs to be acutely aware of the product or service innovations planned to be offered to customers so that suitable information can be collected and analyzed to determine operational and strategic directions as well as risks to loss of market share. In contrast to disruption theory, the Resource-Based View of the Firm takes a broader and inward focused approach examining how the organization can be more efficient and effective by understanding its own strengths and weaknesses.

Resource-Based View of the Firm (RBV)[12]

The RBV analyses the myriad of resources available to an organization, which can be utilized in an infinite number of ways. It assumes that competitive advantage arises from utilizing resources better than competitors (Penrose, 1959). Many writers contributed to understanding resources:

- Resources should be widely defined (Daft, 1983).
- Resources have short-term and long-term strategy uses (Barney et al., 2001).
- Endowed (historical) resources may have beneficence (Barney, 1991).
- Resources are the internal strengths and weaknesses of an organization (Wernerfelt, 1984).
- Common resources can assist survival if exploited to create competitive parity (Hirshleifer, Glazer & Hirshleifer, 2005; McKelvey, 1982).
- Resource attributes (abbreviated VRIN[13]) fall into two pairs (Barney, 1991). Valuable and Rare (among current and potential competitors), measure if a resource or capability can support a competitive advantage. A valuable resource can exploit opportunities and neutralize threats

and improves effectiveness and efficiency (Barney, 1991). The other pair, Inimitable and Non-substitutable, measures if a resource can be sustained against competitors.

Verbs are used by many of these authors to describe how resources are used without distinguishing between them. Table 2–3 identifies the

Table 2–3 List of commonly used verbs associated with resource uses together with uses and examples.

Verb	Resource Uses	Examples
Recognize (Prusak & Davenport 2001)	The identification, acceptance and appreciation of resources	• Meetings to determine employee know-how • Attempts to reduce information/ knowledge silos • Workflow studies • Encouraging knowledge/ information brokers
Allocate (Ohmae, 1982)	The action or process of distributing scarce resources	• Goals (effectiveness criteria) • Reserve or withhold • Apportionment • Limiting or making consumption difficult • Budgeting • Capital budgeting • Contingencies • Brand and image
Develop (Wernerfelt, 1984)	The advancement or evolution of resources	• Automation of support systems • Interfaces for customers and suppliers • Education, training including on-the-job training • Job rotation • 'Stretch' performance targets
Augment (Teece, Pisano & Shuen, 1997)	The supplementation or multiplication of resources	• Modify existing operations • Reprograming • Acquisition • Alliance • Outsource • Consulting expertise
Deploy (Johnson, Scholes, Whittington, 2008) [Exploit, Barney, 1991]	The effective and efficient positioning of resources	• Make available • Prepare in a specific manner • Utilize features • Extend use • Ensure engagement
Leverage (Hamel & Prahalad, 1993)	The influence or ascendancy over resources	• Extend brand or image • Obtain returns or other benefits • Obtain equity or loans

commonly used verbs, describes the corresponding resource uses and provides examples relevant to the managerial accountant.

Apart from the Barney (1991) framework of four resource attributes, there is no RBV model. A model developed by the author uses the distinction tangible/intangible (Grant, 1991) and places resources in a process that consists of identification, classification and comparison with competitors, checking and bundling. In determining elements of the model, four processes implied by the literature were recognized:

- Resources are separated into tangible and intangible[14] (Grant, 1991), although there are many others (e.g., renewable and non-renewable).
- Resources are heterogeneous (Barney, 1986, 1991). Otherwise they have no value, so organizations will have different resource mixes and therefore different strategies.
- Resources should be evaluated by their interplay with market forces (Collis & Montgomery, 1995) and competitors (Barney, 1991).
- Resource position is the product of time, historical origin and the industry (Rumelt, 1984, 1991; Barney, 1991).
- Resources need to be assembled into bundles to be useful, and the relationships between strong and weak bundles explored although individual resources may act as a catalyst (Wernerfelt, 1984).

They are depicted in Figure 2–3, which acknowledges that classifications other than physical, economic, reputation, technology and human can be substituted.

Equally, there is no template for the model to support resource analysis. Table 2–4 suggests that individual resources can be tested for their strength and weakness, and then rated on the impact (high, medium or low) on the organization.

The major limitation of the RBV theory is ambiguity. The four resource attributes (VRIN) identified by Barney (1991) appear to collapse into valuable making the others superfluous (Hoopes, Madsen & Walker, 2003). Although the social aspects of the organization (e.g., interpersonal relations, culture and reputation among customers and suppliers) are recognized as increasingly important, they remain beyond the ability of an organization to systematically manage (Barney, 1991). Another problem is the lack of attention to the changing (deteriorating) value of some resources. Finally, since causal relationships are unclear, contributions from external factors (e.g., industry, economy) that require other frameworks such as industry structure (Porter, 1998) may be overlooked.

The managerial accountant can use the RBV in two ways. The first is to identify resources in the important causal relationships that contribute to creating value for the organization. They may be resources necessary for short-term strategic goals or long-term resources necessary to control and monitor implementation of strategic plans (Nixon & Burns, 2012).

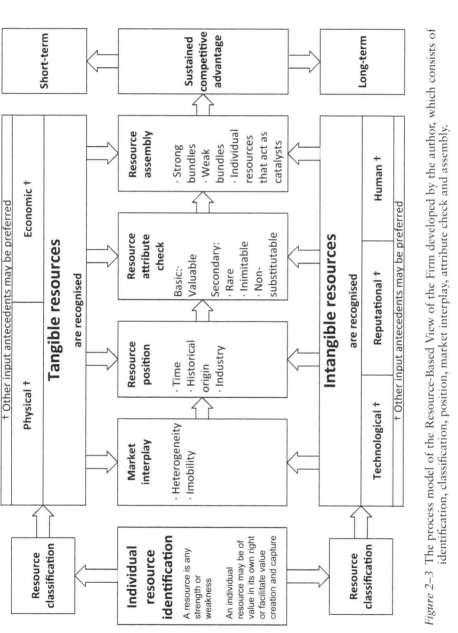

Figure 2–3 The process model of the Resource-Based View of the Firm developed by the author, which consists of identification, classification, position, market interplay, attribute check and assembly.

Table 2–4 Resource analysis template to identify the individual resources and show strength, weakness and impact.

Broad Resource in RBV	Element*	Specific Resource (Specific to Organization/Topic/Issue)		
		Resource Strength	Resource Weakness	Impact: (H)igh, (M)edium or (L)ow
Tangible	Physical			
	Economic			
Intangible	Reputational			
	Technological			
	Human			

*Various elements have been proposed by commentators. The PERTH Analytical Framework is more informative than the dichotomous tangible/intangible often used.

Others may be unproductive, for example, the consumption of costly resources, unnoticed waste and unproductive activities undertaken by the organization (Anderson, 2007). The second is that it may prompt the managerial accountant to consider whether humans have been decentered and redesign accounting information systems for more routinely informed managers, or investigate ambiguous causal relationships that impact strategy (Henri, 2006; Reed & DeFillippi, 1990). However, the RBV theory no longer stands alone. Its limitations have been addressed by extending its focus to capabilities and competencies.

Resource Conversion into Capabilities and Competencies Theory

As noted earlier, Resource Conversion is a synthesized theory. It allows RBV to stand on its own by moving the various extensions called capabilities and competencies into a separate theory that recognizes that resources are transformed. Although some resources can be used as is, it is more likely that their conversion to capabilities and competencies will produce competitive advantage because external demand conditions, competitor actions and public policy on strategy will be taken into consideration (Conner, 1991; Makadok, 2001). Capabilities arise when resources are accompanied by instructions[15] on their use (Felin & Foss, 2009). Selected capabilities can become dynamic capabilities or a competency.[16]

A dynamic capability is an additional capability to purposefully adapt its resources (integrate, build and reconfigure) to address rapidly changing environments (Teece et al., 1997). A competency is an internal activity an organization performs with proficiency. It implies expertise, excellence and effectiveness. A core competency[17] is the combination of multiple resources, knowledge and skills that allow an organization to distinguish itself in the marketplace (Prahalad & Hamel, 1990). It delivers unique value to customers. Prahalad and Hamel (1990) suggest that core competencies fulfill three criteria: (1) They potentially provide access to a wide variety of markets; (2) they make a significant contribution to the perceived customer benefits of the end-product; and (3) competitors find the product or service is difficult to imitate. Core competencies are developed over time and span more than a single product. For example, Honda has a core competency in small four-stroke engines. A distinctive competency arises when the core competence is unmatched by rivals, has potential for being the cornerstone of the organization's strategy, and can produce a competitive edge in the marketplace.

Thus, the earlier model of resources from Figure 2–3 is now expanded in Figure 2–4 to include capabilities and competencies. It retains Barney's (1991) concept of sustained advantage, which occurs when value creation and capture occur, which is above the threshold. Threshold refers to capabilities needed for an organization to be able to compete in a market (Lin & Wu, 2014). That is, they enable market survival because most rivals have them. For example, any organization needs to be able to offer products or services, accept customer orders, process transactions, and deliver a suitable product or service. While threshold capabilities are important, they do not themselves create competitive advantage nor do they provide the basis for superior performance. It is necessary to go beyond the threshold and possess capabilities and competencies that competitors will find difficult to imitate, but which customers value. A sustained competitive advantage is obtained when the organization is (a) implementing a value creating strategy not simultaneously being implemented by its current or potential competitors and (b) when these other organizations are unable to duplicate the benefits of this strategy (Barney, 1991; Coyne, 1986).

A limitation of the Resource Conversion into Capabilities and Competencies theory is the uncertainty over value and imitation. On one hand, the organizational can direct its resources are directed toward processes and strategies that are valuable and difficult to imitate. On the other hand, the results may prove to be imitable even without purchasing knowledge (Barney, 1991). There is also the possibility that during the process, the organization may become difficult or resistant to change and thus ossify developing 'core rigidities' (Leonard-Barton, 1992). So, the process does not guarantee results.

The managerial accountant can be guided by the leveraging approach proposed by Hamel and Prahalad (1993). They suggest concentrating

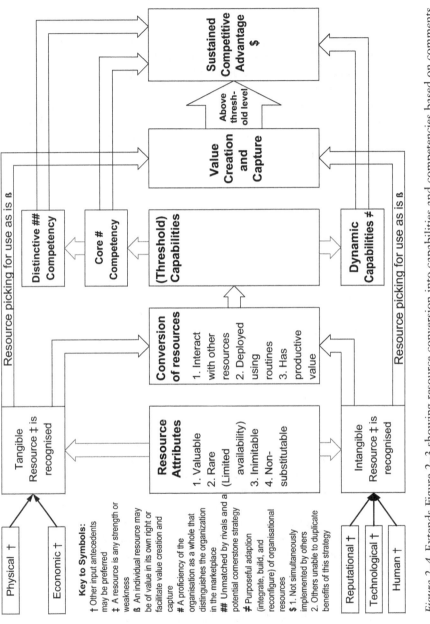

Figure 2–4 Extends Figure 2–3 showing resource conversion into capabilities and competencies based on comments by later writers, including Felin and Foss (2009), Prahalad and Hamel (1990) and Teece et al. (1997).

resources to serve a few consistent goals, usually targeting customers to obtain convergence. This may involve upgrading resources to achieve faster learning or better access to knowledge both inside and outside the organization. The managerial accountant can also seek to multiply the relative value of complementary or different resources by blending or balancing for effectiveness. Finally, the managerial accountant will continue their conservation role by recycling, sharing, co-opting or protecting resources by considering return, as well as the risk of value loss or damage. As Earl and Hopwood (1980) point out in another context, on many occasions, providing new information is a de facto catalyst for change, and information about capabilities and competencies encourages managers to focus on areas under their direct control.

2.4   Conclusion on a Pan-theoretical Approach to the Managerial Accountant's Compass

The role and responsibilities of the managerial accountant include being familiar with the major theories that inform managerial accounting. Individually, the ten theories span the range of issues that confront a managerial accountant in providing operational and strategic advice and assistance to non-accounting managers. Their areas of complementary integration and convergence are summarized in Table 2–5, which both provides a quick reference to commonly used managerial accounting theories and is set out to enable pan-theoretical connections to be made. (The process of making pan-theoretical connections was described in the introduction to this chapter).

Although the theories have been separately discussed, this was a matter of convenience, not their intended manner of their use. There is some overlap in theories, and together they offer greater insights than when used individually. So, managerial accountant should make use of more than a single theory in conducting analysis, making recommendations and executing decisions. Together, the theories offer a means to avoid copying competitors.[18] As noted in the introduction to this chapter, there is always the possibility that an underlying common foundation between different theories may be discerned, which can be used in analyses. This is preferable to attempting to create a meta-theory, which would inevitably omit obscure or simple theories which may potentially be beneficial while being a time-consuming exercise without a certain outcome. The observant managerial accountant may, over time, come to recognize the theories that are critical to the success in their role and responsibilities. The managerial accountant may wish to explore other theories that provide organizational insights.

The theories contribute to the managerial accountant's compass in three ways. They show the importance of defining goals, and their limitations are represented as boundaries. For example, they make clear that the

Table 2–5 Managerial accounting theories set out for pan-theoretical connection.

Perspective	Issue	Theory	Closely Related Theory	Alternative Perspective
Economic	Changes over time to both supply and demand	Price Change theory	Wealth theory	Governance
	Transforms resources into desired products and services	Wealth theory	Price Change theory	
Governance	No single way to structure or make long- or short-term decisions	Contingency theory	Resource-Based View of the Firm	Value
	Cultural rationales for actions	Institutional theory	Principal–Agent theory	
	Potential for loss of economic value from the actions of managers	Principal–Agent theory	Institutional theory	
	Interest groups that are interested in the organization	Stakeholder theory	Principal–Agent theory	
	Costing whether information and enforcement economic tasks are better performed by organizations or in the market	Transaction Cost approach	Resource-Based View	
Value	Divides new products into disruptive or sustaining	Disruptive Innovation Process theory	Resource Conversion theory	Economic
	Identification of financial and non-financial resources to support organizational strategy and examine a manager's actions with resources	Resource-Based View of the Firm	Contingency theory	
	Allocation, deployment and leveraging of capabilities and competencies	Resource Conversion theory	Resource-Based View of the Firm	

purpose of the theory is to assist analysis as well as the interpretation of results. They emphasize the importance of using methods and making models guided by the theories. For example, they make clear that the choice of theories is well-established in managerial accounting. Applying the theories involves the non-accounting managers so developing collegiate relationships is also important as implementation assistance may also be necessary. Finally, the theories are influenced by context. The discussion of the economic approaches particularly emphasized the importance of aggregate and contextual factors. For example, the application of theories is influenced by the geographical location, industry sector characteristics, and trends and particular events. The managerial accountant's compass is thus compatible with the major theories used by managerial accountants. The managerial accountant uses the discourse of concepts and classifications in working with theories and in their collegiate relationship with non-accounting managers.

Notes

1. Robbins (1935) also suggests, by inference, that transferring wealth from rich to poor would not increase total satisfaction. Thus, other remedial approaches are necessary such as integration into the international division of labor (Reisman, 1996).
2. Its maxims are (1) each individual maximizes his or her preference given some constraints, and (2) the actions of all individuals are interdependent. Given perfect and pure competition, these two maxims will determine resource allocation and income distribution.
3. Smith (1776) accepted there were some responsibilities for government. They included defense of the nation, public works (infrastructure such as roads and bridges), universal education, the enforcement of legal rights (property rights and contracts) and criminal matters such as the punishment of crime. It is arguable that Smith (1976) would add public transport to this list on the grounds of making it easier for trade and markets to operate.
4. Inflation indicators such as the consumer price index report movements in the general level of prices for a basket of products and services, but the effects of price changes are specific. Even with low inflation (e.g., 2%–3%) what appears to be a modest increase in sales can actually be a decline. While most prices changes are increases, competition and economies of scale can lead to reductions (e.g., the prices of computers and electronics). Prices are ratios of value. Value comes from the subjective utility that people get from various products or services.
5. Economists (e.g., Marshall, 1890) prefer the term 'goods' to emphasize that the focus is an inherently useful to society and relatively scarce tangible item (e.g., an article, commodity, material, merchandise, supply, ware or resource). 'Product' or 'service' is used across these chapters to emphasize the factors of quality, market, and that it may be physical or virtual.
6. Reasoning from a price change or price movement will be erroneous. Instead, determine whether a shock to supply or demand occurred and which way the curve shifted. Hall and Hitch (1939) observed that organizations not only equate marginal revenue and marginal cost but fail to consider the elasticities of their position on the demand curve. Keynes (1939) also observed that calculation of short-term marginal cost or of marginal revenue should determine price policies. Both considered that this was not normal practice in the organizations they studied.
7. Red tape refers to onerous formalities and excessive bureaucracy in processing applications that increase costs and delay completion.
8. Green tape refers to time-consuming bureaucratic methods and processes relating to environmental concerns usually resulting from having to deal with multiple independent authorities with different requirements.

9. A theorem or proposition is a statement that is not self-evident but can be proved by a chain of reasoning referencing other accepted truths. It may embody a greater principle. The Transaction Cost theorem owes its debt to the Coase theorem, which states that where property rights are concerned, the parties do not necessarily consider how the property rights are granted if they can trade to produce a mutually advantageous outcome (e.g., financial compensation may be offered to an aggrieved party for the activities of the offending party in lieu of the offending party directly addressing the problem). Coase assumed that in completely competitive markets with no transactions costs, an efficient set of inputs and outputs to and from production-optimal distribution are selected.

10. Four broad organizational structures arise from market, business and historical factors: (1) centralized, where decisions are made on behalf of organizational units who are bound to accept (and in some cases, fund) them; (2) decentralized, where decisions, control and funding is assigned to the individual organizational unit to ensure speed and responsiveness to the market (There may be limited leveraging of expenditure or there may be higher capital or operating costs.); (3) dispersed, where organization units are required to fulfill organization-wide standards when making their decisions; and (4) federal, where organizational units co-operate to achieve critical mass and maximize value, but there are differences in return, risk, technology and support between them.

11. These may occur through overlooking the requirement to perform them having not been included in the costing, or it may be that no residual contract monitoring in-house employment group was retained after outsourcing occurred.

12. RBV uses the term 'firm', which is preferred in strategic management as equivalent to an organizational unit.

13. For Barney (1991), the order is significant. If a resource is considered a substitute, then it must be neither rare nor inimitable. These attributes follow from the prerequisite that resources in an organization are logically heterogeneous and immobile (Barney, 1991). This contrasts with Porter (1990) who considers this unsatisfactory.

14. Tangible resources have physical or economic properties. Intangible resources are non-physical: reputation, technology and human which include the latter include culture, the training and expertise of employees, their commitment and loyalty, as well as intellectual capital (Hall, 1992).

15. Instructions are procedures that allow repetition of actions that involve multiple people whose actions are interdependent. They are the primary means by which organizations accomplish tasks. Feldman and Pentland (2003) distinguished between the ostensive or ideal routine and the performative or actual practice (Dionysiou & Tsoukas, 2013). Instructions are also known as performance programs (March & Simon, 1958), routines (Feldman & Pentland, 2003), standard operating procedures (Cyert & March, 1963) and decision rules for their use.

16. A competency can either be specific or broad. An example of a specific competency is the specific skills and expertise of just-in-time inventory control. It is restricted to a single organizational unit. Broad competencies are both inherently multidisciplinary and cross-functional. For example, competence in continuous product innovation requires contributions from managers with expertise in market research, new product R&D, design and engineering, cost-effective manufacturing, and new product market testing.

17. An organization may have more than one core competency in its resource portfolio, but more than two or three core competencies are rare (Prahalad &

Hamel, 1990). A core competence may be the knowledge and experience of managers that results in their organizational unit outperforming its rivals. A core competency should have a greater positive impact on its market position and profitability.

18. The managerial accountant will be cautious in imitating other organizations or comparison groups with regard to Porter's (1990) generic strategies of low cost leadership or niche-differentiation (e.g., Haunschild & Miner, 1997), organizational structure (e.g., Fligstein, 1985) and organizational processes (e.g., Massini, Lewin, Numagami & Pettigrew, 2002). Imitation does not necessarily reduce risk owing to differences in organizational history and circumstances (Porter, 1990).

3 Concepts and Classifications Discourse of the Managerial Accountant's Compass

The aim of examining the discourse of concepts and classifications is to show they have a place in the managerial accountant's compass. Managerial accountants negotiate and construct meaning with non-accounting managers using written and spoken discourse, narrative and rhetoric. Concepts and classifications support the four methods of managerial accountant's compass discussed in Part IV. For easy recognition in this chapter, concepts and classifications are in *italics* and there is description of them so the ways in which discourse can use them is clarified. Discourse is a socially conditioned process that can determine, not just reflect, reality, being itself determined by the existing social conventions and power relations. But there is not just one discourse in an organization.

3.1 Discursive Perspective in Accounting

Discourse in accounting can be generally described as focusing on representing economic events in a purportedly objective way. To do this it renders many of its processes and states in economic language (Gorz, 1989). Some of those processes claim they do so with a uniform representation but the failures from a Ponzi scheme (e.g., Madoff stock and securities fraud, revealed in 2008) or distortion in financial statements (e.g., Enron) suggest otherwise. These also reveal that much of the quantification work of accounting is supporting this representation (e.g., during interactions). This description of lack of control over ends is equally true for managerial accountants although they have more freedom of choice of the methods and models. Nevertheless, the discourse that occurs is about its methods and processes as its outcomes. Given the economic consequences of accounting (Zeff, 1978) discourse theory suggests attention to reification in discourse (Seidman, 1992) or the fallacy of misplaced concreteness. In managerial accounting, this occurs where calculations, analyses and associated recommendations produced by the managerial accountant for managers (a social relation) are transformed into relations between things (material objects). A second reification can occur by allowing the space and time of accounting (e.g., periods[1]) to distract its functions as a social institution (Takatera & Sawabe, 2000). Reification is a judgment, so this is something for the managerial accountant to be aware, and thus reflection forms part of the managerial accountant's compass.

A discourse view also prompts attention to accounting information. It is produced because it should be informative and thus useful to assist decision making and one feature of this is its independent or objective status. Again, discourse theory suggests information is often framed as narrative.[2] shared in the form of a story, uses figures of speech (e.g., metaphor), draws on archetypes and myth[3] (Oliver & Snowden, 2005). There have been some attempts to extend narrative to claim accounting makes myths (e.g., Rubin, 2007), but the general difficulty with them is their broad description, which is contrary to the anthropological analyses typified by Evans-Pritchard (1937). The production of calculations, analysis or recommendations occur in a sequence surrounded by human expectations and behavior. Non-accounting managers can be influenced so their understanding and accountability are guided along the lines of the accounting 'facts' provided. This has the advantage of reducing their challenges, while making them contestable to other narrative. In addition to focusing on the calculations, analysis or recommendations, the story may also retrospectively justify the choice of accounting methods and processes. The managerial accountant may therefore find themselves accepting other constructions of the figures or recommendations as there are other ways to express the realities of the organization. This can be as simple as introducing qualitative factors, or looking for disconfirming information. These are practical responses since they may also be proposed by the non-accounting manager.

The managerial accountant can also use discourse creatively. Framing (Goffman, 1974) can be used by the managerial accountant to recognize that non-accounting managers interpret what is going on around them through their primary frame of physical and socially driven occurrences. It has wide application since it affects how information interpreted, processed and communicated and viewed through the lens of efficiency (Hopwood, 1984). Two consequences are already known. Non-accounting managers may regard the accountant as an under-laborer ('bean counter') who provides some useful information but is not authorized to make "value judgements on the goals of decision making" (Power & Laughlin, 1992: 115). Non-accounting managers may also challenge the managerial accountant's claim that accounting discourse represents the organization to itself (Hopwood, 1987). These may lead to accounting information having a place in organizational politics, so at a local level, there is interdependence between language, power and reality.

The other aspect of discourse is rhetoric. Rhetoric aims at persuasion by structuring discourse (Cicero, 1948). It uses rhetorical or stylistic devices (Aristotle, 2004) to convey to the audience a new idea or meaning, signal incongruity or provide anecdotes, or retain attention. Rhetoric devices can always be interpreted in various ways, but their aim is to produce a convincing and desirable version of reality so the recipient is persuaded to commit to that version (Potter, 1996). Rhetoric is usually associated with recurring themes within the particular industry but can also deal with the temporality (Dunmire, 2008). For the managerial accountant, one of the most effective uses of rhetoric is asking questions (Heinrichs, 2017). This can be with an awareness of the rhetorical stake and interest (Edwards & Potter, 1993) that is, how interest is managed to minimize it appearing as a vested interest. Here the managerial accountant has an advantage as they can use the earlier role attributed to them as impartially presenting the figures or recommendation, albeit, in a helpful manner. However, the discourse of the managerial accountant and the non-accounting manager is locally produced (Sacks, 1992) and can only be shown by examining their conversation, so those analyses cannot be accomplished here.

Bourdieu (1998) proposes another view of discourse, which can be applied to accounting. Its calculations, analyses and recommendations are a special form of knowledge, known as symbolic capital, in which honor, prestige or recognition can be marshaled by individuals for credibility and authority, in this case, using the veracity of the figures.[4] Of course, calculations, analyses and recommendations can be challenged. However, any challenge must overcome the existing weight of their presumed veracity and the established processes that produce them. This weight is present irrespective of whether they are the product of a situated (Suchman, 1987) calculation by a human or machine. Two forms of symbolic capital confront each other. The non-accounting manager relies on their detailed knowledge of operations and years of experience, while the managerial accountant relies on their methods and models drawn from the discipline of managerial accounting. One possible resolution lies in the use of narrative. Aerts (1994) suggests that narrative is used defensively, with negative performance explained using the accounting concepts and classifications and positive performance using cause-effect terminology. Callon (1998) suggests more general concepts from economics are annexed, which can give the appearance of objectivity (e.g., market which uses the measurability concept of local currency used by accountants). Macintosh, Shearer, Thornton & Welker, (2000) use Baudrillard's concepts of simulacrum and hyperreality[5] to suggest that as a universal measure for everything money enables artifice as other judgments (e.g., usefulness is ignored). Roberts (2009) considers the preparers themselves. He points out with reference to the global financial crisis, market participants believe their own calculations (e.g., performance, risk, horizon) owing to their insider knowledge and expertise. These discourses may be durable even through the discussion was transient. In this respect, the managerial accountant is often producer and interpreter of information that others consume. The use has a dual aspect. There is personal self-interest (e.g., wealth accumulation, retention of job security) and organizational visibility (e.g., espousing goal congruence with the organization).

This view of discourse has limitations. A materialist view of language is specific to the particular society and interactions. So, later discussion of concepts and classifications are only general observations requiring application to a specific context to situate the intended meaning, defend shortcomings in analysis and identify the particular asymmetries between participants in their interactions, including their cognitive and social resources. Some views of discourse consider the struggle and conflict in society should be reflected in discourse (Macdonell, 1986). This requires discourse to be assessed for its political effects. Again, this is specific to the circumstances and the discourse, so it is not possible here. The functional analysis proposed by Barker and Galasinski (2001) certainly shows the construction of infinite variation but even a microanalysis (e.g., Garfinkel, 2002) of the production of social order in institutions requires actual study of how non-accounting managers and managerial accountants conduct themselves which is not possible. What is clear is that discourse is contingent, situated, produced and managed by them using concepts and classifications as well as terms from related disciplines so differences in their use of language can be discerned.

In summary, discourse in accounting communicates and constructs reality. It uses socially constructed categories to describe practices and set boundaries (Meyer, 1986) which are revealed when they are reached (Garfinkel, 2002; Winch, 1990). While accounting uses specialized concepts and classifications, it also uses ordinary language with them so meaning and understanding cannot occur without considering the cultural and social factors on the use and interpretation of language across contexts (Wittgenstein, 2009). So, accounting discourse needs to have regard to conventions, norms and rules falling under the general rubric of cultural knowledge. More importantly, accounting discourse can serve a multiplicity of functions or purposes. Thus, it cannot be investigated independently of other considerations, for language is woven across all human activities and behavior. This can guide the managerial accountant in their use of accounting discourse. They need to be aware that the information they provide gains its meaning from the day-to-day practical affairs and preoccupations of the non-accounting managers for whom it is produced. Discourse is not uniform, but many different activities or applications, so each occasion has to be analyzed afresh and not generalized. This is consistent with Wittgenstein who did not believe it was possible to suggest any methodology or general findings as does structural or Foucauldian discourse. The other consequence for the managerial accountant is the possibility of resistance. This can be more than rejection of the calculations or recommendations but challenges that discourse in managerial accounting does not properly represent the value of labor both in terms of knowledge and exploitation and places greater emphasis on technology.

This is not to suggest that the managerial accountant abandons the concepts and categories but uses this chapter to consider how they form a practical discourse.

Taking a discursive view begins with considering the discussion above. It suggests four issues with managerial accounting discourse. They arise out of taking the view that accountant's use discourse to presents a view of reality judged by non-accounting managers, and it leads to further negotiation. The first is the discursive consequences of the assumed coordination function of accounting as the language of business which assumes financial performance is real and comparable. Second, the availability of many overlapping concepts and classifications in managerial accounting is used to show the need for simultaneous multiple classifications. Third, it shows that despite its orientation to the future, managerial accounting remains connected to financial accounting. Finally, the discourse is moving from cost classification to cost management.

3.2   Discursive Consequences for Communication With Accounting as the Language of Business

Accounting (financial and managerial) is described as the language of business. It is reified as formatted financial and non-financial information about past activities, the economic performance of its current operations, and plans for its future operations and strategy. This information is provided to non-accounting managers so they can determine whether the organization is operating satisfactorily and develop plans of action if it is not meeting its goals (Larsen, 1952). Through a common format, organizational units are coordinated and cohesively act as an organization. These outputs are reciprocally regarded by the non-accounting managers who receive them. While senior management may have a mechanical stimulus and response view, the managerial accountant participates in an interpretive process which may also consider source information and past knowledge of performance. So, the language of business is not a single discourse. This has four consequences for the managerial accountant using the discourse of accounting: the possibility of ambit claims on meaning, the presence of constraints on meaning which can be imposed or lifted, the effect of terms clustering together, and problems with discourse in new situations.

Accounting terms are used for their breadth of meaning. While definitions for accounting terms can easily be found in online searches or in specialized accounting dictionaries they are not necessarily used or understood in that way. Three cases of discourse are considered. First, the common approach of selecting accounting terms that are a general description to take advantage of their indefiniteness. A notable example in managerial accounting is *costs*. Although it historically describes expenses in manufacturing frequently is to refer to all payments and expenditure, traditionally the managerial accountant avoids this in two ways: by elaborating the specific form of cost (e.g., *direct cost*), or by giving the account in the chart of accounts/general ledger (e.g., *sales advertising*). However, when faced with discourse at a general level, the managerial must respond either by acknowledging the ambiguity or qualifying the term and offering their authoritative opinion. The second reason for wide meaning arises from using a term in accounting from another discipline. The foregoing approach will not always succeed where this occurs. For example, *resources* is a reminder that an organization has both tangible resources (e.g., physical and economic) and intangible resources (e.g., reputation, technologies and human), and in certain combinations, they are productive (Wernerfelt, 1984). However, there is a process that determines which become *capabilities*, that is, to adapt resources by focusing on organizational routines to improve short-term competitive position to develop competitive advantage in the long-term (Nelson & Winter, 1982). Managerial accountants need to change their emphasis and articulate assumed relationships and intentions in their discourse. Otherwise communication may be incomplete. Third, some terms have been developed theoretically by their parent discipline without reference to accounting. For example, *strategy* gains its theory and application from extensive development in industrial economics (e.g., Porter, 1985) and organizational leadership (e.g., Eccles, 1993).[6] This illustrates that discourse is partly dependent upon managers choosing some theories and persisting in preferring them. This opens the final consideration, which overlaps some of the earlier discussion. Concepts and classifications in the accounting vocabulary are chosen partly for their shared meaning but are used in an 'account' (Scott & Lyman, 1968). That is, as statements made to explain unanticipated or untoward behavior. But they may also be deployed in with a proactive or creative intention (Firth, 1995). Discourse thus involves the selection of terms to gain an advantage. The presence of ambiguities and existence of terms at different levels of generality allows them to be used to advantage despite constraints.

Constraints refer to acceptable uses of managerial accounting calculations, analysis or recommendations. The most ubiquitous constraint is the constraint imposed by the stated purpose for requesting or producing them. This implies a goal and discourse will straddle the goal and the resulting calculations, analysis or recommendations. Another common constraint that affects every decision maker, from the owner of a small start-up to the CEO of a global conglomerate is their understanding of the nuances of accounting. Of course, non-accountant managers do not necessarily approach the managerial accountant to seek advice, and this constraint needs to be considered when making such numbers available. Even when they do, non-accounting managers may lack sufficient confidence to ask or pursue questions that would elicit new or contextual information relevant to decision making. Although some terms are defined in the accounting standards, non-accounting managers are not constrained by accounting concepts and classifications, unless they are party to complying financial statements. Discourse may feature inexactness as well as ambiguities as non-accounting managers make sense of and share accounting information. Again, the managerial accountant may be reluctant to provide corrections immediately believing that further discussion may lead to clarification and potentially better outcomes. This is a matter of judgment. However, the managerial accountant would want to point out any ambiguities of the concepts and classifications and the erroneous conclusions that may be drawn from providing the numbers. While ultimately responsibility for decisions rests with the decision makers, the managerial accountant has a duty to inform, counsel and advise where departures from accounting rules known as Generally Accepted Accounting Principles (GAAP) are acceptable. For example, the accounting discourse associated with internal decision making uses different criteria because it does not make economic sense for future. The managerial accountant will therefore be sensitive to the impact of constraints, while encouraging the use of a rigorous accounting concepts and classifications.

Clustering accounting terms together may introduce ambiguities. One possibility is the intended relationship between them may not be constant. Two examples illustrate this. Traditional cost accounting analyses begin with the concepts of *labor, materials* and *overhead* (Church, 1995).[7] Some changes between them may be nonlinear although it is convenient to treat them as linear. The Cost-Volume Profit (CVP) analysis avoids traditional gross profit to emphasize *operating income* and *contribution margin.* The CVP assumes that all costs are classified accurately as either fixed or variable. The clarity of these definitions understates the difficulty in making judgments. A related possibility is an apparently favorable calculation, analysis or recommendation, which is meaningless. For example, calculating that selling an investment realizes a capital loss when it may make a gain in the future. A major issue in managerial accounting is the calculation of *unit costs* from which erroneous decisions can be made. In his discussion of *common* and *joint* costs,[8] Wells (2006) comments that where overheads are included this may lead to incorrectly identifying *unit costs*. Similarly, using a *transfer price* allows profit to reside in the seller or buyer organization unit where they are controlled or related entities. However, *transfer prices* may be set, which do not represent the costs incurred (Gox, 2000). Related terms include the expenses associated with product development, manufacturing and assembly, transportation and warehousing expenses, and product obsolescence. Another cluster of related terms occurs with budgeting. Comparison of planned performance (*budget*) with accomplishments (*actual*) introduces *variance.* It is apparent from Klemstine and Maher (2013) that the concepts and classifications of manufacturing costs and budgeting have changed little since the 1950's,[9] so the managerial accountant can concentrate on identifying superficial understanding and probing silences from non-accounting managers, which may arise during discourse. Thus, terms can cluster because they are part of a calculation (e.g., in its formula) or appear together in analyses and recommendations, and when terms are related, there can be ambiguities. There are also problems in applying old terms to new situations.

Managerial accounting terms gain some ambiguity when used in new situations outside their origin in manufacturing. While there are similarities with merchandising (e.g., inventory) and the service sector (e.g., work-in-process), those operations have a quite different character. In any case, there are major differences between old and modern manufacturing. The roots of managerial accounting lie in large-scale industrial manufacturing[10] from the mid-eighteenth century (Garner, 1954) where the product range was very limited (e.g., the model T Ford), and the focus was cost accounting.[11] By the twentieth century, there was a second focus: management control (Kaplan, 1984). So, ambiguity takes two forms: multiplication of meanings, and its obverse, non-absolute meaning. The result is that meaning is the subject of discourse. For example, a supervisor's cost may be direct where they intensively oversee production of a particular product, but indirect where they only generally monitor a group of products.[12] Another form of ambiguity occurs with the application of terms. *Cost categories* are populated from the situation to which they are applied. The direct cost originated with (both short and long run) product costing (Edwards, 1958; Horngren & Sorter, 1961; Moss & Haseman, 1957). For example, in the transport industry, fuel (petrol, diesel, LPG) should be a *direct cost*, while fuel purchased by a lawyer who has an office is an *indirect cost* (Gibbs, 1958). Thus, some discourse depends upon point of view, and this can produce a range of candidate numbers. For example, there is no single figure for *product cost*. For the factory accountant, it will refer to those costs associated with manufacturing the product. For the marketing manager, all *advertising (or promotion) costs* are added to the *manufacturing costs*. For the sales manager, *distribution costs* will also be added. For the quality manager, the *cost of warranties* and *cost of returns* will also need to be added. Product cost also varies for a particular customer. There are similar choices with cost reduction. For example, to reduce the costs of quality (quality management) requires a total cost viewpoint (Deming, 2000). However, it has not been widely adopted partly because it other costs are far easier to reduce (e.g., *procurement costs* and *distribution costs*). It also incurs new costs (*setup costs* and *transition costs*) if the production system is re-engineered (Hammer & Champy, 2006). In the earlier discussion, *cost* was found to be used generally, but *cost* is also used as a substitute for other terms such as 'price' (the monetary sum asked by a seller) and 'value' (the extent to which a good or service is perceived by its customer to meet her or his needs or its ownership worth) as well as for expense. Thus, the managerial accountant using cost accounting terms in discourse outside manufacturing should anticipates some difficulties in discourse with non-accounting managers. There are two instances of new terms in managerial accounting: *activity-based costing* and *sticky costs*.

Activity-based costing (ABC)[13] illustrates the social conditioning of the managerial accounting discourse. The ABC retains existing arrangements with direct costs and focuses solely on indirect costs. It deliberately changes the indirect cost focus from *cost object* as a product (or service) to activities, that is, processes. Compared to the traditional *broad average costing*[14] approach, under ABC *indirect* costs are calculated by considering the *resources* consumed by particular processes (or activities)[15] Cooper (1988a, 1988b, 1989a, 1989b) in the United States showed the advantage of ABC was its better incentives for performance. Later discussion (Cooper & Kaplan, 1991, 1992) showed there were high organizational costs to implement and operate suitable systems. A scaled-back version, known as *time-driven ABC* (TDABC), is less resource intensive (less information, less computations and less reliance on technology).[16] The discourse of cost allocation is changed to cost per unit of time, and time taken and the practical capacity of committed resources and their cost. Partly this shift addresses the implementation difficulties reported by managers (Kaplan & Anderson, 2004). Partly it responds to the need for *profit*, an important aspect of discourse, as implementation costs were high (Kaplan & Anderson, 2007). The discourse on TDABC across industries appears to be about its merits, the impact of unused or idle time on calculations, and the use of multiple time drivers and their interaction (Siguenza-Guzman, Van den Abbeele, Vandewalle, Verhaaren & Cattrysse, 2013).

The other recent addition to concepts and classifications is *sticky costs* (Anderson, Banker & Janakiraman, 2003). They propose that as activity changes, the response by managers to costs is asymmetric. That is, managers increase resources when volumes increase but are reluctant to reduce them (or reduce them less) when there is a decrease in volume, output, or activity. It has implications for short-term decision making. Managers are reluctant to act owing to the transaction costs of altering resource levels and uncertainty whether the reduced demand will continue. In terms of a discourse on profit, lower cost savings results in a greater decrease in earnings. The issue for managerial accountants is that *sticky costs* mean that *variable costs* are less variable on their downside. Although the *sticky* cost model has been questioned in recent years (e.g., Balakrishnan & Soderstrom, 2009), partly owing to the limitations on making inferences about cost management information from the financial accounting system, there is a lag before taking action. Differences to this outcome may lead the managerial accountant and non-accounting managers to highlight specific industry or organization characteristics (e.g., provisions for job security under enterprise-labor agreements). While this is consistent with some studies (e.g., Subramaniam & Watson, 2016), single industry studies find little or no sticky cost behavior, so the discourse may center on the conservatism of the managerial accountant (Fasarany et al., 2015).

Managerial accountant and the non-accounting managers both construct and negotiate their accounting concepts and classifications in the language of business, recognize the possibility of a wide variety of meaning, be aware of constraints, identify terms that cluster together, and be cautious in applying existing terms to new applications. The effort to overcome ambiguity in discourse and clarify its application to the particular industry and the organization (and in some cases, in the particular organization unit) requires further discourse. These concerns also apply to managerial accounting classifications.

3.3 Discursive Problems of Individual Uni-dimensional Multiple Classifications

Managerial accounting uses a variety of uni-dimensional approaches to both allocate resources and evaluate their use. It lacks an equivalent single integrated classification to financial accounting.[17] Instead it relies on a variety of methods and processes to generate information about planning and controlling. There are a few instances where classifications are paired together. For example, the pairing of the individual classification *cost behavior* (comprising *fixed*, *variable* and *mixed*) with another individual classification *cost assignment* (comprising *direct* through cost tracing and *indirect* through cost assignment) creates two dimensions. Combining them creates the two-dimensional matrix shown in Figure 3–1.[18] There are several compatible paired combinations. For example, product and period costs are similarly paired with absorption and variable costs in Table 3–3.

While a two-dimensional taxonomy of classifications is an improvement over a uni-dimensional classification, it is still incomplete. Many other classifications or dimensions could be added. For example, the manufacturing stage where the cost is incurred, who bears responsibility

		Cost behavior	
		Variable cost	Fixed cost over the relevant range
Cost assignment	Cost tracing	Direct and Variable	Direct and Fixed
	Cost allocation	Indirect and Variable	Indirect and Fixed

Figure 3–1 Pairing of cost behavior and cost assignment in a two-dimensional taxonomy.

for controlling the cost, or the types of relevant costs in decision making. Some accounting textbooks (e.g., Anthony, Hawkins & Merchant, 2011) strongly advocate multiple cost classifications to clarify thinking and facilitate communication. They offer two reasons. First, the ability of the managerial accountant to invoke multiple classifications simultaneously or successively can reveal much about costs in the organization. Second it helps non-accounting managers understand that costs are multi-dimensional giving them confidence to effectively manage costs. However, this raises the question, what are the other cost classifications? A scan of the literature shows, authors typically identify around five cost classifications (e.g., Kaplan & Bruns, 1987). However, this is far below the maximum available. When assembled together, the total count of cost classifications is 13 using the cost object as the organizing principle, while the actual number of individual costs is 40. Table 3–1 summarizes the managerial accounting classifications in a uni-dimensional format based on identifying the cost object known to the author. The only overlap is capitalization classifiable both as a relevant cost and an accounting treatment. The table is annotated with explanatory comments to make it more immediately comprehensible.

Table 3–1 Uni-dimensional managerial accounting cost classifications together with individual cost elements based on identifying the cost object.

Cost Object (that is, purpose)	Cost Classification Elements (Note 1)
Accounting for costs (typically manufacturing product costs)	Manufacturing (comprising direct material, direct labor, manufacturing overhead)
	Non-manufacturing (comprising selling, general and administration expenses)
Time perspective	Historical (that is, actual) costs
	Standard costs (usually per unit)
	Budgets (usually amounts per time period)
Assignment of costs to cost object (traceability)	Direct costs (traceable)
	Indirect costs (allocated)
Behavior also known as *function* of costs (in relation to volume/activity). Cost behavior is viewed in terms of *total costs* or *unit costs*. Both approaches are used, but they are not interchangeable.	Fixed over the relevant range (remain constant in total)
	Variable (proportional to activity)
	Mixed (also known as semi-variable)[19]
	Step-function (costs change at discrete points for which the relevant range is narrow)
	Curvilinear (also known as nonlinear) cost (which varies with the volume of activity, but not in constant proportion, e.g., where there are discounts)

Cost Object (that is, purpose)	Cost Classification Elements (Note 1)
Decision making where different economic costs are recognized under different conditions (relevant costs)	Capital cost (capitalization)[20]
	Imputed or opportunity cost[21] (measurement of foregone benefit)
	Incremental cost[22] (relevant to the option selected)
	Marginal cost[23] (a special case of differential cost because it is the cost of one unit)
	Differential cost (difference between options, usually annualized)
	Committed costs (a sunk[24] cost such as depreciation is one type of committed cost)
Manufacturing stage	Raw materials (as inputs to the manufacturing process)
	Work-in-process (sometimes called work-in-progress, but in both cases, abbreviated WIP) is *direct (raw) materials*, *direct labor* and *overhead manufacturing costs* incurred for products that are at various stages of the production process
	Finished products (also known as finished goods)
	Cost of goods sold (COGS) known as cost of sales[25] (COS) in merchandising organizations
Engineering and process improvement	Total cost of quality (sum of resources used in activities to prevent poor quality, appraise the quality of products or services, and test, fix, scrap or reimburse for quality failures, whether internal or external)
	Kaizen costing[26]
Accounting treatment	Capitalized (but then expensed using depreciation)
	Expensed as earned (also known as period, costs), which reduces retained earnings
Prepare financial statements (Function)	Product costs (inventoriable) costs associated with producing a finished product
	Period (expensed) costs necessary to operate during a fiscal period
Determining the proper amount[27] and assessing unused capacity impact on fixed costs or cash flow concerns	Engineered costs (have a clear connection with output)[28]
	Committed costs (an investment or obligation that cannot be avoided except by incurring further costs)
	Discretionary costs also known as programmed or managed costs (expenses that can be curtailed or eliminated in the short-term without an immediate impact on the short-term profitability)
	Working capital (funding an organization's day-to-day operations)

(*Continued*)

Table 3–1 (Continued)

Cost Object (that is, purpose)	Cost Classification Elements (Note 1)	
Cost responsibility	Cost center (costs are charged for accounting purposes)	
	Revenue center (earns revenue as well as incurring costs)	
	Profit center (directly responsible for generating its own revenue with its managers making decisions on product pricing and operating expenses)	
	Investment center (measured against its utilization of capital as well as revenue and expenses)	
Degrees of managerial influence over a cost item (Controllability)	Controllable cost	These are always assessed with reference to a specific manager
	Non-controllable cost	
Valuation	Replacement cost[29] (present cost to replace with the same or equal value)	
	Market value[30] (selling price of the item)	

Note 1 Costs in financial statements are associated with either the *product*, or the *period* in which they are expensed.

Table 3–2 Three bases for identifying costs.

	Cost Bases		
	Absorption (Full)	Responsibility	Option
Source data	• Historical or estimated future	• Historical or estimated future	• Estimated future, may have historical information
Basic cost concepts	• Direct costs • Indirect costs	• Controllable • Non-controllable	• Variable • Fixed
Supplementary cost concepts	• Capitalized costs • Product costs • Period costs • Absorption costing[32]	• Engineered • Discretionary • Committed includes sunk	• Semi variable • Step-function • Curvilinear • Opportunity or imputed • Replacement
Other costs for manufacturing	• Raw materials • Work-in-process • Finished goods • Cost of goods sold		

In addition to classifying cost objects in the uni-dimensional way shown above, they can be recast with their cost bases (absorption or full costs, responsibility costs and alternate choice costs).[31] Table 3–2 summarizes the costs in these three bases for identifying costs.

Classifying is thus an important aspect of discourse. It is a specific practice that may sustain or subvert particular relations between the managerial accountant and non-accountant managers. Discourse with unidimensional classifications has the advantage of emphasizing a particular characteristic making it the focus of attention. Combining classifications allow the managerial accountant to highlight multiple dimensions and discourage non-accounting managers from compartmentalizing their thinking when discourse is confined to one dimension. Although the concepts and classifications use the vocabulary of managerial accounting, there are many connections with financial accounting.

3.4 Discursive Connection of Managerial Accounting With Financial Accounting

Managerial accountants adopt the discourse of financial accounting to determine performance. They use net worth from transactions and profitability over a period of time. Net worth is reported on the balance sheet (statement of financial position) and profitability on the income (profit and loss) statement. Managerial accountants express this as the distinction between *product costs* and *period costs* (also known as period expenses). A *period cost* cannot be capitalized into the prepaid expenses, inventory or fixed asset accounts but is immediately treated as an expense. Discourse between the managerial accountant and non-accounting managers therefore centers on what are advantageous classifications. To inflate *product costs*, classification will favor those *direct costs* (e.g., *direct labor* and *direct materials*) and *indirect costs* (e.g., *manufacturing overhead*), which relate to the acquisition and production of products. To inflate *period costs* the operating expenses of *selling costs* and *administrative costs* will be used. There are four consequences for discourse. First the definitions in the chart of accounts provided by the managerial accountant are brief so they need to explain their financial implications of classifying *operating costs* as *manufacturing costs* or *non-manufacturing costs* to non-accounting managers. For example, the managerial accountant will frustrate some attempts to loosen definitions by pointing out that *product costs* can no longer be counted once the product leaves the production line (e.g., *distribution costs*). Second practice of deliberate or accidental misclassifications between *product costs* and *period costs* and within them will misstate *product costs* and *period costs*. As a result, the managerial accountant will recheck this financial information before using it. For example, misstatement of *indirect costs* can affect the apparent attractiveness of outsourcing. Third the attempt to shift the some of the expenses of creating new products or improving existing products to existing product costs. Since these are not part of the production of current products, the managerial accountant will treat them as operating expenses either in *variable operating expenses* or *fixed operating expenses*. Finally, every *cost allocation* of *indirect costs* among products method is arbitrary. As a result, the managerial accountant will cost a range of options to anticipate the convincing arguments that non-accounting managers are likely to proffer for their preferred allocation method. For example, apart from fixed and proportional allocations, several indirect cost rate calculations can be systematically determined by dividing an indirect cost by a cost object (e.g., sales revenue or area occupied). These consequences have even greater potential impact on the financial position of the organization where customers have the choice of customizing their order by selecting from many products or services. Of course, deliberately misclassifying manufacturing costs as non-manufacturing costs to minimize income tax is illegal. However, recent examples from the banking and motor vehicle industry suggest the use of non-allowable classifications was not a deterrent.

Table 3–3 shows the operationalization of *product costs* and *period costs* with reference to manufacturing a product using the two different costing methods (*absorption* or *variable* costing). Finished goods when placed in inventory, may be accounted for by either allowing all costs of production (*absorption costing* also known as full costing or traditional costing), or only considering the costs of production that vary with output (*variable costing* also known as direct costing or marginal costing). Table 3–3 shows the difference between the two methods is in the treatment of *fixed manufacturing overhead costs*.

The managerial accountant uses multiple classifications to perform multiple calculations. Both costing methods are usually calculated because *variable costing* is used by internal managers for decision-making purposes, while *absorption costing* provides information used by external parties (primarily creditors, but also auditors and government agencies)

Table 3–3 Absorption versus variable costing for product and period costs.

Costing Method		Cost Classification	
Absorption (Full)	Variable	Cost Assignment	Cost Behavior
Product cost	Product cost	Direct labor	
		Variable manufacturing overhead	
	Period cost		Fixed manufacturing overhead
Period cost			Variable selling and administrative expenses
			Fixed selling and administrative expenses

as well as internal managers. Each has unique benefits and limitations. Absorption costing provides a more accurate accounting of net profit, particularly when sales occur in a period after production. *Variable costing* provides a better understanding of the effect of fixed costs on net profit because total fixed cost for the period is shown on the income statement as well as net operating income, which may approximate the cash flow. Since *variable costing* does not assign fixed cost to units of products, the production costs cannot be truly matched with revenues. That is, there are distinctions but also relationships between product and period costs. Figure 3–2 summarizes both the distinction and the connection in the staged transfer of costs between the *inventory* and *cost of goods sold* accounts based on *product cost* or *period cost*. Product costs (also known as production costs) are expenses that an organization incurs in acquiring raw materials and manufacturing a product. *Product costs* are initially treated as inventory so they do not appear on income statement until the product is sold. Once the product is sold, these costs are transferred to *cost of goods sold* account. All other expenses an organization incurs that are not product costs are period costs. *Period costs* remain separate from *product costs*. So, an organization does not need to wait for the sale of products to recognize them as expense. They arise during a specific accounting period. According to Generally Accepted Accounting Principles (GAAP), all *marketing costs*, *selling costs* and *administration costs* are treated as *period costs*. The managerial accountant distinguishes between *absorption costs* and *variable costs* to improve the *product cost* accuracy, so that non-accounting managers can set prices. Simon, (2015) identifies the central place of price in determining profit by tracing its antecedents (innovation, value, customer awareness and understanding, and the use of alternatives to shift consumption to higher-priced products). Therefore, the managerial accountant will be mindful that Simon (2015) considers that very few companies will achieve long-term success with a low-price strategy.

Despite their internal focus, the managerial accountant is aware that their calculations, analyses and recommendations may be used in financial accounting. This is apparent from discourse that is likely to take the form of narrative describing the circumstances behind making the calculation which place the figures at its center. Since a narrative is also an account, the figures do not stand by themselves. They are likely to be framed to bolster success and pre-empt unfavorable interpretations. The managerial accountant may be the instigator of the discourse or respond to it. Their argument will depend upon the understanding shown by non-accounting managers of both financial statements and their commitment to operational imperatives. This suggests that a large proportion of the managerial accountant's time should be devoted to discourse to validate the information they use for calculations, analyses and recommendations. Another task in their discourse is uncovering confusion, ambiguity and

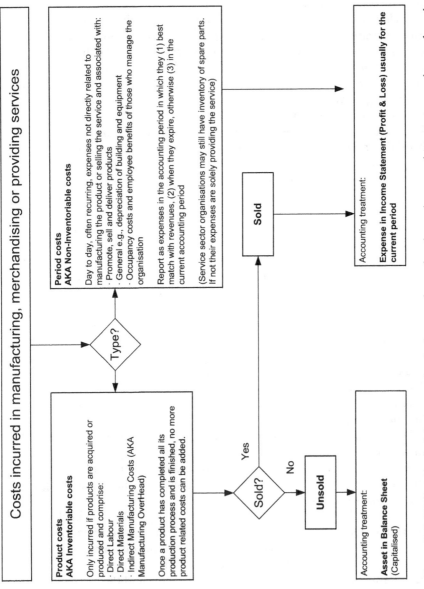

Costs incurred in manufacturing, merchandising or providing services

Product costs
AKA Inventoriable costs

Only incurred if products are acquired or produced and comprise:
· Direct Labour
· Direct Materials
· Indirect Manufacturing Costs (AKA Manufacturing OverHead)

Once a product has completed all its production process and is finished, no more product related costs can be added.

Period costs
AKA Non-Inventoriable costs

Day to day, often recurring, expenses not directly related to manufacturing the product or selling the service and associated with:
· Promote, sell and deliver products
· General e.g., depreciation of building and equipment
· Occupancy costs and employee benefits of those who manage the organisation

Report as expenses in the accounting period in which they (1) best match with revenues, (2) when they expire, otherwise (3) in the current accounting period

(Service sector organisations may still have inventory of spare parts. If not their expenses are solely providing the service)

Type?

Sold?

Yes

No

Sold

Unsold

Accounting treatment:

Expense in Income Statement (Profit & Loss) usually for the current period

Accounting treatment:

Asset in Balance Sheet
(Capitalised)

Figure 3–2 Distinction and the connection in the staged transfer of costs between the *inventory* and *cost of goods sold* accounts based on product cost or period cost.

well-meaning misjudgments used by non-accounting managers making accounting-related decisions. The related issue of performance and control is discussed in Chapter 8, which is introducing the managerial accountant's compass. In some instances, reframing discourse around cost management will highlight misconceptions about financial information and ensure non-accounting managers take decisions informed by insights from the managerial accountant.

3.5   Discursive Escalation of Cost Classification to Management of Costs

Cost accounting, managerial accounting and cost management have all resulted from initiatives in large organizations. A notable contributor is the DuPont Company,[33] which spanned diverse manufacturing and selling activities was a centrally managed but functionally decentralized organization. It focused on budgets to coordinate its strategy, and this required it to develop planning, controls and accounting policies (e.g., investment return) to determine new investments, maintain working capital and finance new capital investments (Chandler, 1977; Flesher & Previts, 2013; Johnson, 1975).

This approach to managing costs contrasts with cost accounting (also known as historical cost accounting[34]), which determines costs at the time of the original transaction using systems and methods that have already established cost structures[35] and cost standards.[36] Cost accounting uses specific methods and processes. They include job costing, process costing, standard costing, activity-based costing, throughput analysis, budgetary control, marginal costing, cost–volume–profit analysis, uniform costing, inter-firm comparison standard costing, and stock counts. There is a broader approach to costing known as cost management. It involves managers planning and controlling with the objective of continuously improving the operations and strategy organization by improving the information available for decisions. It has a deliberately future orientation, with the aim of

- Measuring the cost of resources in major activities;
- Eliminating non-value adding costs;
- Determining efficiency and effectiveness of major activities;
- Evaluating new activities that can improve future performance; and
- Using proven methods and processes for data reduction,[37] make assumptions explicit, combine quantitative and qualitative data, and consider constraints.

One of its initial concerns was with manufacturing activities. Subsequently, it was extended to analyzing the non-manufacturing processes of an organization to identify activities that can be eliminated or improved to maximize the value added in relation to its current and proposed markets.[38] This broader approach is referred to as *Activity-Based Management (ABM)* where managers use their understanding of and insights from business processes and cost behavior to improve operational and strategic decisions (J. A. Miller, 1996). The main cost management methods it uses include:

- Suitable forms of activity-based management. These examine costs more broadly to improve operations and re-assess strategy.
- Responsibility accounting. Each organizational unit is identified as a cost center (if the manager is held accountable for costs incurred in the organizational unit), a revenue center (if the manager is held accountable for revenues incurred in the organizational unit), a profit center (if the manager held accountable for revenue and costs attributed to the organizational unit) or an investment center (if the manager is held accountable for profit and the invested capital used by the organizational unit to generate its profit where the investment options include payment as bonus, reinvest in R&D, distribute to shareholders or use for expansion).
- Analysis of performance reports. These contain information on the budget flexed for a period (e.g., month and year to date) together with the actuals for same period (e.g., month and year to date) and the variance for same period (e.g., month and year to date). Ideally, there is a hierarchy of performance reporting so that the performance of each organizational unit is part of the performance of the next higher organizational unit, and this relationship means it is possible to 'drill-down'[39] to find details.
- Organizational unit reporting allows common costs to be re-allocated. Often costs that are traceable to an organizational unit at a higher level become untraceable at a lower level. If so, they should be included for investment evaluation but excluded for performance evaluation.
- Value engineering to reduce costs and achieve a quality level that satisfies customers. It combines process improvement and cost reduction through a systematic evaluation of all aspects of the value chain.
- Activity-based responsibility accounting. It focuses on activities that drive the costs and revenues across organizational units and includes nonfinancial measures of operational performance. All activities are assessed against three questions: (1) Is this activity necessary? (2) Does this activity add value? (3) Can this activity be improved?
- Overhead cost reduction to arrive at a cost that is fair and reasonable.
- Devising a combination of lead and lag indicators.[40] A lead indicator should provide an early warning whether plans are on track and is measured more frequently than lag indicators because its focus is

on short-term performance. Typically, it is captured at the level of individual processes. A lag indicator is a broad measure of financial outcomes resulting from earlier management decisions and should reveal an already commenced pattern or trend. Lead and lag indicators should be selected because they display a demonstrated cause and effect between them, and they are closely associated with organizational goals and strategy.

- Profitability analysis of customers. Several levels will be selected (e.g., an organizational unit, market segment, geographical region, distribution channel or customer) to determine how serving a customer will cause activities to be performed and costs to be incurred.
- Gain-sharing plans as part of an incentive system for managers and employees to improve their performance on operations. Their key feature is specifying a formula for sharing cost or productivity gains between the organization and its managers/employees.

These cost management methods have a wider focus than cost accounting. They move beyond products/services, are not limited to cost reduction, and accept that precise cost figures may need to be replaced with estimates, indicators and judgments, which can be tested for their utility. They involve the managerial accountant in assessing the current situation, deciding on the form of the investigation, reporting findings and considering implementation. All these can be the subject of discourse between the managerial accountant and non-accounting managers to negotiate priorities and resourcing. While it is not possible to specify the tenor of the narratives used nor the plotting to establish credibility (Weick, 1995), the inevitability of organizational change and competing interests mean discourse is unlikely to be brief and participants will display competence to formulate dramatic stories (Czarniawska, 1997), which can challenge other points of view as myths (Gabriel, 1995), even taking advantage of ambiguities (Eisenberg, 1984). That is, the story can be the bearer of differences and cultural conflicts with managers singling out and rearranging apparently objective features of the organization.

3.6   Conclusions on Discourse for the Managerial Accountant's Compass

The managerial accountant has a discursive role and responsibilities. Since there is no single accounting discourse, this means the information (numbers and commentary) has multiple meanings in the organization, particularly among different organization functions (e.g., sales and production). This meaning may be expressed in narrative and rhetoric. In effect, narratives will compete, but the best storyteller may not necessarily win given prior circumstances and power relations associated with the coordination arrangements. While the managerial accountant has an advantage, they too are subject to the same power relations. These may negate the discursive advantages of familiarity with the language of business, understanding the subtleties of concepts and classifications, appreciating the connections between managerial and financial accounting, and potential weaknesses or pitfalls in the information they supply. Moving from cost accounting to management of costs is both a semantic change and a work effort change. It requires the selection of methods and models that can improve cost efficiency, so the managerial accountant will use discourse to justify their approach of different and advanced methods and models. They also need discourse to describe the opportunities they find to improve costs. Their discourse overlaps but is different to the discourse non-accounting managers have with financial accountants. So, their role and responsibilities depend on formal and informal communication, and they use different discourse, while still falling within the language of business.

Since their role and responsibilities emphasize the future, misunderstandings and oversights can be catastrophic for the organization, as well as their career. The managerial accountant will be aware when using new or different to expected concepts, classifications, methods and models they need to be delicate with their discourse: checking the judgments they make about the accounting understanding of the non-accounting managers and their intended use of accounting information. These conclusions impact the managerial accountant's compass in two ways. Overall, the managerial accountant's compass needs to be sufficiently general to allow discourse to construct and negotiate the detail in applying it. In addition, the managerial accountant's compass needs to provide a context for discourse though suggesting openings and avenues for discussion. Using their understanding of narrative, rhetoric and reification in discourse, the managerial accountant can be sensitive when providing information to non-accounting managers. This may compensate for any lack of guidance on what is expected of them and reluctance of non-accounting managers to admit gaps in their understanding. The next chapter expands this to consider information needs, methods of analyzing information and drawing conclusions from it.

Notes

1. Chambers (1986, 2006) gave two examples of time being simultaneously treated as the present folding past and future into it (depreciating the past purchase price and future selling or scrap value), as well as time inversion for comparison (by using present value calculations to bring estimated future options to the present).
2. Any way of representing a series of events as a sequence that moves from a point of beginning to a finishing point.
3. Kolakowski (1989) gives three reasons for modern myths: (1) time is fleeting and meaningless, (2) values are contingent and ephemeral, and (3) they make the world is continuous even though it presents as discontinuities.

Myths overcome the apparent indifference of the world, and then manage-rial accounting contributes to them through rejecting a true cost, objective benchmark or ideal process.

4. The Marxist claim that identity is multiple, subject to change and contingent (Hall, 1996) is accepted, but Covaleski, Dirsmith, Heian, and Samuel, (1998) and Cataldo and McInnes (2011) find for accounting it is bound up with intellectual heritage and accounting's distinctive role in society rather than other personal behaviors.

5. In postmodern discourse simulacrum is the replacement of reality and mean-ing with symbols and signs, so human experience is more than an unsatisfac-tory imitation or substitute; it is artificial. The hallmark there is a lack of critical self-awareness. Hyperreality is used to emphasize that the represen-tation lacks the original referent. Baudrillard (1994, 1998) argues that the process of social homogenization, alienation and exploitation constitutes a widely applicable process of *reification,* which includes commodities, tech-nologies, as well as discourse.

6. Neoclassical economics examined imperfect competition (Chamberlin, 1933; Robinson, 1933). This dual parentage led to the structure–conduct–perfor-mance (SCP) theory attributed to Mason (1939) and Bain (1951). Market concentration was analyzed in relation to market power and the rate of profit (Bain, 1951). Barriers to entry determined industry performance (1956). These were developed from empirical studies in petroleum (Bain, 1944–1947) and manufacturing (Bain, 1954).

7. Overhead, sometimes abbreviated OH, are the costs required to run an orga-nization, but which cannot be directly attributed to any specific business activity, product, or service. Overhead is also known as *burden* or *indirect* costs. Overhead is more accurately described by detailing its nature: manu-facturing overhead (overhead costs incurred in the manufacturing process); selling overhead (costs incurred by the sales function), administrative over-head (overhead costs incurred in the administration of the organization) or general overhead (depreciation, insurance, licenses and government fees). General and administrative expenses appear in the income statement below the cost of goods sold (cost of sales). Or they may be integrated with sell-ing expenses (in which case they are clustered together as selling, general and administrative expenses). In Chapter 7 on decisions, the fully classified income (profit and loss) statement shows a more informative approach. Over-head is treated differently under activity-based costing (or time-based activity costing) as it is separated into a cost hierarchy to eliminate the dependence on volume. Drucker (1954: 37) describes overhead as "what the accountant lumps together . . . the very term reeks of moral disapproval – contains the most productive resource, the managers, planners, designers, innovators". The managerial accountant should be aware of the perjorative discourse of accounting.

8. An expense a firm incurs as a whole that cannot be assigned directly to any particular product, organizational unit or segment of the business. Where costs are common to more than one cost objects (e.g., several products, processes, activities, organizational units, territories) but cannot be traced to them individually, it is not possible to separate the cost or contribution between the beneficiaries accurately. Joint costs arise where a product or service simultaneously benefits two or more cost objects up to the point where they become distinct.

9. My colleague Dr. Rodney Coyte suggested *Activity-Based Costing* and *sticky* costs should be added as recent and important expansions of the concepts and

classifications of managerial accounting. To those I would add 'cost management'. They are discussed in the following paragraphs.

10. There are many conjectures why costs became central to accounting. One is the amount of capital residing in fixed investments of plant, equipment and in-house transport facilities (Garner, 1954, Chatfield, 1971). Another is the need to recognize the declining value of the asset (depreciation). Johnson (1981: 513) sees it as an early form of information to make "short-run production decisions". However, it remains unclear why large firms began to allocate costs between products and periods.

11. Many reasons are suggested for cost accounting becoming managerial accounting. Johnson and Kaplan (1987) suggest costs lacked the information to plan production capacity. Miller and O'Leary (1987) suggest it was to monitor performance. The International Federation of Accountants (1998) suggests by 1965 planning and control information enabled decision analysis and this resulted in managerial accounting that focused on process analysis and cost management by 1985 and value creation by 1995.

12. Cost objects that are the purpose costs are accumulated and can be identified as a cost category (e.g., direct materials and direct Labor), or cost pool (when indirect), which have a cost driver.

13. In Germany, a form of ABC had already been used following World War 2 where it was designated flexible standard costing (Schilbach, 1997). In *grezplankostenrechnung* (GPK), only variable costs closely associated with the product are charged to the cost object in product costing. It supports short-term decisions (e.g., make versus buy, production planning, pricing of arms-length sales and internal transfers) and can guide long-term decision making. Different fixed costs are subtracted from *contribution margin* to produce a layered contribution margin analysis.

14. Broad average costing uniformly distributes costs across all products or services. It assumes that all products or services are alike in their consumption of resources with reference to the cost object. Provided there are only a few products or services and no variation in their consumption of overheads costs will be accurate otherwise overheads cost figures will be misleading.

15. Under ABC care is needed to ensure the activities chosen are representative of resources consumed. Usually, higher volume products will have lower variable costs, while smaller volume products will receive higher and more variable costs than conventional costing.

16. Instead of estimating the proportion of time spent on various activities, Time-Based ABC requires a manager to estimate (1) how long it takes to complete one unit of an activity and (2) the cost per time unit of the resource, (3) the unused capacity after multiplying the total number of units of activity by the unit activity cost per time unit (Kaplan & Anderson, 2007). An advantage of time-based ABC is that it encourages activities falling in the same classification to be examined to see if they are different. For example, the setup time for manufacturing may be short for certain products, but extensive for complex products requiring precision manufacturing.

17. The integrated framework is the basic accounting equation of assets = liabilities + owner's equity is based around the economic effects of financial activities in a business, which is then expanded by showing the accounts that make up owner's equity. The components in the expanded accounting equation differ between sole proprietorship and corporation. For a sole proprietorship: Assets = Liabilities + Owner Capital + Incomes − Expenses − Withdrawals. For a corporation: Assets = Liabilities + Owner's paid-in Capital + Revenues − Expenses − Dividends − Treasury Stock. Neither assets nor liabilities are expanded further. The expanded accounting equation makes visible (1) the impact on equity from

net income (increased by revenues, decreased by expenses) and (2) the effect of transactions with owners (drawings, dividends, sale or purchase of ownership interest).

18. The two-row/column spanning top and left headings, and separate column and row headings distinguish it from a 2 x 2 matrix. In a 2 x 2 matrix, the axes are chosen so that the most desirable outcome is in the upper left quadrant and the least desirable outcome is in the lower right quadrant.

19. Mixed costs should always be decomposed into their component variable costs and fixed costs.

20. Capitalized costs include plant and equipment (formerly called fixed costs) but also materials and supplies, cost of work-in-process, and finished goods.

21. An invisible cost is a cost that is not incurred directly, as opposed to an explicit cost, which is incurred directly. It is also known as an implied cost.

22. The composition of total cost is described by identifying the contributing factors or cost items. Any increment is determined by the contribution of the cost factors, not necessarily by single units.

23. The increase or decrease in the total cost of a production run for the next unit or one additional unit of volume or output. The purpose of analyzing marginal cost is to determine at what point an organization can achieve economies of scale. When only one additional unit is being considered, the marginal cost may equal incremental cost. Cost-Volume Profit is an example of marginal costing.

24. Sunk costs are costs that have been incurred that cannot be recouped.

25. Cost of sales uses the same cost classifications of manufacturing: direct labor, direct materials, and overhead, but may add the cost of the *sales commissions* associated with a sale. *Cost of sales* is calculated either as (1) an adjustment the cost of the goods purchased or manufactured by the change in inventory during a given period, or (2) add the cost of goods purchased or manufactured to the inventory at the beginning of the period and subtract the inventory of goods at the end of the period commonly shown as beginning inventory + purchases – ending inventory.

26. It is the process of continual cost reduction that occurs after a product design has been completed and the product is now in production. It focuses on reducing the cost of raw materials, better procurement, effective waste management and continuous product improvement.

27. Expenditure can be classified as based on the proper or appropriate amount to spend, deemed a matter of judgment. In part, this depends upon whether there is unused capacity.

28. These are synthetic costs because they are constructed logically as expected costs from the components of each item using a specific method. For example, a time study is used to determine the expected labor time of a particular product, which is then converted to a cost.

29. A replacement cost is the actual cost to replace an item or asset. This may arise because an item or asset has been irreparably damaged or destroyed or has to be re-valued. The comparison is with a substantially identical new item or asset at its pre-loss condition. Replacement cost does not equate to the 'market value' of the item and is typically distinguished from the 'actual cash value' payment, which includes a deduction for depreciation. Market value is market value is its price at sale.

30. According to Koller, Dobbs and Huyett (2010), market value depends upon (1) whether the organization's value is driven by growth or return on capital, (2) its generation of cash flows (not rearranging liabilities and risk), (3) the competence of the managers and the strategy, and (4) stock market expectations where the organization is traded (e.g., through public listing).

31. The minimum number of options for alternate choices is two, so one option should always be retaining the status quo.

32. Absorption or full costing refers to the full costs of producing a product or service being assigned to the product or service. It contrasts with variable costing (by measuring direct material, direct labor and manufacturing overhead) and shows the costs of maintaining capacity during the period as fixed overhead costs as expenses for the period.

33. The DuPont analysis is a common form of financial statement analysis that allows the dominant elements of profitability to be identified by usually comparing return across organizations in terms of three ratios: (1) profitability (measured by profit margin); (2) asset efficiency (measured by asset turnover) and (3) financial leverage (measured by equity multiplier), although adjustments to components can be made based on industry characteristics (Soliman, 2008). Two other relationships are equally popular. (1) Hayzen & Reeve (2000) decompose change in profit into: profit (productivity variance, and price recovery variance); productivity (capital utilization variance, and efficiency variance); quantity (Percent change in product quality, and Percent change in resource quantity); and Price (Percentage change in product price, and Percent change in resource price). (2) Percentage (e.g., materials, overhead, wages) of sales is also used. This analysis is secondary to the managerial accounting costing discussed above.

34. Historic cost emphasizes the distinction from original cost from its replacement cost, current cost, or inflation-adjusted cost.

35. Cost structures are the types and relative proportions of fixed and variable costs at the level of the organization, organizational subunit, geographic region, product or service group, customer or product or service line.

36. A predetermined or estimated cost is used as target cost and basis for comparison with the actual cost. It is derived from time and motion studies; historical data analysis or approximations.

37. These include suitable forms of activity-based management, business process re-engineering, life cycle management, value chain analysis and target costing.

38. A market is a place for buyers and sellers to transact. A market is successful where there is information symmetry, people are spending their own money, public goods are under provided, and quality is transparent. Ideally, the operation of markets should reallocate resources to achieve improved outcomes.

39. Access more detailed data at lower level. It is either at an intermediate aggregation (e.g., data for a geographical region) or the original transaction from a source document.

40. The balanced scorecard is one example of a performance report that combines lead and lag indicators. However, it is neither balanced nor a scorecard. It lacks a theoretical justification for its four categories and their measures. For example, an organization has many stakeholders, not just customers and in some industries, the 'customer' stakeholder does not exist; there are no stakeholders for the financial and internal business process perspectives, and the innovation and learning perspective are internal business processes whose stakeholders exist across the organization.

4 Importance of Information and Communication to the Managerial Accountant's Compass

The aim of establishing the importance of information[1] to the work of the managerial accountant is to show its place in the managerial accountant's compass. Information supports the four methods of managerial accountant's compass discussed in Part 4. Previous chapters have taken the availability and understanding of information for granted. This chapter examines the responsibilities of the managerial accountant for selecting, compiling and providing information in a form that is customized to both the characteristics of the decision to be made and the knowledge and expertise of the decision maker(s). The managerial accountant routinely distinguishes between financial and non-financial information, understands its properties or attributes, and uses the source documents to validate information. More importantly, the managerial accountant remembers that non-accounting managers need accounting documents that can be readily understood and will often assist by explaining the document in a 'walkthrough' of the figures and their meaning for decisions.

4.1 Communication with Non-Accountants by the Managerial Accountant

The managerial accountant will recognize that that they primarily communicate with non-accountants. This has seven implications. First the choice of analytical framework will be justified both for itself and in reference to other options not selected, and then explained. An analytical framework may be a formula, equation or arrangement of factors. Second, the starting values used and substituted into the analytial framework will be made explicit. This may require two or more sets of calculations where using a low, high and typical number gives significantly different results. Third, any assumptions used in the analysis will be stated together with a description of their use and the reason for making the assumption. Similarly, where the managerial accountant relies upon external information, they will describe its source, veracity and limitations. Fourth, all intermediate workings will be shown in full together with any intermediate analytical framework and the method used for making any estimates.

In practice, this means that the managerial accountant will carefully format their calculations to ensure that they avoid ambiguity and repetition. One approach will be to use templates[2] so that managers become familiar with the layout and can readily understand it. Fifth, the calculated result will not only be stated, but it will be qualified in terms of the units used (e.g., labor hourly rate in dollars) together with any suffix (e.g., favorable or unfavorable in the case of cost variances). Sixth, the meaning of the result will be explained and related to the purpose or circumstances initiating the analysis. Finally, the managerial accountant will seek feedback from the non-accounting manager.

To communicate with non-managers, the managerial accountant will consider the best means of communication. In selecting a means of communication, the managerial accountant will first determine their knowledge management strategy: codification or personalization (Hansen, Nohria & Tierney, 1999). Codification is the making of a record. Personalization is person-to-person contact to share experiences and knowledge. Table 4–1 outlines communication options in combination with the codification/personalization strategy.

Table 4–1 divides communication into two options. Hansen et al. (1999) in the *Harvard Business Review* suggest that the choice of communication strategy should be based on the industry, goals and business operations. If an organization's products are standardized and mature,

Table 4–1 Communication options for the codification/personalization strategy.

		Communication Strategy	
		Codification	*Personalization*
Formality	**Formal**	Memo* Report* E-mail* Letter* Contract or agreement*	Discussion† Interview† Meeting† Phone call (Traditional or Skype)†
	Informal	Handwritten note Diary or day journal note (electronic or handwritten) Bullet notebook[3]	Chance meeting (e.g., water cooler, cafeteria, canteen) Ad hoc query requesting advice or assistance Lurking (overheard conversation)

Notes
* Supported with calculations or analyses.
† Scheduled appointment

and if people rely primarily on explicit knowledge, then they recommend codification (e.g., Dell Computer Company). If an organization's products are customized and innovative, and if people rely primarily on tacit knowledge, they recommend personalization (e.g., McKinsey Consulting Organization). However, the choice is not that simple. Codification should be used where there is a possibility that later there will be debate about what was said, or whether it was said at all. One solution for the managerial accountant is to continue with personalization but follow-up with a written confirmation (e.g., e-mail). This sequence appears professional if the managerial accountant is aiming to position themselves as a trusted advisor. Maister, Green & Galford (2001) describe the trusted advisor as someone who builds trust, sells (recommendations) the right way, manages effectively, and resolves disputes equitably.

The managerial accountant can succeed as a trusted advisor by using communication to gain the trust of top management before proposing advice and providing assistance. Maister et al, (2001) suggest that becoming a trusted business partner can be expressed in the following equation: Trustworthiness = (Credibility + Reliability + Intimacy)/ (Self-orientation). That is, build credibility by listening empathetically and separating rational from emotional issues. The aim is to help managers frame the problem in a way that can be solved in the short term and then partner with them to craft a detailed solution recognizing they may need to carefully manage expectations. To ensure reliability, the managerial accountant will always be renowned for delivering consistently and excellently. The aim is to show they are mindful of senior management needs and expectations by providing advice and assistance that anticipates those needs and expectations. To foster sound interpersonal relations the managerial accountant will communicate professionally but sensitively as with a close friend or family member. The aim is to share concerns and work through all issues whether professional or personal in a way which leaves the senior manager grateful for the advice and assistance and willing to seek further collaborations. Finally, the managerial accountant will show they are oriented to the others not themselves. The aim is to show that what you do and say benefits senior management and the organization, if necessary to your detriment in time or expense. One way of doing this is to always be transparent with motives, demonstrate flexibility, show openness to change, remain dedicated and passionate yet humble. Maister et al. (2001) also recommend humility to overcome self-defeating problems of self-control. To structure communication they recommend using a five-step process (engage, listen, frame, envision and commit). Improving communication thus builds a foundation for the managerial accountant to demonstrate to non-accounting managers how they add value to information.

4.2   Adding Value to Information

There are a variety of approaches to value. Smith (1976) identifies two. Exchange value measures worth, one of which may be money. Use value is the satisfying power of a commodity. While information has value, it is not inherent in it, nor is it carried by the message it provides. Therefore, the information has the potential for value. Its context is equally important. This is separating the its use from the effect of its use (Machlup, 1979). The managerial accountant who recognizes this will demonstrate to non-accounting managers the potential in information and make an effort to present it in a form that enables its use rather than its dismissal as having no value, or simply ignoring it. Feldman and March (1981) observe that organizations provide incentives for gathering more information that is optimal and this results in information users becoming overloaded. Ackoff (1967) had previously gone further and claimed many managers asked for information although they had no plan for its use. An early study of value in information by Taylor (1986) is the clearest approach because it was based on an extensive study. It suggests there are four value-adding processes: organizing information arranges information so it can be used effectively;[4] analyzing information is examining in detail; making judgments is drawing conclusions, while the decision process selects an action. Table 4–2 identifies the value-adding and non-value adding processes in using information. It identifies the related subprocesses for both. Taylor

Table 4–2 Comparing value-adding and non-value adding processes with commentary.

Value-Adding Process	Subprocesses	Non-Value Adding Processes	Subprocesses
Organizing	• Grouping and labeling information based on their attributes • Comparing and contrasting noting similarities, associations differences and relationships • Ordering information according to a given criterion • Formatting to represent the form of information but not its substance	Recognizing Standardization Displaying	• Attending to information • Formatting information using standard templates or proformas • Presenting information to be viewed (subject to permission)

Value-Adding Process	Subprocesses	Non-Value Adding Processes	Subprocesses
Analyzing	• Noticing absences • Interpreting/ appraising • Separating/ differentiating (distinguishing) • Comparing and identifying interrelationships, trends and patterns • Evaluating including logic • Validating • Aggregating • Integrating/ synthesizing • Extrapolating • Addressing unanticipated results	Filtering Comprehending Conjecturing	• Selection and exclusion • Investigating • Familiarisation • Forming hypotheses or hunches
Judgment	• Devising options • Assessing options • Determining advantages/pros/ strengths • Determining disadvantages/ cons/weaknesses	Recalling Defining	• Retrieval for availability • Determining meanings • Checking availability and suitability of meaning
Decision	• Matching goals • Negotiating/ bargaining • Compromising • Selecting/choosing	Explaining Defending	• Meeting • Discussion • Resolution

was one of the earliest commentators to recognize that some processes add value irrespective whether that is recognized by any accompanying definition. However, in some decision contexts, apparently non-value adding processes may improve productivity, for example through the recognition heuristic (Goldstein & Gigerenzer, 1999).

Using Taylor's (1986) value of information approach, the managerial accountant will recognize that all information has potential value but is context dependent. Effort spent in understanding how the information will be used can suggest to the managerial accountant the processes they should perform that will make its value apparent to non-accounting managers. In addition, by differentiating between the information and the resources that process, transmit or contain the information, the managerial accountant can increase the probability that their info is useful to non-accounting manager. That information can be financial or non-financial.

4.3   Distinguishing Between Financial and Non-Financial Information

The managerial accountant will assemble four kinds of information to investigate any problem or opportunity. The basic distinction is between financial and non-financial information. Outside accounting, there is some debate over the meaning of 'financial information' that leads to overlapping definitions.

In accounting, the strict definition confines financial information to information sourced from the reported financial performance of an organization, for example, from its financial statements, its disclosure notes and other financial communications to the market and its regulator. Examples are the values of assets, liabilities, equity, revenue and expenses. The format of presentation is governed by accounting standards for reporting. Non-financial information is thus information available from sources other than financial statements produced as part of financial reporting even though it may be expressed in monetary amounts.

Outside accounting, broader definitions apply. Financial information is any information expressed in monetary terms irrespective whether it is sourced from financial statements produced in accordance with accounting standards or from other sources including non-accounting systems (e.g., advertising budget for a particular sporting team to carry the brand of the organization; an estimate of loss of sales from a natural disaster). There are three kinds of non-financial information. It is non-monetary numbers (e.g., quantities of shipments). Second it may be words for description (e.g., locations of customers), or to express grades or categories (e.g., high income or poor risk). Finally, it may be numbers can be stripped of their monetary characteristics and expressed as proportions e.g., market share). The managerial accountant will make clear which definition they are following since many of the figures they use can ultimately become part of financial statements.

Financial and non-financial information can be presented in various formats. Usually, it is summarized in reports using tables with monetary amounts, but it can be displayed visually in a single-dimension chart (often to compare differences), shown as a plot (locating a point in a two-dimensional Cartesian space as a relationship between two or more variables), or as a graph (to diagrammatically show a mathematical function). The managerial accountant will consider the needs and preferences of recipients in assembling information. This may lead to some negotiation where additional effort is required to initially produce the report, but it will then be regularly produced. However, information has other dimensions, apart from the financial non-financial dichotomy.

4.4 View Information as Multi-dimensional

In addition to their preoccupation with financial information, the managerial accountant will also be concerned with its other aspects and these are referred to as dimensions. These broader views of information can affect the initial selection or review of information. This ensures that the managerial accountant is aware whether there is any lack of balance or limitations. The six dimensions are paired as quantitative versus qualitative, external versus internal, primary versus secondary, time horizon (past, present, future), operational versus strategic and evaluation versus prediction.

Another means of distinguishing financial and non-financial information is to refer to quantitative and qualitative information. Quantitative information is expressed with numbers. Qualitative information is expressed with words, symbols or stories. Using both kinds of information has two advantages. First, measures of the characteristics or attributes are typically necessary for analyses. Second, relationships between information are likely to be perceived. Typical examples of the four kinds of information are provided in Table 4–3, which is arranged so the financial and non-financial is in the columns and the quantitative and qualitative is in the rows.

Table 4–3 Frequently used examples of the four kinds of information separated into two axes. Columns are divided into quantitative and qualitative information. Rows are divided into financial and non-financial information.

		Type of Information	
		Quantitative	*Qualitative*
Financial (Note 2)	Appearing in the four financial statements	• Assets ($) • Liabilities ($) • Equity ($) • Revenue from operations ($) • Investment income ($) • Profit (Loss) ($) • Tax paid ($) • Provision for bad and doubtful debts • Borrowings ($) • Valuation of inventory ($)	

(Continued)

Table 4–3 (Continued)

| | | Type of Information | |
		Quantitative	Qualitative
Non-financial	Is not required to appear in financial statements	• Share price information for publicly listed organization ($), often made available on the organization's website in real time • Comparative financial information, e.g., for 5 years	• GAAP applied to transactions • Financial accreditation using credit rating agency (e.g., Standard & Poor's) ranging from 'AAA' to 'Junk'.
	Sales	• Forecast sales revenue for period ($) • Actual sales revenue for period ($)	• Product sales forecast (number of units sold) • Customers (Number) • Brand awareness (%) • Price point of products (e.g., high, medium, low)
	Production	• Total value of production for period ($) • Work-in-process ($) • Unit cost for production ($)	• Product mix • Purchases for manufacturing (Tons) • Employee productivity (e.g., product produced per day) • Factory and machine capacity
	Support	• Cost of desktop and laptop computers ($)	• Conditions of access and use of information and communications technology
	Corporate	• Capital investment proposal including cost/benefit analysis ($)	• Mission statement • Vision statement • Strategic plan • Standard Operating procedures • Organization chart with organizational unit names • Job or position descriptions • Contingency plans for disasters

Note to table: The examples are sourced from Oliver (2012). This table uses the strict definition of financial information from the text. A $ symbol indicates a monetary measurement. A % symbol indicates a measurement by percentage or proportion.

Table 4–3 shows the wide range of information provided by the managerial accountant requires many sources and many different types of information. This is further explored in the section on integrating and aggregating information.

The managerial accountant expects to find information from many sources. The basic sources are external and internal to the organization. Important external sources include:

1. Government agencies such as the Federal/Central Reserve Bank for monetary policy and inflation rates as well as the Consumer Price Index (CPI)
2. The national parliament for economic policies including annual budget, which sets taxes and rates
3. Credit ratings (e.g., Standard and Poor's; Dun & Bradstreet)
4. Industry information provided by major employer associations (e.g., Chamber of Commerce) and specific industry associations (e.g., Mining Council)
5. Stock exchanges and commodity exchanges
6. Publications of international bodies and foreign countries (e.g., UN, World Bank; US Treasury; China Trade Representative)
7. Secondary sources of information include business newspapers (e.g., (London) *Financial Times, Wall Street Journal, Australian Financial Review, The Australian Business Review*), business magazines (e.g., *Forbes, The Australian Deal*) and journals (e.g., *Academy of Management*). They contain reports of business activities, interviews with business identities and commentators, comments on business activities, opinions on business activities and business trends.
8. Historic information can be sourced from academic libraries and, specialized libraries associated with industry associations.

Internal sources of information arise from both discussions with functional managers as well as documentation. They include

1. Board and senior management reports, including summaries of performance, prior decisions, plans and proposals
2. Reports from operations (e.g., sales, costs, profitability) reported both as financial information and as commentary from managers on performance
3. The official strategy of the organization as reported in the approved strategy document as well as official announcements and presentations to employees and external parties
4. Specific analyses (e.g., to identify and assess the resources of the organization; capital budget with its analyses and supporting documentation)
5. Documentation from projects (e.g., proposals, specifications, plans)

Primary versus secondary sources of information refers to the closeness of information to its source. Primary sources are original material that provides the original data. As noted above many external organizations are primary sources because they produce useful and original information, and much internal information is also primary as it comes directly from the original transaction (using source documents). Secondary information is based on primary sources. Most newspapers and magazines and books are secondary sources. They provide useful summaries and commentaries as well as descriptions of trends, developments and predictions. There are also tertiary sources that introduce and summarize both primary and secondary sources. Some are reputable such as refereed handbooks and encyclopedias. Those that are aimed at mass circulation are written for broad audiences who are unfamiliar to the topic so they may oversimplify or be narrowly selective. The managerial accountant will be aware of all three because it is likely that managers with whom they interact will be familiar with such material.

Managers have different information time horizons (past, present, future). So, the managerial accountant will also consider both the operational and strategic aspects for the short medium and long-term, as part of giving a range of options. Operational information deals with today and this period. Operational information is used to answer such key questions as

- How are we going to satisfy customer orders?
- How do we get the raw materials (for manufacturing, mining or construction), inventory (for merchandising) or labor (for services)?
- How can we improve efficiency?
- How can we reduce costs?
- How can we maximize profitability?
- How do outperform our competitors?

Strategic information refers to information that enables the organization to plan ahead for five or more years. Specifically, strategic information is intended to give competitive advantage to the organization. This information is therefore an amalgamation of separate streams or sources of information, most of which will be sourced externally from the organization.

The clearest guide to strategic information was given by Peter Drucker (1964) who emphasized that strategy was mainly about opportunities and to do that it was necessary to have information about opportunities that were additive (more fully exploiting existing resources), complementary (something new which can be combined with the existing business), and breakthrough (which changes the fundamental economic characteristics of the business). Strategic information is used to answer such key questions as

- Who will be our future customers?
- How will we reach those customers? (What channels will be used?)
- What do we need to do no to be ready for our new business direction?
- What is likely to go wrong with our plans?
- How is customer value incorporated in the price set and communicated? (Simon, 2015)

Table 4–4 gives an indication of the information that is operational and strategic.

The managerial accountant will closely link the time horizon of information with decision making. One reason is their concern with cause and effect. Many outputs or outcomes such as growth of the organization, increased shareholder value for owners, and greater market share result from improved products and services for customers. Therefore, in considering the types of information required, the managerial accountant will want to get as wide a range of information available as possible to get early (weak) signals about looming problems and opportunities. This is explored in Part III on decision making.

The final dimension is evaluation versus prediction. Much information collected and analyzed in the organization is for evaluation. It makes costs visible and is used in assessing control or governance. Information can also

Table 4–4 Information time horizon for operational and strategic information.

	Strategic	Operational	Impact on Stakeholders
Reason for the information	Converts the mission statement, which is a broad vision, into specific plans and projects that can be measured	Implements the strategic vision into specific and measurable short-term targets, for example, day, week, fortnight, month	Most stakeholders are reliant on general purpose reports, although creditors may be able to obtain specific reports as a condition of providing resources.
Time horizon	2–5 years and longer	Typically, monthly aggregation to year	Most stakeholders will expect their information at the same interval as financial statement reporting, that is, half yearly with continuous disclosure.
Organizational focus	Organization-wide (often called the strategic business unit)	Functional unit	Organizations will be reluctant to release detailed information to stakeholders owing to its value to competitors. Segment reporting may be used.
Source of information	Mostly external to the organization	Entirely and directly from inside the organization and its individual functional units	Organization will need to officially release information. Usually in conjunction with financial statements.

(Continued)

Table 4–4 (Continued)

	Strategic	Operational	Impact on Stakeholders
Types of information	National (government) reported figures such as inflation, employment and consumer confidence Key indicators on market share, market growth, margin and raw material (input) costs	Production and sales volume in units Costs, revenue and profit in financial terms Variances between budget and actual performance	Stakeholders will expect financial and non-financial information. Information will be aggregated, although some specific information may be provided for locations or projects.
Users	Board Senior management team	Individual managers and supervisors	Some tailoring to stakeholders is likely to be necessary owing to their particular interests or power.
Uses of the information	Setting direction based on socioeconomic trends and expected competitor actions	Compare actual achievements to the short-term targets	Stakeholders may use the information to assess the market as well as to challenge the organization on its achievements or failings.
Major documents and reports	Strategic plan Financial statements Forward estimates Program and project plans	Budget Capital budget Weekly and monthly production/sales reports Quality assurance report	Stakeholders will use both financial statements and supplementary information provided by the organization, as well as seek information from other formal parties (e.g., regulators) and informal parties (e.g., non-profit advocacy bodies).

be used for prediction. It attempts to shape expectations and considers user needs. These are closely associated with the methods for analysis. Many are based around the financial statements either directly or recast as common-size and use trend analysis, ratio analysis, indices, percentage change measures, and benchmark figures to consider cash flow and performance. The managerial can use these as well as specific statistical analyses for costing and activities, but this will involve making a choice between summarized information or detail that requires aggregation and integration of information.

4.5   Aggregating and Integrating Information

The managerial accountant aggregates and integrates information to present information that delivers greater value than its components possess individually. The managerial accountant will always attempt to combine information to increase confidence and detect apparent anomalies. Five forms of aggregation are common:

1. Aggregating to give the 'bigger picture'. This may occur where totals are lacking or are unreliable. Estimates may be formed from proxy data. For example, imported volumes may be added to internal volume and estimated competitor volume.
2. Triangulating to use multiple sources of information to 'fill-in the gaps' or make sense of phenomena. For example, unexpectedly low Christmas sales may be explained by external factors such as low consumer confidence and predicted interest rate increases when competitors experienced a similar downturn.
3. Combining existing information to create meaningful new measures. This may use existing data or be the prelude for advanced statistical analysis. For example, an organization that decides to use the DuPont return on equity measure will assemble information for its three different dimensions (operating efficiency, asset use efficiency and financial leverage).
4. Aggregation to produce new, high level summary measures. Typically, these are averages, indexes or ratios. For example, the average customer order value in dollars or the gross sales per employee.
5. Aggregation to present different information together. Many summary reports contain line items that do not have an arithmetic or logical relationship but are simply presented together for convenience and ease of review. For example, Kaplan and Norton (2001) suggest that the Balanced Scorecard should be connected with strategic objectives in a cause-and-effect relationship. This leads to a hierarchical balanced score card that is cascaded down through the levels of the organization so that managers are all being measured in relation to the highest level strategic objectives.

In addition to adding value to information by aggregating and integrating information, the managerial accountant can make recommendations to improve systems and processes associated with capture and use and storage of the information. These may make information more valuable in the future through revealing new correlations or trends.

Detailed examples are provided in Table 4–5, which also groups the information grouped by the method showing that different information is needed to fulfill different purposes or goals. Frequently, both appear in routine and ad hoc reports used by managers throughout the organization. Mostly, information is provided in the form of reports, schedules and statements. Other forms may be just as important, if not more important. For

Table 4–5 Types of information (financial and non-financial) sub-grouped by source (financial statements), other internal routine and ad hoc reports and separated by method (making costs visible, improving performance, evaluating performance, and creating and capturing strategic value).

Method	Type of Information		
	Financial		Non-financial
	Financial Statements	Other Reports and Including Internal	Routine and Ad Hoc Reports
Quantitative — Making cost visible	• Cost of goods sold ($) • Raw materials and consumables used ($) • Selling, general and administrative expenses ($) • Employee benefits expense ($) • Non-cash expenses, for example, depreciation and amortization ($)	• Contribution margin ($) • Direct labor rate ($ per hour) • Cost of quality ($) • Reduction in cost base ($) • Cost allocation base rate as a labor rate ($)	• Cost allocation base (e.g., machine hours) • Product mix (units) • Sales (units) • Inventory (units) • Effective income tax rate (%) • Productivity (e.g., number of deliveries) • Customers (number) • Common sizing of financial statement • Regression equation • Customer satisfaction (e.g., faults per 1,000 units)
Quantitative — Improving performance	• Cash and cash equivalents ($) • Assets ($) • Liabilities ($) • Equity ($) • Issued capital ($) • Revenue ($) • Other income ($) • Distribution costs ($) • Gross profit before tax ($) • Reserves ($) • Net income after tax ($)	• Product selling price ($) • Operating income ($) • Accounts receivable ($) • Market share ($) • Sensitivity ($) • Employee productivity ($) • Warranty costs • Financial analysis ratios (e.g., liquidity)	• Setup time (hours/batch) • Allocation base rate as units (e.g., machine hours; units of production output; direct labor hours, direct materials usage) • Breakeven point (e.g., units) • Batches (number) • Machine hours • Direct labor hours • Raw materials (e.g., weight in kilograms) • Product and segment proportion (%)

Method	Type of Information		
	Financial		Non-financial
	Financial Statements	Other Reports and Including Internal	Routine and Ad Hoc Reports
Evaluating performance	• Property, plant and equipment ($) • Investment assets ($) • Trade and other receivables ($)	• Financial budget ($) • Infrastructure budget ($) • Variance ($)	• Production budget (units) • Variance (units)
Creating and Capturing value	• Share price ($) • Financial performance trends for a 5-year period ($)	• Strategic outcomes ($) • Customer preference/demand ($)	• Customer satisfaction/loyalty (%) • Brand awareness (%)
Making costs visible *Qualitative*	• Grade (e.g., excessive, within tolerance or lean)	• Costs versus sales (proportion)	• Cost pattern (e.g., direct, indirect) • Cost behavior (variable, fixed or mixed)
Improving performance	• Financial performance or profitability rating (e.g., high, medium or low)	• Financial value risk of the organizational evaluation (e.g., large, medium or small) • Price point (e.g., high, medium or low)	• Standard operating procedures • Corporate culture • Employee morale • Organization chart and organizational unit names • Job or position title • Employee knowledge • Employee co-operation

(Continued)

Table 4–5 (Continued)

Method		Type of Information		
		Financial		**Non-financial**
		Financial Statements	*Other Reports and Including Internal*	*Routine and Ad Hoc Reports*
Evaluating performance		• Financial control (flagged items) • GAAP applied to transactions	• Financial accreditation • Valued assets (list) • Reliability of financial records (validation)	• Responsibility centers • Risk management objectives • Compliance with legislation provisions • Terms and conditions • Security arrangements for protection of assets
Creating and capturing value		• Strategic plan	• Goals • Intangible value • Perceived synergies	• Innovation • Long-term advantage • Brand name(s) and product/service reputation • Strategic vision statement • Urgency for action

Note on abbreviations:

A $ symbol indicates a monetary measurement. A % symbol indicates a measurement by percentage or proportion. Other descriptors shown in parentheses after the entry indicate measurement of units or a count by number.

example, one form of information is stories. Stories are valued by managers and employees because they embody values and describe consequences associated with planning, or setting goals, and devising methods to achieve those goals as well as how implementation is monitored and discrepancies between expected and actual performance are judged. Stories show that financial and non-financial information can be effectively combined.

The managerial accountant will recognize that the information needs of non-accounting managers and employees cannot be collapsed into a simple summary. The diverse of information required should be explored in terms of time, financial or non-financial, and attributes or properties. Table 4–6 uses time focus to identify seven broad financial information needs of managers. There is no column showing the kind of report where this information is likely to be found as a relational database system can make data available in many different reports at different levels of detail. Instead the common sources of information are identified to suggest where the information originates.

Table 4–6 Seven broad financial information needs of managers matched with common sources of information and the time focus.

Broad Information Need	Focus	Dimension	Time Period (day, month, quarter, 6 months, year)	Source of Financial and Non-financial Information
Compliance	Statutory reporting and penalties	Lodgment compliance Process quality assurance Infringement detection	Past (last and corresponding period, previous 5 financial years)	Internal controls Management control system External audit
Project and initiatives	Services	Schedule Quality Cost	Past (last and corresponding period) Future (short term and long term)	Project reports General ledger
Organization value	Pricing	Market value (if listed) Notional pricing (if unlisted)	Past (last and corresponding period) Future (short term and long term)	Public announcements Subscription and consulting reports
Profitability	Current and prospective	Sales revenue Cash takings	Past (last and corresponding period) Future (short term)	Transactions Bank statements

(Continued)

Table 4–6 (Continued)

Broad Information Need	Focus	Dimension	Time Period (day, month, quarter, 6 months, year)	Source of Financial and Non-financial Information
Risk	Financial	Solvency and leverage	Current (short term) Future (short term and long term)	Bank statements Lender obligations (contract) Balance sheet assets
	Business	Reliance on product range Reliance on customer base Dependence on innovation Vulnerability to competition	Current (short term) Future (short term and long term)	Sales ledger Debtors ledger Customer surveys Competitor intelligence
Return on investment	Within the organization	Bond earnings Hurdle rates	Past (last financial year, previous 5 financial years) Future (short term and long term)	Internal calculations Industry benchmarks Economic data
	Compared to alternatives	Bond earnings Hurdle rates	Past (last financial year, previous 5 financial years) Future (short term and long term)	Internal calculations Industry benchmarks Economic data
Return to owners	Drawings	Amount and frequency	Past (last financial year, previous 5 financial years) Future (short term and long term)	Requests Ledger

4.6   Properties or Attributes of Information

Managerial accountants need to judge the quality of information they gather and use because users and recipients of information provided by the managerial accountant will also assess it. This view from quality management is the degree to which information meets their needs. The quality of information can be judged by its attributes. The attributes of data are also known as characteristics (English, 1999) and dimensions (Wang & Strong, 1996). However, according to the *Oxford English Dictionary*, attributes are also known as properties or qualities. There are many potential attributes and many classifications of attributes. Two hierarchical classifications are discussed as they provide two different groupings of attributes that emphasize different aspects of the information:

1. Qualitative characteristics that are oriented to primary users of financial statements
2. Four-way classification oriented to the type of information

Other classifications use different category names or combinations (e.g., Laranjeiro, Soydemir & Bernardino, 2015), but the Accounting Conceptual Framework (2006, Chapter 3) with its description of the qualitative characteristics of useful financial information is a useful starting point because it divides them into fundamental and enhancing characteristics. The fundamental characteristics support the full disclosure of economic phenomena to assist users make resources allocation decisions for the information to be useful. This implies ethical accounting practices performed by ethical accountants, which is explored in Chapter 10. Verrecchia (1983) shows that knowing information is withheld results in conjectures about its content and reason for omission. The usefulness of information that is relevant and faithfully represented is enhanced if it possesses the qualitative characteristics of comparability, verifiability, timeliness and understandability. Table 4–7 summarizes the attributes stated in the Conceptual Framework.

The Accounting Conceptual Framework recognizes there are constraints with information. The major constraint is cost. Decision-useful information imposes costs on providing financial information that include:

*   Collecting information
*   Processing information
*   Verifying information
*   Disseminating information

The benefits of providing information should outweigh costs, and this principle is incorporated in the managerial accountant's compass. The managerial accountant may need to sacrifice one or more enhancing qualitative characteristics where it is essential to reduce the cost of collecting and presenting information provided the fundamental characteristics are unaffected. Costs can be understated by using untested assumptions, unproven or incorrect methods, estimates without insights into uncertainties that discount risk, or costs from early analyses before details of the scope and effort have been established (Oliver & Walker, 2006). A cost

Table 4-7 Summary of the attributes and their detail from the Conceptual Framework with examples.

Attribute		Detail	Examples
Fundamental	Relevance	Predictive value	• Develop expectations about the future • Maintain or expand current level of operations • Repay debt • Pay dividends in the future • Amount, timing and uncertainty of future cash flows
		Confirmatory value	• Confirms or contests past or present expectations • Provides feedback to help users assess accuracy of past predictions and decisions especially of operating activities • Ratio analysis helps make decisions about resource allocation (e.g., liquidity and solvency)
	Faithful representation	Complete	• Depicts the economic substance of the transactions, events or circumstances • Economic substance is not the same as legal form
		Neutral (unbiased)	• Not intended to adduce a particular behavior or result • Allows judgments and estimates in conditions of uncertainty provided inputs are the best available information at the time
		Free from material error	• Materiality sets a threshold • Rounding • Expensing small expenditures of non-current assets

	Attribute	Detail	Examples
Enhancing	Comparability	To facilitate identification of similarities and difference between economic phenomena to make resource allocation decisions	• Two or more pieces of information • Between different years of the same organization or between different companies • Requires check of same or consistent accounting principles and methods
	(Independent) Verifiability	Direct verification Indirect verification	• Classifying, characterizing and presenting information clearly and concisely (without simplifying) • Use appropriate recognition and measurement methods
	Timeliness	Available before it ceases to be relevant so is still capable of influencing decisions	• Encourages efficient capture/collection and preparation • 'Latest' information is task dependent. • Some information remains timely beyond the reporting period (e.g., used for trends).
	Under-standability	By a proficient use (reasonable knowledge of business and economic activities)	• Still capable of influencing the decisions users make based on the information • Classifying, characterizing and presenting information clearly and concisely will aid understanding

should always be substantiated and where uncertain stated as a range of values. The same caveats apply to calculating benefits.

A four-way classification is proposed by Wang and Strong (1996, Appendix D) for analyzing information. It covers the same attributes discussed by others (e.g., H. Miller, 1996; Strong, Lee & Wang, 1997; Parker, Moleshe, De la Harpe & Wills, 2006) for traditional and internet communications. However, it too uses a hierarchy to group the information attributes. Table 4–8 uses four features of the information.

Table 4–8 Information attributes (also known as properties, dimensions or qualities).

	Information Attribute	Explanation	Broad Impact on Managerial Accounting Decisions
Intrinsic	Accuracy	Degree of correctness and precision with which information represents states of the real world	Information may need to be independently verified.
	Objectivity	Degree to which it is unbiased, unprejudiced or impartial	Depends upon the choice of source
	Believability	Degree to which information is accepted as true, real or credible	Depends upon content and source
	Reputation	Degree to which information is trusted or highly regarded	Depends upon the content and source
Context	Relevancy	Degree to which information is applicable and helpful for the task at hand	Information may be relevant but lacks other attributes
	Value added	Degree to which information is applicable and helpful	Depends on the task or purpose
	Timeliness	Degree to which information is up-to-date and has not been delayed	Depends upon the specific task
	Completeness	Degree to which information is not missing	Completeness may require different levels of detail

	Information Attribute	Explanation	Broad Impact on Managerial Accounting Decisions
Context (*continued*)	Amount	Degree to which quantity or volume is appropriate	Depends upon the availability of information
Representation	Interpretability	Degree to which information is in appropriate language and units	Depends upon information definitions conform to standards
	Understanding	Degree to which information is clear without ambiguity	Comprehension assisted by clarity
	Consistency (Format)	Form considers the recipient and their use. Frame is the context for interpretation.	Proven or agreed formats will assist communication, aiding comprehension and expediting a response.
	Concise	Degree to which information is compact without being overwhelming	Completeness and brevity go together
Accessibility	Accessibility	Degree to which information is available, easily obtainable or quickly retrievable when needed	Knowledge of its availability and capability to acquire it require efficient systems.
	Security	Degree to which information is protected from intentional and unintentional human acts	Interception by any intelligent opponent may reduce its value or allow undue advantage to be gained.

Table 4–8 gives a total of 15 attributes. This emphasizes that managers use many factors to judge whether the information provided by the managerial accountant is satisfactory. The production of information consumes precious resources it may not be possible to optimize satisfaction with all attributes. The managerial accountant will also appreciate that the attributes are related. A delay may occur before accurate information is produced reducing its timeliness, or accessibility may limit the information considered. The managerial accountant must make trade-offs and advise the recipient (manager) what trade-offs have been made and how they affect the usefulness of the information provided. In some cases, these trade-offs concern source documents.

4.7   Use Source Documents for Costing and Control

The managerial accountant has a long preoccupation with making use of records (e.g., Ashton, 1925).[5] An accounting source document (or more often, source document) is the original record containing the details that substantiate a transaction entered in an accounting system. That is, it evidences economic dealing has occurred. There may be more than one source document necessary to support transaction. For example, purchase of merchandise requires the supplier's invoice supported by the receiving organization's purchase order and a receiving ticket. Accounting source documents are required for

- Verifying transactions (e.g., on a month-to-month basis)
- Any financial audit (e.g., end-of-year financial statement sign-off by the auditor)
- Satisfying the regulatory requirements (e.g., taxation)

The source documents for common economic events are listed in Table 4–9. They are an original and objective report of the economic activity represented by a transaction. Usually there are several source documents associated with a transaction, so internal control should identify all the source documents; otherwise there is the possibility of fraud. For example, manufacturing issues a single purchase requisition for the raw materials it needs to complete its job-orders for the next period. However, some of those raw materials are used each day and therefore each allocation for the day requires a separate source document. Source documents are sometimes referred to as the 'paper trail'. A paper or 'electronic' trail gives a step-by-step documented history of a transaction. It enables an auditor to trace the financial information from general ledger to the source document (e.g., invoice, receipt, voucher, ticket). The presence of a reliable and easy to follow audit trail is an indicator that internal controls exist for source documents.

A source document includes some basic particulars about the transaction. So ideally, the source document usually contains the following information:

- Name and address of the organization selling the product (or service)
- Date of the transaction and sometimes the time
- Type of transaction (sale, refund, deposit)
- Description of a business transaction (e.g., product and quantity)
- A specific amount of money in numerals (e.g., $1,201.57)
- To whom the transaction was made (organization and any representing individual)

- Amount of any taxes
- Any of the special terms and conditions of the transaction (e.g., discount, payment and delivery details)
- An authorizing signature or equivalent confirmation for payment or acceptance of product or services

Table 4–9 Source documents for economic events.

Economic Event	Source Document	Possible Use by Managerial Accountant
Cash received by the organization	Cash receipt, cash register tapes, bank statement, bank deposit form	Understand banking efficiency using Bank Deposit form. The original is provided to the bank with the copy retained by the organization.
Cash paid by the business	Check (cheque) butt ATM or EFTPOS receipt Bank statement Payroll records Canceled check (cheque)	Sales receipt efficiency in recording product or service payment from customer. The original goes to the customer with the copy held by the organization. Purchase receipt efficiency in recording product or payment by the organization to suppliers. The original is provided by the supplier to the organization.
Organization gives credit to customer.	Sales invoice Credit note Debit note	Sales invoice efficiency in recording product or service details and the amount owing to the organization by a customer. The original goes to the customer with the copy held by the organization. Credit note controls when correcting an overcharge on an invoice (e.g., making an adjustment for goods not supplied), or accepting goods returned with or without restocking fee. Debit note controls when correct an undercharge in the invoice.
Organization receives credit from a supplier.	Supplier's original invoice Supplier's statement, Supplier's debit note Supplier's credit note Credit card receipt Credit card statement	Purchase invoice efficiency in recording product or service details and the amount owned by the organization to suppliers. The original is provided by the supplier to the organization. Supplier's statement efficiency stating invoices unpaid at a particular date are within credit terms and/or settlement discounts. Credit card receipts efficiency and control over transactions on a credit card supported by a periodic statement.

Accounting source documents to substantiate a transaction come in many different forms depending upon the transaction.[6] Table 4–10 identifies source document by common transaction with users.

Occasionally, no source document is available. This may occur where the transaction does not generate a source document (e.g., depreciation). In those cases, the managerial accountant will create a memorandum or worksheet, which is then authorized (or counter-signed) by a more senior accountant. The second possibility is that the source document is not received (e.g., an invoice is lost in the mail). Here the solution is to request a replacement (duplicate). Some organizations require source documents (e.g., petty cash claims) to be supported by written document, known as a voucher, which requires a certification from who incurred the expenditure that it was for organizational purposes as well as describing the expenditure.

The source documents for the different cost assignments are listed in Table 4–11. Usually job-order cost accounting requires that records are kept for each job order. That is, details will be kept of raw materials used, labor and overheads for each job order. There is some flexibility in the recording. For example, some organizations still use the individual job documents described in Table 4–11 to authorize the release of materials for production. Other organizations prefer a summary sheet where details are recorded on multiple lines. For example, the time sheet records labor over a period of a week and after authorization by the supervisor, then go to the pay clerk for payment. Yet other organizations have two systems, where one document records the total amount for the effort (e.g., the employee time sheet shows their hours for the pay week), and there are other documents which are specific to the job (e.g., the employee fills out a ticket for each job order showing the number of hours worked on that job during the shift for the day). The managerial accountant often finds that many different but overlapping systems have germinated in an organization. Careful investigation may explain why different costs are available for the same cost object.

The managerial accountant uses a wide variety of source documents to obtain information for cost analyses and related purposes. In designing processes, or entire systems, the managerial accountant will investigate whether source documents can be combined or eliminated.[8] The managerial accountant will also use source documents to discover whether they are being listed in non-value-adding registers or compiled into non-value-adding reports. Registers are often a sign that documents can be lost but do not prevent the loss. Reports also often proliferate in numbers and complexity to satisfy power or status needs, or as a reaction to a previous loss or failing. As always, the main question the managerial accountant will ask is, 'What does the manager do as a result of getting information?'. Preliminary answers may suggest that source documents should

Table 4-10 Source document used to substantiate common transactions with common users.

User	Transaction	Source Document	Managerial Accountant's Uses
Investor	Share issue	Stock (share) holding certificate	Proper recording in the accounting system where there are systems and processing concerns
	Dividend	Dividend check (cheque) Dividend statement	
Creditor	Bank deposit	Bank deposit slips/forms Check (cheque) canceled Check (cheque) stubs Bank statements	Proper recording in the accounting system where cash flows need investigation
	Borrowings	Notes (unsecured, debenture)	
Customer	Quote	Price and availability quote	Proper recording in the accounting system where there are inventory or stock quantity discrepancies
	Sale for cash	Receipts for goods purchased with cash Receipts for cash received Cash register tapes	
	Sale on credit	Sales invoice Credit card receipts	
	Dispatch of product	Packing (dispatch) slip Consignment note/shipping document	
Supplier	Order	Purchase invoices Credit note/ invoice	Proper recording in the accounting system where there are costing concerns
	Purchase on credit	Credit card receipts Suppliers invoices Suppliers statements Good received slip	
	Dispatch of product	Packing (dispatch) slip Consignment note/shipping document	
Employee	See Table 4-11.		

Table 4–11 Source document for the different cost assignments.

Cost Assignment	Source Document	Explanation
Direct materials	Materials requisition record showing • Part number • Description • Actual quantity supplied • Actual unit cost • Actual total cost	Cost of materials supplied to a specific organizational unit
Direct labor	Labor time sheet showing • Employee name • Specific tasks/jobs • Time spent (hours and minutes)	Usually weekly showing time spent on jobs and time spent on general duties (e.g., cleaning, maintenance, training)
Manufacturing overhead	• Budget for normal costs* • Standard costs* *Based on prior year transaction totals	Cost allocation bases and cost drivers guide the identification of costs.
For job orders	Job cost record AKA job cost sheet • Direct material • Direct labor • Manufacturing overhead	Accumulates all costs for a specific job
Selling costs*	• Payroll records for commissions and bonuses paid • Invoices for advertising purchased • Expense claims approved for promotions and other events	There may also be transport invoices for product promotions.
Administrative costs*	• Payroll records for service and support employees including head office employees • Operating lease or loan repayment records for vehicles and invoices for their running costs • Rental, lease or loan repayment records for premises • Invoices from councils for property rates • Invoices from utilities for water, gas and electricity	
General costs*	Approved worksheets for depreciation and corresponding journals and postings	These should be subject to internal audit checks

* Under activity-based costing, the four-category cost hierarchy (unit level costs, batch level costs, product sustaining costs and facility sustaining costs) will be substituted for the selling, general[7] and administrative costs.

be redesigned to at least avoid overlap, or ideally, reduce the amount of information collected. Before this occurs, the output should also be considered.

4.8 Communicating With Output Documents: Report, Statement, Schedule or Proposal

Accounts produce an infinite number of outputs, some to prescribed formats, but many are the left to the judgment of the individual accountant. The managerial accountant communicates in writing and orally using numbers, words and diagrams and has done so for a hundred years (Garner, 1947). Minto (2010) suggests all writing can be improved by a three-step approach (1) state the situation, (2) describe what makes the situation less than the ideal, and (3) answer how it can be fixed providing supporting evidence. The managerial accountant who adopts this approach to communication can communicate effectively and simply to gain understanding and persuade acceptance by non-accounting managers.

In managerial accounting, the word 'statement' tends to be reserved for making a declaration of something to be true or correct. Managerial accounting also uses the four common financial accounting statements[9] to use past performance to create forecasts and make estimates. In managerial accounting, the word 'report' tends to be reserved for written records or summary directed at someone in authority who will make a decision and identifies the issue and explains it. In managerial accounting, the word 'schedule' is a list of amounts and balances by period, which is then summarized in other reports or statements. A proposal is a document written to a manager, board or committee to assist them make a decision on expenditure or investment to benefit an organizational unit or activity. It is usually persuasive and explanatory as there are usually competing proposals. But there is no hard and fast rule that distinguishes them. So, documents can be labeled 'report', 'statement' or 'schedule'. They cannot be distinguished on the basis of their production for the reader to make operational decisions and strategy decisions.

Most managerial accounting reports allow non-accounting managers to monitor performance throughout an accounting period.[10] As noted earlier, information is time sensitive, so reports may be sought quarterly, monthly, weekly or even daily to allocate resources or ensure react quickly to competitor actions. A broad categorization of tabular reports[11] used by the managerial accountant is given below as an introduction.

- The income statement, or more strictly the operating income statement, lists all revenues generated and expenses incurred by an organization or an organizational unit. This report is the most important report available to managers, as it shows the profit or loss generated by the organization's operations.[12]

- Cost reports show expenses for products. They may be a job-cost report for a batch of the product or job order as well as reports for specific costs such as prime cost, conversion cost, manufacturing cost report, non-manufacturing costs report, quality cost report, cost of goods manufactured (statement or schedule), cost of goods sold (statement or schedule) an, a contribution margin income (statement or schedule). Or, it may be a process cost where continuous product is produced (e.g., oil, fuel). Cost reports allow analysis of expenses, while the product (or a project) is in progress so managers can correct areas of waste before costs escalate. They may also show total costs and unit costs.

- Inventory report is produced where an organization has a physical inventory that it holds for sale. Inventory reports show usage, stock levels, obsolescence, damage and shrinkage. Inventory reports can draw attention to the costs incurred by ordering inventory as well as associated costs for storage (warehousing), distribution and readying for sale (e.g., inspection, cleaning).

- Procurement reports (in both manufacturing and merchandising) can identify cost of raw materials, shortages, usage and waste. The information may indicate excess holdings as well as stockouts to enable costs to be determined.

- Labor cost reports provide costs for both labor and overhead costs. This enables comparison of labor costs in assembly lines, factories, branches or shops within the organization to identify improvements or give rewards for meeting specific financial performance goals.

- Budget reports can be used organization-wide and at various organizational unit levels by managers and supervisors to analyze actual revenue and expenses for a time period. Comparison to prior years and budgeted amounts gives a difference (variance) and gives insight into the expected day-to-day operations.

- Sales reports are useful in their own right as well as to match with production (for manufacturing) or inventory (for merchandising). This helps identify higher-earning products or branches in the organization with potential for further improvement as well as low-profit margin products and branches where effort should also be focused.

- For businesses which sell on credit, an Accounts Receivable Aging report is a critical tool for managing cash flow. This report ages the customer balances by how long they have been owed, typically current, 30 days late, 60 days late and 90 days late, or more. A manager can use the aging report to determine if a particular customer, customer group or all customers are outside the organization's collection (payment) policy. The accounts receivable aging may also highlight whether debt collection is adequate.

In preparing reports, the managerial accountant will ascertain whether information that reports strategic direction and day-to-day operations will also be used to evaluate operational performance. If so, it is likely that operational managers will change their behavior possibly with harmful effects on the organization. The behavioral consequences of information are discussed as part of decision making in Chapter 7.

4.9 Limitations of Information

Information by itself is meaningless. As noted in Chapter 3, it is part of discourse, so information does not stand by itself. Even if the preparer is not present, their role and responsibility for preparing the report is always salient. The circumstances of the organization and the manager's own organizational unit act as a frame of perception guiding interpretation (Goffman, 1974) and even revealing propensity for taking risks (Kahneman & Tversky, 1984). In addition, the organizational incentives influence their understanding and action. So, the managerial accountant will realize they cannot expect the information they present to be understood the same way they do. It is necessary to important to be selective in choosing a source, qualify the information, anticipate questions and provide a guiding interpretation. Even so, the information itself often has three limitations. It may rely on non-uniform measures and bases compromising comparability. Second, the information may be incomplete or only available for limited periods, so it has gaps. Third, it may have been originally collected for other purposes, so it may use non-standard definitions or approaches, which affect its quality. Therefore, the aggregation and integration may be superficially credible.

The managerial accountant will also want to respect any confidentiality and security issues that arise from either the volume of data or the sensitivity of so much data across the organization being available in one place. There may also be privacy issues, so the information should be stripped of all identifying elements (e.g., name, address, age). This can be partially overcome by allowing summary figures to be investigated. This is known as 'drill-down' capability. It ensures the integrity of the information preserved because the same underlying data used in the calculation is then made available for inspection and verification. The managerial accountant will also apply continuous learning to their provision of information, so they can make improvements to its attributes bearing in mind its fundamental qualitative characteristics.

4.10 Conclusion on the Use of Information in the Managerial Accountant's Compass

The role and responsibility of the managerial accountant is selecting, analyzing, presenting and communicating information to non-accounting managers. The value-adding processes give the managerial accountant criteria for anticipating the potential value that a non-accounting manager will see in the information and therefore the kind of assistance they can provide that will be well regarded by the non-accounting manager. A major responsibility is providing quantitative (financial and non-financial) information, balanced with qualitative information in either routine output documents or customized documents. Because the managerial accountant is across the organization, they can view information as multi-dimensional. The six dimensions are paired as quantitative versus qualitative, operational versus strategic, external versus internal, primary versus secondary, time horizon (past, present, future), and evaluation versus prediction. This requires the managerial accountant to select information from a wide pool and justify those choices. In addition, they are responsible for aggregating and integrating information. In doing this, the managerial accountant must be aware of the limitations of information as well as reflect on the way it is likely to be used. To do this requires understanding of its properties or attributes, to fulfill the further responsibility of ensuring the information meets the needs of its audience who are usually non-accounting managers and employees. Much of the output prepared by the managerial accountant uses source documents to obtain costing and control information. These too have limitations and the non-accounting manager may not be aware of them. This may necessitate them providing a 'walk through' of the figures and their meaning.

With the review of resources available to the managerial accountant complete, the next part contains three chapters: role and responsibilities (Chapter 5), critical success factors (Chapter 6), and decisions (Chapter 7). Chapter 5 identifies the role and responsibilities, abilities and skills of the managerial accountant.

Notes

1. 'Information' is conceptually distinguished from 'data' to emphasize that recipients make meaning from what they read, see or hear (the data) by processing, organizing, synthesizing or structuring them. Data are the symbols, numbers, diagrams and images (still and/or video), which are the representation of stimuli and the content of communication (Zins, 2007). Similarly, knowledge is the combination of understanding, experience, skill, expertise or capability that resides in an individual and is tacit (Polanyi, 1966) or may be expressed explicitly as propositions or procedurally. Many discussions suggest they can be arranged in a hierarchy (e.g., Ackoff, 1989), but this fails to recognize the personal nature of knowledge.
2. A template is a calculation set out in rows and columns, which have headings (or captions) on columns and labels for rows.
3. The bullet notebook is a system of rapid logging (Carrol, 2018). It uses five modules: titles (topic), monthlies, dailies, future and collections. It has an index that links them. It uses bullets to arrange any bullet point into one of three categories (task, event or note).
4. Common methods are by location, alphabet, time, category and hierarchy, but this overlooks the process that is responsible for creating value.

5. Managerial accounting was pioneered in mercantile, textile and railway organizations. Mercantile operations required internal accounting for the purchase or trading of commodities and their eventual conversion into saleable products that were subsequently transported to major markets in cities in Europe. Coordination and decentralization required improved information (e.g., Spraakman, 1999). Textile mills used raw materials and labor to make fabrics. Internal accounting was used to assess the efficiency with which they used their inputs (e.g., Gourvish, 1972; Tyson, 1992). Railways required significant investments of capital over long periods of time for the construction of the permanent way (track) suitable for carrying freight. Once operational, they handled large volumes of cash receipts from numerous customers and required internal accounting systems to measure efficiency for moving freight and passengers (e.g., Previts & Samson, 1999–2000).

6. Clarke and Dean (2007: 9) identify an accounting standards shortcoming: the mistaken proposition is that "uniformity of . . . input and processing rules would produce uniform, comparable financial statements".

7. General expenses are operating expenses other than those specifically identified as cost of goods sold, selling and administration expenses.

8. Breadmore (1971: 76–77) suggests there are four generally applicable rules for work reduction, which should govern any approach to problem solving. In order they are eliminate the entire activity under investigation or failing that, as much of it as possible, simplify to remove non-essential aspects, combine forms, activities, jobs to avoid duplication and lastly, automate or mechanize.

9. The four reports are variously named depending upon country and the accounting standard. Revenues, expenses and profits/losses generated during the reporting period appear in the statement of income (USA) or profit and loss (Europe). The assets, liabilities and equity of the entity as of the reporting date are in the balance sheet (USA, Europe) or statement of financial position (Australia). The statement of cash flow outlines the cash inflows and outflows that occurred during the reporting period. Changes in equity during the reporting period are in the statement of retained earnings (USA) or owners' equity (UK, Australia). Simplified reporting applies to small organizations in some countries where lodgment is with the taxation office (Europe).

10. Breadmore (1971: 54) comments on measurement that the three problems with counting are the following: What to count? How to count? When to stop counting? This overlooks the other important question: How often? He recommends counting all the kinds of useful information in a painstaking way on the grounds that the characteristics sought may not be immediately apparent. How to count should be preceded by paper and pencil design to determine feasibility. It is impractical to sample everything, and options from employees can be unreliable so to ensure accuracy of a result statistical sampling should be used after calculating the standard error to determine either the level or error or the number of items to sample (depending upon how values are substituted into the formula) using the formula standard error as a percentage .

11. Graphical reports were very common for many aspects of costs in production systems in the 1940s and 1950s. A variety of examples is provided in Lang (1958) indicating pre-computerisation formats.

12. Weil (2005) shows how alternative accounting treatments of identical economic events can allow different reported income.

Part III

Insights From the Managerial Accountant's Role, Performance, Decisions and Judgments

5 Role, Responsibilities and Personal Qualities of the Managerial Accountant That Inform the Managerial Accountant's Compass

The role or function and responsibilities or tasks or duties of the managerial accountant inform the managerial accountant's compass by highlighting the range of concerns and actions. Professions that control a body of expert knowledge enable its members to charge high prices when assisting a client. Recent studies suggest three possible directions for professions in the twenty-first century. One is that technology may augment professional abilities allowing them to work faster and more thoroughly (Leicht & Fennell, 2001). Or, technology may develop artificial intelligence, which can do the same work better and cheaper (Susskind & Susskind, 2015). Finally, technology may use large datasets that make diagnoses or predict outcomes, thus reducing the need for professional assistance (e.g., Remus & Levy, 2016). Of course, technology has already intruded on routine work with intended and unintended consequences, including reducing the numbers of professionals employed. The implication for the managerial accountant is that they should reflect on how the application and diffusion of technology affects them in terms of their duties (role and responsibilities) and personal qualities (skills and abilities) and how their profession has changed (Langfield-Smith, 2008). (The following chapter addresses the issue of performance and control.)

Managerial accountants could also be described as chief intelligence officers because, apart from senior management, perhaps no one else knows more about the various functions of the organization. The managerial accountant plays a significant role in the decision-making process of an organization, whether by preparing information, validating it, interpreting it or implementing it. They are responsible for the installation, development and efficient functioning of the managerial accounting system and the framework of the performance reports that provide timely and meaningful information about organizational processes and outcomes. Irrespective of their level in the organization, the managerial accountant is competent in framing and asking questions, and suggesting answers. However, as Hall (2010) observes, managers may use the knowledge of the managerial accountant to understand the organization rather than as an input to a specific decision. These different information needs are vary at the different levels of managerial accountant.

5.1   Distinguishing Levels of Organizational Duties From Personal Qualities

The work of the managerial accountant is set out at three broad levels: (1) entry level, (2) intermediate level and (3) senior level. The entry level describes any gender who has no or negligible previous experience in managerial accounting in an organization. The intermediate level describes any gender who has around 5 years of experience in managerial accounting in at least one major organization. Senior-level describes any gender who has wide experience in managerial accounting in several organizations reporting to the chief executive (or equivalent), and who provides leadership in accounting matters. The features of the three levels have been compiled from discussions with accountants and non-accountants in a wide variety of organizations over 10 years. The description of each of the three levels is structured in two parts. The first deals with the job: its commonly used job titles, the line of reporting, an outline of the main responsibilities and key personal attributes. In addition, the key expectations of from non-accounting managers and employees are identified. Some obvious courses of action such as seeking advice and referring queries upwards have not been included as they are not specific to the managerial accountant's role and responsibility.[1] The second part outlines the personal qualities, that is, skills and abilities that allow the managerial accountant to add value to their organization. The managerial accountant can use this information to shape their career in a changing environment where personal sense-making (Weick, 1979) is expected, and uncertainty (Ditillo, 2004) is common.

Clearly, an organization that places a high priority on having quality information on which to make the best-informed decisions possible is likely to have effective managerial accounting practices that guide managerial accountants at all levels carrying out their duties and responsibilities in ways that meet or exceed the expectations of non-accounting managers and employees. One indicator is participation in planning and goal setting. An organization that uses its plans and goals to guide its operations is likely to be able to refashion its plans to take account of changed circumstances. An organization that involves its members in setting its plans and goals is more likely to secure commitment to them and be willing to seek advice and assistance to ensure their accomplishment. For these reasons goals feature in the managerial accountant's compass discussed in Chapter 8. The three levels of the managerial accountant are each discussed separately using the traditional outline format. An organization will format and supplement this to meet their own needs. Each of the three discussions concludes with its relationship to the managerial accountant's compass.

5.2   Entry-Level Managerial Accountant

Job Titles of the Entry-Level Managerial Accountant

- Business analyst, staff accountant, cost accountant, junior managerial accountant, managerial accountant

Organizational Line of Reporting

- To either an intermediate-level or senior-level managerial accountant or accountant

Key Responsibilities

- To establish and maintain appropriate costing models by cost and profit center. This responsibility includes having regard to fixed, variable and overhead costs and their relationships, key performance indicators, budgets, forecasts, trends and other factors which would affect the reliability of the costing model.
- To prepare routine and ad hoc accounting information on a daily, weekly, monthly, quarterly basis and provide it to senior managers. This responsibility includes recording, classifying and certifying transactions, selecting information or evidence, making estimates that are useful and relevant, and interpreting information.
- To conduct additional research, analysis and reporting. This responsibility includes advising the impact of actions on the organization and making appropriate recommendations
- To communicate effectively with the users of managerial accounting information. This responsibility will include both education and persuasion of non-accounting managers.

Key Personal Attributes

- Able to put observations and managerial accounting knowledge into questions to build understanding and agreement
- Easily able to recall all the methods of managerial accounting
- Empathy with the organization and its industry
- Ability to transfer past learning to new problems by generalizing from previous education and work experiences
- Understand how to apply the managerial accounting methods and their limitations
- Understand how the interrelationships are formed between managerial accounting methods and topics
- Working co-operatively with others to gain familiarity with new information and determine its application
- Persuade others by justifying and defending with evidence

Key expectations of the entry-level managerial accountant from non-accounting managers and employees include

- Routinely provide information to managers that satisfy their needs for information concerning:
  - Cost, economy and efficiency of processes and services
  - Effectiveness of processes and services
  - Quality of products and services
  - Ensuring the best use of resources
  - Time taken in creating and delivering products and services to end customers
  - Innovation to enhance the competitive position of the organization
  - Assessing the actions of competitors in the marketplace
  - Ensuring the organization's long-term competitiveness in its industry through better understanding of the organization's operating environment and competition

- Supplement the information with services to non-accounting managers that assist their understanding of the information.
- As requested, engage with the management team in resolving planning and decision-making queries. Planning includes selecting goals, predicting results, deciding how to attain goals and communicating this to the organization. Decision making involves selecting among options.
- Provide information to allow managers to proactively direct and control their operational activities.
- Identify weaknesses in controls and performance and recommend solutions in conjunction with the non-accounting manager.
- Measuring the performance across a spectrum. This includes managing activities that are insourced and outsourced, as well as giving attention to organizational units or the lower functions in the organizational hierarchy.
- Evaluate the adequacy of measures used to evaluate performance of organizational units. These may directly affect customers or be vital to the success of the organization.

The entry-level managerial accountant skills and abilities are quantitative or numerical accuracy, investigation, information literacy, analysis, communication and making recommendations.

Quantitative or Numerical Accuracy

The managerial accountant is expected to be aware how discrepancies[2] can arise in calculations, provide authoritative figures and comment on the values used in calculations. The managerial accountant will also consider the suitability of alternate forms of formulas, equations and ratios, as well as stating ranges and/or probabilities.

Investigation

The managerial accountant investigates an issue under a warrant. That is, she has a sound reason for devoting organization resources to an activity. The activity may have come as an instruction from a manager, a request from a non-accounting manager, or it may be something which the managerial accountant thinks has merit. The resources spent doing the investigation will be in proportion to the perceived importance and urgency. During investigation, the managerial accountant will ensure they obtain a clear understanding of the relevant organization goals and sub-goals for organizational units or functions. Some investigations take on the nature of a project. Where the managerial accountant is dealing with a system design specification and they are involved in soliciting and expressing requirements they will constitute this as a project. Of course, symptoms and requirements are often vague, so the skill of the managerial accountant is in selecting from the available information, and frequently making estimates based on sound reasoning as well as ensuring that all assumptions that would affect the issue are surfaced. The managerial accountant is aware there are different investigations.

Information Literacy

The managerial accountant either collects the base information that they will use or, where it is not available, makes conservative estimates of the information they need. The managerial accountant shows their information literacy in (a) selecting relevant information, (b) identifying any assumptions associated with the information or its use and (c) scrutinizing the information to determine whether it is acceptable or whether additional information needs to be sought. All this is done against a background that recognizes that perfect answer does not exist and some information will always be unavailable. The managerial accountant is aware that uncertainty is not always overcome.

Analysis

The managerial accountant conducts an analysis of the available information. This may require distinguishing symptoms from the root of a problem or opportunity (Kepner & Tregoe, 2013). Analysis answers the following questions: (1) What are the key elements of the problem or solution? (2) What are the relationships between them? (3) How do they combine to add value, resolve a problem, or take advantage of an opportunity? Analysis will always consider the context of the organization. This forms part of the managerial accountant's compass discussed in Chapter 8.

Communication

To obtain information and disseminate the recommendation, the managerial accountant needs communication skills. Communication has three aspects: (1) clarifying the purpose their analysis was undertaken, (2) explaining what their findings mean, (3) making clear its importance and relevance to managers. In communicating, the managerial accountant will offer to actively implement their recommendation to show their confidence in it. The managerial accountant may want to determine engagement is acceptable. They may either make the initial arrangements, for example, conducting a workshop so that everyone is trained on the skills and implementation arrangement, or by using a consulting arrangement allowing the manager to keep day-to-day responsibility for the operation. The managerial accountant excels in communication.

Making Recommendations

Successful recommendations are targeted at managers capable of authorizing change. They describe specific shortfalls of the current arrangements. They show what needs to be done, and how it should be implemented. Supporting information for the recommendation will identify (a) evidence for the findings, (b) the resources needed, (c) proposed sources of the resources, (d) the timeframe for implementation and (e) the costs and benefits, taking into account the time-value of money. The managerial accountant provides clear and practical recommendations.

In summary, the entry-level managerial accountant is expected to be technically proficient but quick to apply their knowledge to organizational issues under the guidance of a more senior manager. That guidance will emphasize clarifying goals, selecting appropriate methods and models, and being aware of their constraints and limitations. In this way the entry-level managerial accountant is able to develop their capabilities by exposure to higher-level roles and responsibilities under supervision of their manager and ideally a separate mentor. Of course, some entry-level managerial accountant role and responsibilities may overlap the intermediate level, depending upon the characteristics of the organization and its circumstances.

In terms of the managerial accountant's compass, the entry-level managerial accountant will master its cardinal points. Although they may remain reliant on advice and assistance to provide them with an understanding of its context, they will begin to understand context through its organization dimension.

5.3   Intermediate-Level Managerial Accountant

As noted earlier, the intermediate-level managerial accountant has approximately 5 years of experience in managerial accounting in at least one major organization so they can show breadth of experience and capability for supervision.

Job Titles of the Intermediate-Level Managerial Accountant

- Accounting manager, senior managerial accountant, systems accountant, senior accountant or project accountant

Organizational Reporting

- To a senior-level managerial accountant or accountant

Key Responsibilities

- To understand the organization's fundamentals and drivers of growth or provision of services. This responsibility will include identifying the currently used key performance indicators and evaluating their effectiveness as representative lead indicators.
- To analyze and assess in detail the effectiveness of key performance indicators, plans and internal controls. This responsibility will include determining how best to analyze and present information making these assessments. It will also consider the adequacy of lead and lag indicators.
- To supply full commentaries for board or senior management reports by proactively identifying past concerns, new matters and emerging issues.
- To implement a full range of performance measures for the business so benefits exceed costs. This responsibility will include clarifying organizational objectives, incentives and performance conditions.
- To improve the manual, semi-automated and automated systems associated with all aspects of key performance indicators, budgets, forecasts and business plans and any related projects. This responsibility will include exploring potential problems or opportunities, ensuring that suitable resources are available at the time required.
- To liaise with line or functional managers and project managers to identify risk/opportunity areas. This responsibility will include partnering with line employees and managers to obtain feedback on findings.
- Supervise entry-level accounting staff. This responsibility will include specific coaching and career development across a full range of managerial accountant knowledge and skills. These will cover established areas and emerging concerns such as big data where local competence may be developed to avoid reliance on experts (Lander 2013). It will also include finding a suitable mentor.

Key Personal Attributes

- Able to formulate questions using available information and knowledge
- Specialist knowledge of at least five areas (key performance indicators, performance evaluation, cost management, resource deployment including asset usage and strategic planning) obtained through hands-on experience
- Proficiency in difficult decision making under uncertainty to formulate complex recommendations
- Practical experience in all the major aspects of managerial accounting (planning, key performance indicators, budgeting, forecasting, compliance and controls)
- Able to accurately filter and evaluate both financial and non-financial information
- Capable of providing a high standard of accurate and timely information within a short time-frame
- Well-developed communication skills to persuade non-accounting qualified managers and employees by justifying and defending with evidence and experience

Key expectations of the intermediate-level managerial accountant from non-accounting managers and employees include:

- Engagement with the entire management team to promptly resolve queries in planning and decision making that become apparent
- Upon request, assist non-accounting managers to direct and control their operational activities
- Address or mitigate weaknesses in controls and performance and set review arrangements to determine whether methods to remedy weaknesses or make improvements have been successful
- Obtain comparative evidence of performance concerning customers and the organization
- Provide targeted commentary on key issues whether information was previously provided. This includes activities that are in-house and outsourced, as well as giving attention to organizational units or the lower functions in the organizational hierarchy.

The intermediate-level managerial accountant skills and abilities are adaptability, abstraction, continuous learning, visualization, modeling, negotiation and familiarity with technology and systems.

Adaptability

The only constant in organizations is change. The managerial accountant will investigate new approaches, overcome obstacles to achieve results, remain flexible after selecting an approach, encourage others to value change, but where necessary, persist in proven solutions and goals in changing circumstances where risk minimization is appropriate. The managerial accountant is always aware of the sunk cost phenomenon.

Abstraction

The managerial accountant abstracts analytical frameworks from instances and examples. One simple method of abstraction is to filter from the model details considered unimportant. Another is to select and use accounting-related concepts and parameters to develop a new analytical framework with an acceptable accounting basis. The managerial accountant will take advantage that abstraction occurs at different levels of detail and can be matched to different layers of management (board, senior managers, tactical supervisors and operational employees).

Continuous Learning

The managerial accountant is both aware of knowledge gaps and acknowledges new information and adjusts their response accordingly. This can occur through setting their own learning goals, making time for their own learning, actively learning by asking questions, asking for feedback and/or advice from more experienced co-workers, observing more experienced colleagues or practitioners, appraising their skill strengths and the areas for improvement, and seeking out and participating in training or education courses. The managerial accountant expands their skills and build new skill-sets as well as maintaining and honing existing skills and abilities through practice.

Visualization

Many aspects of managerial accounting that measure variables over time or relationships between variables are best represented with graphs, drawings and sketches.[3] For example, graphs can be used for cost behavior, least squares regression to separate costs into variable and fixed, cost volume profit including breakeven, and cost variances such as fixed overhead variances. Visualization can reveal whether a function is linear (as is often assumed) or nonlinear. For example, a scatterplot can be used to discover cost behavior. It is can also represent different levels of abstraction (e.g., different levels of variance). The managerial accountant will display their skill in selecting the most appropriate graph and avoiding misleading the reader with poor scaling, labeling or truncation.[4]

Modeling

A model is a selective representation of a system using symbols, algebra[5] or prose notation. The model may be based on an existing formula, prior analysis, or perceived new relationships, and it can be tentatively drawn as it is thought about (Nelms, 1981). The managerial accountant generates a new model by taking the following steps: (1) Select or formulate the analytical framework or method; (2) obtain the relevant information needed or, where necessary, make estimates; (3) state any assumptions made, constraints recognized and risks associated with the results; (4) conduct a comprehensive analysis considering at least three scenarios (best, worst, expected); (5) separate the starting information from conclusions; (6) explain what the analysis means for the organization and (7) document the written solution as an organizational record for future reference and potentially, re-use. The criteria for a good model are that it is relatively simple and focuses on key drivers. The challenge for the managerial accountant is to devise a model that communicates successfully.

Negotiation

The managerial accountant recognizes that positions are negotiated. It involves keen listening, attention to non-verbal signals, rapport building, problem solving, and the ability to clarify and overcome misunderstandings. Sometimes the counterparties will be difficult personalities, and thus emotional control will also be important. In all cases, teamwork with others from the organization is important to ensure important items are not overlooked or downplayed. Where external parties are involved, it is desirable to project a common point of view, which can be difficult with managers from different organizational units. The features of persuasive negotiations are well documented, and many points made by these authors are useful (e.g., Bazerman & Neale, 1992; Cialdini, 2006; Fisher & Ury, 2012; Grant, 2013; Galinsky & Schweitzer, 2015; Kennedy, 2012; Shell, 2006).[6] However only the managerial accountant can determine whether they are likely to work or fail in the particular negotiation. The managerial accountant will always abstract the concerns of the other party from their comments but deliberately explore what is valued by the other party.

Familiarity With Technology and Systems

The managerial accountant will understand systems design, automation of processes, project management and project reporting. The managerial accountant will have hands-on advanced spreadsheet skills (e.g., creating functions, pivot tables and using programing language) and an understanding of enterprise accounting software custom reporting using commands (e.g., XML).

In summary, the intermediate-level managerial accountant will supervise and act as a role model for entry-level managerial accountants. At the same time, the intermediate-level managerial accountant needs to successfully undertake challenging tasks that enable them to seek promotion as a senior-level managerial accountant. So, in addition to being concerned with the five compass points of the managerial accountant's compass, they will be aware of the context of the organization and its industry, having regard to trends and events in society, as well as geographical factors.

In terms of the managerial accountant's compass, the intermediate-level managerial accountant will use the entire managerial accountant's compass (cardinal points and context).

5.4   Senior-Level Managerial Accountant

As noted earlier, the senior-level managerial accountant has wide experience in managerial accounting in several organizations reports to the chief executive (or equivalent) and provides accounting thought leadership.

Job Titles of the Senior-Level Managerial Accountant

- Controller, (executive)[7] director of accounting, (executive) director of finance, chief managerial accounting officer, chief administrative officer, chief operating officer, head of business planning, chief accountant

Organizational Reporting

- To the chief executive officer, managing director, divisional general manager, executive director finance and accounting

Key Responsibilities

- To display leadership in the application of managerial accounting knowledge to establish, coordinate and administer, as an integral part of management, an adequate plan to account for all aspects of operations and strategy. This includes (to the extent required in key performance indicators) leading to the establishment of approved policies for accounts and costing, expense budgets, sales forecasts, profit planning, a program for capital investment, and planning cash flow and financing, together with necessary methods and processes to execute the plans.
- To compare performance with the approved operating plans and standards and to interpret the reported results to all layers of management. This includes the formulation and administration of managerial accounting policy, and the compilation of statistical records, to build a history to allow comparison and trend analysis, and special reports as required.
- To recognize and prioritize the necessity of taking actions where the reputation, risk or viability of the organization is affected
- To consult with non-accounting managers responsible for policy or action concerning any aspect of operations including outsourced

operations. This includes the setting and attainment of objectives. It may require effective policies and procedures having regard for any potential dysfunctional consequences.

- To protect the assets of the business. This includes adequate internal control, proper identification and protection of assets and secure record keeping, including privacy compliance.
- To act as a repository of knowledge concerning cutting-edge methods and make them available to managers by encouraging trials. The managerial accountant will help managers successfully use the methods of managerial accounting to better understand their organizational unit.
- To continuously appraise the political, economic, legal and social forces as well as government influences, and interpret their effect. This includes considering the continuing effects of the post-global financial crisis for operational actions and strategies. It also includes maintaining industry connections and obtaining industry information (e.g., total market size).
- To maintain harmonious and productive collegiate relationships with non-accounting managers in all aspects of managerial accounting. This includes providing proactive advice and assistance, as well as conveying compliance and technical obligations in a constructive manner.
- To directly oversee the managerial accounting function. This includes ensuring systems and processes are adequate, maintaining the ethical culture of accounting, ensuring the timely inter-generational recruitment of appropriately qualified managerial accounting staff. It also requires developing staff skills and knowledge, and ensuring they have appropriate mentors.

Key Personal Attributes

- Able to formulate questions through deduction and from contextual knowledge
- Broad experience in planning, measurement and governance, in a divisional and multi-layered organization
- Capable of comprehending information in a short time-frame and determining the action required
- High degree of communication skills for all layers of managers and employees
- Understanding of the implications of accounting regulation for the organization

Key expectations of the senior managerial accountant from non-accounting managers and employees include:

- Provide information to senior managers which integrates a variety of sources

- Resolve discrepancies and contradictions among the available information, whether or not identified by managers
- Engage with senior managers and the board in strategic planning
- Make decisions with senior managers and the board
- Pro-actively assist senior managers to direct and control their operational activities
- Approve policies on controls and compliance and resolve policy issues arising out of their operation
- Ensure the managerial accounting information provided is reliable and relevant and measures performance across a spectrum
- Ensure that measurement systems across the organization are integrated and produce meaningful information
- Foster an organization culture around any performance-focused goals and (monetary and non-monetary) incentives that avoid producing dysfunctional or unethical behavior

The senior-level managerial accountant skills and abilities are strategic cost management, strategic forecasting and strategic control.

Strategic Cost Management

This is concerned with improving the operations of the organization and making cost management information part of the management information system accessible to managers. The related skills include

- Anticipating the changing costs of resources in existing and new activities that are required to improve future performance
- Maintaining a continuous review of the acceptability of all expenses
- Ensuring that costing measurements provide strategic cost information. These include cost drivers, cost categories, cost pools and cost allocation bases for generating suitable information for cost management.
- Pursing continuous reduction of the operation and maintenance cost of costing systems (data collection), and increasing the benefits to managers (succinct and timely presentation of information to allow effective decision making)
- Encouraging the minimization or elimination of non-value adding costs

Although specific data-reduction statistical processes are commonly used, there are many other useful methods. These include making assumptions explicit, combining quantitative and qualitative data, conducting samples of time-based activity-based management, selective business process re-engineering, life cycle management, target costing, and determining the efficiency and effectiveness of major activities in relation to their value. The senior managerial accountant will ensure that managerial accountants and non-accounting organizational unit managers work together and have the required skills to produce meaningful analyses using proven methods and processes.

Strategic Forecasting

This involves carefully analyzing resources, markets and the industry aimed to determine avenues of competitive advantage in the future. The major skills include:

- Defining and communicating the unique position of the organization
- Recognizing synergies so that its organization sub-units create more value together than they would individually
- Ensuring the hierarchy of indicators of performance that measure the realization of strategy against targets is reliable

Strategic forecasting is closely associated with uncertainty. Although there are many forecasting methods that suggest what the world will look like, managerial accountants often become preoccupied with planning what the world should look like (Armstrong, 2001). To avoid confusing forecasting with planning, there are also useful strategic processes, such as establishing the baseline against which performance can be measured, using a prediction framework and investigating unfavorable outcomes. These require an organization culture that ensures the forecast is realistic, selects the best time to implement strategic decisions, adjusts or reforecasts where trends and events affect the organization, and provides the lender and investors with useful strategic information. The senior managerial accountant recognizes that forecasts do not change behavior and that strategic controls may be gamed.

Strategic Control Over Strategic Plans

This is overseeing the development of policies, guidelines and standards[8] to ensure conformity with controls, and where applicable, consistency between organizational units. The major skills include:

- Ability to rapidly yet rigorously reassess strategy due to unforeseen events
- Associating strategy with responses to disasters that interrupt operations or challenges to the reputation of the organization and its brands
- Awareness of events within and outside the organization that may prevent or facilitate the achievement of strategy[9]

- Recognizing when to conduct ad hoc reviews or bring forward milestone reviews to assess whether the implementation of strategy is occurring successfully
- Ensuring that strategic reviews are commenced and completed in time to allow changes in strategy to preserve resources and maintain competitive advantage

Senior managerial accountant will be aware that the signals from strategic controls require skill to interpret whether there is a strategy drift or failure (Ciborra et al., 2001). Periodic checks of financial controls are necessary to protect the integrity of financial information as it flows from production areas (e.g., manufacturing, merchandising, construction) to accounting. Continuing attention to operational controls is necessary to eliminate waste from production and administrative processes and to improve employee efficiency. These improvements may not occur unless promoted from outside the organizational unit, so the senior managerial accountant may need their diplomacy skills to gain permission to perform these checks, explore assumptions and interpret progress.

The senior-level managerial accountant will also promote generic skills among managerial accountants. These are skills useful in many different business functions and subject matter specialties. Common examples include the ability to complete work by deadlines, solve problems, think creatively (e.g., think laterally to identify different or better ways to do an activity), flexibility (e.g., adapting quickly to new ideas, new technologies, new methodologies and cultural change) and teamwork (e.g., collaborate with a team of people who work in different disciplines, show respect and seek understanding). They be named differently or defined in relation to organization mission or vision (Bowman, 2010). According to Gagné (1984), generic skills require the cognitive strategies of recognizing processes (steps) and principles (guidelines) and thus take time to develop. The senior-level managerial accountant will therefore add a further generic skill: the ways in which managerial accountants attend, perceive, encode, remember and think about business issues.

In terms of the managerial accountant's compass, the senior-level managerial accountant will master both its cardinal and context. Their concern with the future competitive advantage of the organization aligns with the five compass points. Their concern with the environment of the organization translates across to the context of the managerial accountant's compass.

5.5 Conclusions on the Effect of Duties and Personal Qualities on the Managerial Accountant's Compass

The role and responsibilities of the managerial accountant at all levels in the organization can be viewed through the lens of the managerial accountant's compass. All levels of managerial accountant are concerned with all the cardinal points. At the entry-level, the managerial accountant competently prepares information after verifying its veracity, while the higher-level managerial accountants take on the additional responsibility of assessing the implementation utility of the information provided and the need for changes to predetermined actions. All levels of managerial accountant liaise with different levels of managers and employees throughout the organization. Differences arise from the impact of context. The senior-level managerial accountant overlays an industry view and is attentive to trends. One use of context is to assess whether the required skills and abilities are either missing or under-developed in terms of the five cardinal points and the four context points. In some organizations, it is left up to the individual managerial accountant to identify where their skills and abilities can be improved. The managerial accountant who is adept at being proactive therefore gives themselves an advantage.

While there is some overlap in the role and responsibilities at the three levels (entry, intermediate and senior), their common concern with operations and planning for the future mean that they are continually providing information to non-accounting managers in the organization so the managerial accountant's compass is relevant for all three. No matter what the level, managerial accountants are expected to always exercise the highest ethical standards. This discussion of roles, responsibilities, skills and knowledge noted some performance, controls and risk apply to the role and responsibilities. This is considered in the next chapter.

Notes

1. Reasons for referral may include the following: (1) does not fit the existing policy; (2) has information or knowledge implications; (3) needs treatment as an exception; and (4) approval will set a precedent or create future consequences that have financial costs, or for reporting.
2. Common sources of discrepancies include the number of decimal places used in calculations, the use of sensitivity analysis to create best, worst and typical cases, and using different constants (e.g., inflation rates).
3. The informal nature of graphs, drawings and sketches makes them ideal for rapid response and immediate feedback (e.g., Hanks & Belliston, 1990).
4. This topic is well served by both statistical references (Huff, 1954) and visual display guides (e.g., Tufte, 2001). Tufte (2001) provides examples of outstanding large-scale and small-scale statistical graphics, charts and tables that allow a rapid, precise and effective analysis. Huff (1954) discusses the two common kinds of error: (1) misleading interpretations of statistics, and (2) incorrect conclusions and decisions arising using statistics.
5. Algebraic expression of a problem or hypothesis is a matter of practice. A useful introductory guide is Johnson and Johnson (2000).
6. These include the following: Make use of the norm of reciprocity, rank negotiation 'wants' (clearly understand the 'package'), be aware of cognitive biases particularly primacy and anchoring, be prepared to leave the offer on the table for consideration and make the opening offer wherever possible.

7. Using 'executive' emphasizes the position has day-to-day work responsibilities rather than just attending board meetings.
8. These will cover the technical accumulation of costs and allocation of costs-to-products and services, to recover materials, labor and overhead costs, and earn a profit. Senior managerial accountants are skilled in avoiding cost allocation errors, which can result in unprofitable operations being allowed to continue unchecked. The senior managerial accountant will link strategy to operational reports to understand organization costs.
9. This is the skill of monitoring multiple information sources and synthesizing the information to uncover important information ahead of it becoming widely known.

6 Performance Standards for the Managerial Accountant That Permeate the Managerial Accountant's Compass

Performance standards specify expected and acceptable results for completing work tasks and imply the expected knowledge and skills. They take many forms ranging from useless to useful. Vanity metrics neither link to strategic nor operational goals. Two common standards are Key Performance Indicators (KPI's, Kaplan & Norton, 2001) and Critical Success Factors (CSF's, Bullen & Rockart, 1981; Daniel, 1961). KPI's measure achievement across a range of activities. In contrast, CSF's are a limited number (usually three to eight) of key characteristics, variables or conditions that require close and continual attention to bring about high performance.[1] They answer the broad question, "Why would customers choose us?"

However, the customer of the managerial accountant is internal. This distinction was developed by quality management who found those directly connected to an organization, usually (but not necessarily) internal to the organization, also affected acceptance of the product or service (Kelemen, 2003). The CSFs for the managerial accountant, at all levels, apply to their own work and to assisting non-accounting managers (e.g., run their operations, pursue growth or avoid challenges from competitors who may jeopardize it as a growing concern). Performance measures are concerned with achieving goals within constraints and overcoming boundaries such as accounting for costs (Crossman, 1953) or measuring industrial engineering (Musson, 1957) by establishing broader organizational relationships. These are central to the managerial accountant's compass and are examined in terms of CSF's. This selection of performance measures has two implications. The first implication concerns the sphere of use.

Performance measures have two spheres of use. Widely applicable macro-measures used by the managerial accountant determine how well goals are being achieved. These measures can be developed at the organization level and then cascaded down to organizational units if they are profit centers or investment centers. Common macro performance measures used by managerial accountants are the forms of profit (e.g., EBIT, EBITDA or net profit margin)[2] as they have the benefit of relating to the financial statements and may be the performance measure used to determine the CEO bonus. One deficiency is the likelihood they are too coarse for managerial accounting as they aggregate individual organizational units and are subject to challenge based on the principle of controllability of costs. Controllable costs are expenses that can be adjusted in the short term and can be affected by a manager. However, many costs are not readily classified as either controllable or uncontrollable unless they are subdivided. Some are partially controllable because they are shared between two managers (e.g., maintenance costs depend upon the production manager's prudent use of machines and the maintenance manager undertaking adequate preventive maintenance using competent technicians). The other sphere of performance is associated with incentivizing managers and rewarding superior performance for exceeding predefined targets. Although achievements can be used as the base for rewards (e.g., Atkinson, 1998) generally different measurement systems are used to avoid them being gamed and ensure that it identifies the manager's contribution to the organization's results (Kauhanen & Napari, 2010). Where the advice and assistance provided by managerial accountant improves organizational unit performance, they will want to clarify how their contribution is judged if its implementation depends upon approval by the line manager.

The second implication concerns changes in products and services. To reduce costs, organizations attempt to produce and/or sell high volumes of products or services. The result is that products or services are at different stages in their life cycle. However, product and service life cycles themselves can be truncated (e.g., iPhone X) or extended (e.g., the original Mini car). The managerial accountant will be sensitive to changes in life cycle as it has consequences for financial reporting (e.g., capital budgeting) and cost management (e.g., demand). In addition, once the products or services produced by the organization are no longer similar in terms of resource use, cost assumptions must be re-examined, and this requires the managerial accountant to allocate time to investigate. The managerial accountant therefore needs to have a program of work associated with any CSF's they are expected to achieve, so that they continue to provide accurate and timely cost information, which captures not only what has been done, but what has not been accomplished and what has gone wrong.

In the following discussion, eight CSF's are proposed. This is at the high end of the number discussed earlier. There are two reasons for this. Some organizations see the satisfactory execution of routine activities as mitigating risk. CSF's numbered 1 to 3 protect and exploit the advantages inherent in current arrangements. These ensure a preoccupation with costs and productivity (CSF #1), improving existing products and processes (CSF #2), and ensuring availability by reducing the cycle time to market. There is also a cultural or behavioral aspect (CSF #3). Many organizations have change forced upon them (e.g., banking sector) or are experiencing digital disruption (e.g., Sears, Walmart response to Amazon). CSF's numbered 4 to 7 highlights understanding the customer and ensuring strategic improvement. Each CSF is accompanied by several key questions suggested by practicing managerial accountants. This distinction echoes the central importance of information discussed in Chapter 4.

The CSF's proposed are a guide to performance but can be placed in the larger context of control. Some views of controls in managerial accounting use Foucault's methods (Kendall & Wickham, 1999). They argue that performance is analogous with discipline and punishment (Hopwood & Macintosh, 1993). They discuss the genealogical view that takes chance and error as producing relations of power and locate cost accounting in this method and demystify the claims accounting makes to objectivity and neutrality. They take the later archeological approach, which takes an identifiable period marked by special events and discourses discontinuous with the preceding and succeeding periods to suggest that the power arises through enclosure with space, the body and time. Hopper and Macintosh (1993) illustrate this with Geneen's financial controls at ITT commenting that the monthly operating report was the cornerstone of control with its discourse of reporting and explanation. They quote Geneen's rationale for having controllers report directly to him as leader, while still providing their findings to the local manager. However, accounting did not remain the sole control. Roving product line managers who had to sell their ideas to line managers. Moreover, the managers were not under day-to-day control. Consequently, the view of performance and control outlined here takes the ethnomethodological view (Garfinkel, 2002) that this knowledge is available to the participants, and social phenomena should be studies on their own grounds and revealed in their own terms. That is, knowledge about performance evaluation assists managerial accountants make decisions about their practices and helps their commonsense reasoning in concrete situations. So, the CSF's described are generic and each concludes with a set of key questions to allow them to be re-described for other applications.

6.1   CSF#1 Preoccupation With Costs, Efficiency, Economy and Productivity

The global financial crisis reminded organizations they operate in a worldwide economy. This leads to continued attention to costs, efficiency, economy and productivity. Cost pressures may arise from the fundamentals of commodity supply and demand (e.g., higher prices obtained by producers leading to capacity investment, attract new entrants and the search for substitutes ultimately resulting in lower prices before any further rise in prices),[3] or in the supply chain (e.g., retailers forcing manufacturers to contain or even reduce costs).

Efficiency is another aspect of cost containment. It is concerned with input or utilization of resources in relation to outputs. By working with managers, the managerial accountant can suggest what costs require attention and what actions are necessary to reduce costs. This may involve better understanding of fixed and overhead costs to eliminate unproductive activities, such as scrap and rework to make essential activities more productive by aligning them with customer needs, or by focusing in on costs previously thought not to be material. While costs are a critical measure of efficiency, any improvements will only be viable if the definition, measurement and assignment of costs are up-to-date with operations.

The managerial accountant has a dual interest in the economic consumption of resources: actual benefit obtained and adequacy of controls over resources. Economy ensures frugal and judicious expenditure on material resources. In some cases, the managerial accountant will remind managers that resources are scarce and their future provision cannot be taken for granted. The managerial accountant will also remind managers that, under continuous improvement, the goal is reduced consumption if the use of the resource is essential.

Finally, the managerial accountant is concerned with productivity trends over time. The managerial accountant will explore which activities cause productivity to fall, using both financial and non-financial information, with regard to the outputs and the inputs required, and processes utilized. The managerial accountant will take productivity into account when calculating the prices customers are prepared to pay for a product or service. For example, to validate target costs, the managerial accountant will subtract the target operating income from the target price determined by sales and marketing organizational function. This can be a difficult area as graphs of trends may fluctuate and require estimates and judgment particularly where the expectations of resellers and customers change suddenly.

This CSF can be framed around the contribution of the managerial accountant to costs, efficiency, economy and productivity, by answering key questions such as

- What are our most critical products/services and their associated appeal?
- How do our costs compare with our competitors?
- How can we improve our understanding of fixed costs and overhead costs?
- How can managers meet the challenges of existing and prospective local and international competition with improved productivity?

6.2 CSF#2 Ensuring Improvements to the Quality of Products, Services and Systems

Improvements through quality may be achieved by continuous improvement (Deming, 2000) or by radical redesign also known as 'breakthrough' (Juran, 1995). The Total Quality Management (TQM) movement aims to exceed customer expectations rather than provide just acceptable products or services and thus obtain future sales. A by-product of this approach is the elimination of defects and the improvement of tolerances to reduce variation. The quality of the raw or component materials is paramount for ensuring continuity of production and this is heightened under the Just-In-Time (JIT) approach to inventory. The managerial accountant can identify various costs of quality, including the costs of maintaining product or service quality, costs of servicing customers, finished goods rectification or repair costs to enable supply, and warranty costs as well as revenue benefits of TQM (e.g., from greater customer loyalty). These are usually handled in conjunction with the ISO9000 standard, which is usually framed around process improvement and thus can become an ongoing responsibility of the managerial accountant.

Process improvement should routinely occur. The managerial accountant can contribute to the continual search for increases in efficiency and productivity by reducing waste, improving quality and managing costs to ensure that the customer's expectation of quality is satisfied by building it into the production or administrative process (Deming, 2000). They can also assist with radical redesign to avoid delays and bottlenecks that arise when the work to be performed exceeds the available capacity (Hammer & Champy, 2006). This should result in a dramatic short-term improvement to revenues from relieving capacity and other constraints associated with the delays and bottlenecks, and increase the output from introducing a new set of business processes. In both cases, the managerial accountant can prepare or review quantifications of proposed costs and benefits as a specific option or a range of options.

This CSF can be framed around the contribution of the managerial accountant to improving quality, by answering key questions such as

- What quality does the customer expect from our products and services?
- How does our quality compare to our competitors and similar industries?
- Is it possible to lower costs, while retaining the same quality level as competitors, or is a lower quality acceptable to customers?
- Are there advantages in performing activities at a higher quality level to competitors without increasing cost?

6.3   CSF#3 Awareness of Behavioral or Human Responses to Information and Decisions

Behavioral accounting is an approach to the study of accounting that emphasizes its psychological and social aspects. It is concerned with (a) the way that managers and employees react to information available to them, (b), the impact of uncertainty or unfavorable events on managers and employees, and (c) those decisions that produce dysfunctional consequences in managers and employees. Dysfunctional consequences are outcomes that are abnormal, impaired or maladaptive. Managerial accountants should be aware of the behavioral aspects of managerial accounting, because there may be dysfunctional consequences from providing information or influencing decisions.

Management control systems prefer to approach attitudes and behavior in terms of goal congruence. That is, trying to ensure that organizational units (and individual managers) align their own performance with expressed goals of the organization (Caplan, 1971). Goal congruence is usually attempted at all levels of management. Principal–Agent theory (discussed in Chapter 2) explains why boards and senior management need to offer incentives to managers to zealously address stated organization goals, having regard for organizational effectiveness. Goal incongruence occurs when individual goals take precedence over organization goals. It manifests itself as pursuing either self-interest on behalf of their own organizational unit (e.g., reducing organizational unit's costs but passing on the consequences to other organizational units) or personal self-interest[4] (e.g., maximizing their incentive rewards). It may not be sufficient for dysfunctional aspects to be outweighed by the functional aspects since it can still be detrimental to cash flow. However, dysfunction is not the only cause of poor performance.

Everyone involved in decision making not just the managerial accountant is susceptible to cognitive biases, motivations and organizational/industrial social psychology. Some are beneficial, but some produce erroneous decisions (Birnberg, Luft & Shields, 2007).[5] Beneficial biases and heuristics save time in searching for information and weighing the available information. However, they frequently lead to poor outcomes (Kahneman, 2012). Two common biases often work together. While relying on one fragment of information (anchoring), other information is neglected (e.g., probabilities). Biases partly explain differences in human judgment and decision making and can reflect motivation, in particular, the motivation to have positive attitudes to oneself (Hoorens, 1993). Ignoring other sources of information, particularly contradictory or opposing information, can be the result of hubris (over-confidence bias). While Kahneman (2012) is pessimistic on overcoming biases, Gigerenzer (1996) suggests that since probability and calculus are not ordinary part of decision making, special effort must be directed toward using them. One approach is to pause and reflect, that is, developing a questioning attitude looking for new perspective (Kahneman, Lovallo & Sibony, 2011). Specifically, the managerial accountant can employ three strategies: (1) search relentlessly for new disconfirming evidence, (2) reframe or flip the issue to reveal whether a positive or negative framework is being covertly used and (3) consider repurposing familiar items. The advantage is that this allows knowledge and experience to be generalized and applied to future situations and further develops the skill.

This CSF can be framed around the contribution of the managerial accountant to overcome behavioral or human responses to information and decisions around key questions such as the following:

- Is the process for setting goals productive or counterproductive?
- Are individual employees and managers adequately consulted on what they are expected to contribute to the goals?
- Are key plans associated with strategy (e.g., operating budget) likely to produce dysfunctional consequences?
- Do capital budgets for projects recognize the likelihood of delays, and is there a realistic contingency?
- Are attempts to motivate desirable performance likely to be gamed (that is, using understanding of the system to manipulate rules and processes meant to protect a system to achieve desired outcome)?
- Are evaluations based on past performance or events that overlook unique factors?
- Are corrective actions expected to attain expected performance levels likely to be thwarted?

6.4   CSF#4 Moving to Managing Costs from Calculating Costs

Management of costs requires managers and the managerial accountant to establish stable relationships between costs and activities allowing overhead costs to be more precisely allocated to products, services or customer segments. Although this can be done with various forms of activity-based costing, it is not essential provided the focus is on managing activities to reduce costs and improve customer value (Kaplan & Cooper, 1998). This requires the managerial accountant to become involved in all aspects of an Accounting Information System (AIS).

The managerial accountant encounters two kinds of AIS. The traditional AIS uses a historical cost accounting perspective. It is primarily concerned with the cost of individual products and services. The modern AIS is a broader accounting and management system that provides managers with information to plan and control the activities of the organization (Cooper & Kaplan, 1992). Both can unnecessarily consume the time of the managerial accountant if it is not integrated with transactional or operational systems, which use information from the general ledger. Otherwise there is the possibility of discrepancies in reports being due to timing or period cut-off differences that consume unproductive time to manually reconcile.

This emphasis on cost management represents a significant shift in the role of the managerial accountant. Instead of an information production role, they have a process or activity improvement role that attends to opportunities to automate the information system to provide online reporting and 'what-if' decision support to users (Bonczek, Holsapple & Whinston, 1980). The managerial accountant will therefore want to ensure any AIS enhancement or replacement to handle costs flexibly in many dimensions (Berliner & Brimson, 1988). Although decisions are ultimately taken by the line manager in charge of the organizational unit, the managerial accountant has a role in making sure that the improved information flow is consistent, timely and useful.

This CSF can be framed around the contribution of the managerial accountant to improving both the visibility of costs with multiple dimensions and understanding costs answering such questions as:

- What is the cost of resources utilized in undertaking the organization's major activities?
- What are the non-value adding costs in products or services and in all aspects of administration and management?[6]
- To what extent are costs controllable?
- What is the relevant range for fixed costs?
- Can indirect costs be made direct costs?
- How efficient, effective and productive are all major activities performed in the organization?[7]
- How can new activities improve the future performance of the organization?
- For the AIS: Are costs being efficiently accumulated? Is the behavior of costs clear? Have all costs been properly assigned? What is the timing of costs? Is the responsibility for controlling costs clearly allocated?

6.5 CSF#5 Commitment to Availability-on-Demand by Reducing Commencement and Completion Process Times

Costs are substantially influenced by the time taken to complete a task or a set of activities. Savings can be made directly from the lower input costs, or improved inventory turnover and quicker realization of revenue provide cash flow synergies. These can be assessed using their costs as well as non-financial information. Together, they can guide process improvement or redesign and suggest avenues for innovation, particularly where there are contractual obligations.

The managerial accountant investigates a range of process times. Duration or completion time is measured from several perspectives: (1) for the organization: as the product cycle time to create and bring to market a product or service; (2) for operations: as the throughput time to complete production of a product or service; (3) for the customer: as the time taken between placing an order until the product or service is delivered; and (4) the useful life of the product or service may also be added where warranty or extended guarantees are offered. In some cases, improving cycle times becomes urgent through sudden changes in consumer expectations (e.g., motor vehicle warranties), or new different and better competitor products coming to market (e.g., the first iPhone), so this should always be on a watching brief.

This CSF can be framed around the contribution of the managerial accountant contributing to reduced cycle time (or improving throughput) by answering key questions such as

- Has the product or service availability expectations of our customers changed?
- Has the delivery expectations of our customers changed?
- Is continuous improvement sufficiently shortening timeframes?
- Do customers now replace their products and services more or less frequently?

6.6   CSF#6 Customer Value Orientation

Understanding what constitutes value to the customer is a major source of competitive advantage. Customer value is the difference between what the customer gives (e.g., costs in terms of payment, time to obtain, effort learning to use, maintaining/updating and disposal) and what the customer receives (e.g., features, usage, reliability, care and usage instructions, brand and reputation, and after sales parts and service availability). As such, it encompasses both tangible and intangible benefits.

Organizations know that consumers are now well-informed owing to search engines being available on smartphones and WIFI, allowing access almost anywhere. From the point of view of costs, the organization should understand how to create better customer value for the same or lower cost than competitors' or create equivalent value for a lower cost than competitors'. In some cases, the organization can benchmark against competitor products. In other cases, the organization can use industry opportunities to understand competitor costing methods. Where this is not possible, consulting experts with greater knowledge may be engaged.

This CSF can be framed around the contribution of the managerial accountant to understanding customers, by answering key questions such as

- Who do the most important customers need?
- What alternative offering would immediately appeal to customers?
- What substitutes could customers consider?
- How can we better deliver value to customers in the short and medium term?

6.7   CSF#7 Support Innovation in Products, Services and Systems

Innovation has many definitions. There is the totally new invention or design. For example, the touch-screen smartphone eliminates the dedicated separate keyboard. This form of innovation receives attention from the media and governments without any acknowledgment of the risk and likelihood of exhausting its funds before the design is complete and its operation is efficient.[8] There is improvement in processes. For example, internal combustion engines turn off when stationery and restart automatically, or use less cylinders at low speed. This form of innovation is frequently overlooked. There is repurposing of already known or discovered products (e.g., the non-permanent glue used for sticky notes). This form of innovation also receives little attention. While the managerial accountant is not responsible for innovation of products or services, they can support and encourage it by providing relevant information during planning, development and implementation.

This is vital in industries where there are vigorous competitors, overseas penetration, or low barriers to entry for new competitors. Organizations cannot rely solely on customer loyalty so there needs to be a constant flow of new and improved products and services to attract and retain customers. For example, the history of the British motor vehicle industry shows many innovations (e.g., the Alec Issigonis Mini, the Rover SD1, the Aston Martin Lagonda series 2 with its cathode ray dashboard, the Jensen FF with four-wheel drive and anti-lock braking, and the farm-town oriented Range Rover). However, it is also characterized by many failures, notably in not recognizing and protecting intellectual property value, underfunding new models and mismanaging operational changes. To support innovation, the managerial accountant is concerned with evaluating options for research and development, analyzing investment (capital budgeting) to improve return where there is an associated project, and assisting non-accounting managers understand their development and implementation costs and income.

This CSF can be framed around the managerial accountant contributing to innovation, by answering key questions such as

- Does the budget match the workplan allowing for delays during the development period for the innovation?
- Does the budget match the workplan allowing for delays during testing and certification of the innovation?
- Is the quality and delivery schedule reliable for any outsourced components or services for the innovation?
- Has the proposed pricing of any resulting product or service been compared to existing and new competitor products or services, and is it regularly reviewed?

- Will the innovation be capable of incorporating new technologies and likely advances in the current technology as they become available?

6.8   CSF#8 Cross-Functional Perspective

One of the early recommendations from knowledge management was the need to overcome knowledge silos in organizations. Knowledge silos refers to hoarding uncommon knowledge and specialized experience, and resisting sharing it (Rubenstein & Geisler, 2003: 142). Managerial accounting can be accused of catering to specific organizational functions and sub-units without trying to discover their similarities and synergies. This is understandable since one of the principles of the managerial accountant is 'different costs for different purposes' (Fess, 1961). So, it is understandable that information requests and analyses would be treated independently. But this is often inappropriate in today's context. The value chain (and value network) remind the managerial accountant to consider all the functions within it to ensure that value to the customer is adequately considered. For example, a sales function that offers greater discounts for higher volumes to meet sales targets (which must be delivered before a deadline such as Christmas) may cause the production function to work extra shifts, which will incur additional costs. A cross-functional perspective can enable the managerial accountant to understand relationships between revenue and costs, or output and outcomes.

This CSF can be framed around the managerial accountant contributing to a cross-functional perspective by answering key questions such as

- Are there similar cost objects and drivers in more than one organizational unit?
- Are there common activities in the value chain which are handled differently?
- Does the organization hierarchy/structure and arrangement of organizational units facilitate a cross-functional perspective or are special efforts required? and
- How can the barriers to sharing accounting information across organizational units and sub-units be reduced to benefit the organization?

6.9   Conclusions on Critical Success Factors for the Managerial Accountant

The critical success factors for any particular managerial accountant depend upon their organizational circumstances and personal qualities. They are the basis for proactive identification of problems, opportunities and developing a range of viable options. Their common element is using both financial and non-financial information that support the decisions and judgments of non-accounting managers. This implies they ensure that the information they provide is well understood by non-accounting managers. There is also an element of luck. The domestic and international economy and governing arrangements may provide a stable environment that favors the decisions that are implemented. Table 6–1 summarizes the eight CSFs discussed. Using the attributes of roles and responsibilities discussed in Chapter 5, it summarizes the knowledge (procedural and declarative), primary skills (learned behaviors) and abilities (inherent qualities) of the managerial accountant in relation to in the CSFs. Table 6–1 is then reviewed to consider some implications for the managerial accountant.

The CSF's place responsibility on the managerial accountant to use an AIS that provides information about performance, cost of quality and cost management. In some cases, the organization can fund an expensive

Table 6–1 Summary of knowledge, skills and abilities associated with the identified CSFs.

	Critical Success Factor	*Knowledge*	*Skill*	*Ability*
1.	Preoccupation with costs, efficiency, economy and productivity	Processes and methods	Accurate and quick calculations	Search out relevant information
2.	Ensuring the improvement of the quality of products and services and systems	Statistical processes and methods	Graphical display of information and recommendations	Creativity in formulating options
3.	Awareness of behavioral or human responses to information and decisions	Cognitive biases and motivation	Anticipating consequences	Attention and sensitivity to manager's reactions
4.	Moving to managing costs from calculating costs	Suitable AIS	Gaining confidence	Fostering short-term change
5.	Commitment to availability-on-demand by reducing commencement and completion process times	Full costing and pricing analyses	Costing of different process options	Creativity in formulating options
6.	Customer value orientation	Value and customer choice analyses	Making trade-offs	Understanding the relationship with the customer
7.	Support innovation in products, services and systems	Strategy and technology	Technical understanding	Trial and error patience and diligence
8.	Cross-functional perspective	Conditions to successfully apply processes and methods	Integrating, aggregating and presenting information	Making sufficient time available

integrated system endorsed by consultants. This does not mean that a managerial accountant in organization without an Enterprise Resource Planning (ERP) system is any less effective. Manual and semi-automated systems can collect and adequately process information, and specialized external assistance can overcome knowledge or skill gaps. The most important factors are that the managers can rely on output from the AIS particularly as the organization evolves and the managerial accountant can show non-accounting managers how they can use information obtained from the AIS based on collegiate relationships with all organizational units.

CFS's make clear the importance of the managerial accountant influence over information gathering and analyses for planning, implementation, defining and measuring successful competitive advantage. However, the CSF's lack any framework for this. The managerial accountant's compass offers a framework that guides the application of knowledge, acquisition and use of skills and the development of abilities to fulfill the CSF's. Decision making and judgment that were briefly noted as part of CSF's receive detailed attention in the next chapter.

Notes

1. Some authors suggest that critical success factors enable achievement of objectives (Parmenter, 2015). Consequently, a Key Performance Indicator (KPI) is a measure that quantifies management objectives, along with a target or threshold, and enables the measurement of strategic performance. In other words, CSFs are the cause of success, whereas KPIs are the effects of actions.
2. EBIT or Earnings Before Interest and Taxes can be readily determined from the Profit and Loss/Income Statement. EBITDA or Earnings Before Interest, Taxes, Depreciation and Amortization Depreciation and Amortization may, for example, be included in Cost of Goods Sold and as part of General & Administrative expenses on the Profit and Loss/Income Statement and can be cross-checked with the Cash Flow Statement. The difference between EBITDA and EBIT of capital-intensive industries (e.g., mining and infrastructure) is significant as depreciation expense and capital requirements are high.
3. The managerial accountant and production/sales managers will need to be able to successfully navigate the lag between investor enthusiasm (irrational exuberance), expanding raw material availability, production of refined material and components, regulator uncertainty (e.g., taxation) and eventual product availability. For example, current bottlenecks in supply of battery equipment using lithium, cobalt and nickel for the automotive industry, which competes with hardware technologies (laptops, tablets, smartphones), have encouraged buyers to finalize 5-year supply contracts (Montgomery, 2018).
4. Of course, in some cases this will result in breaches of fiduciary duty. It is legal duty to act solely in another party's interests. Parties owing this duty are called fiduciaries. The individuals to whom they owe a duty are called principals.
5. Cognitive biases differ from logical fallacies. A logical fallacy is an error in logical argumentation (e.g., using a circular argument, making a personal attack). A cognitive bias is a genuine flaw in processing information (e.g., focusing only on information that is readily recalled).

6. Non-value adding activities are those that can be eliminated without any deterioration in the product or service quality, performance or perceived value by the customer. Many statistical and routine reports are non-value adding. Many intrusive interactions with customers are regarded as non-value adding by customers after they have made online purchases from organizations with well-thought-out transaction systems.

7. A danger in a narrow focus for activities is the risk that activities that have no financial added value to the organization are eliminated or not supported. The tendency of performance management systems to overlook activities that have an implicit value that is not embodied in any financial value in a product or service can have repercussions. For example, a workplace that provides a pleasant environment may attract and retain the best staff, but this will not be evident by any additional value to the product or service. Again, this stresses the need for non-financial information to be used when making decisions that have an organization-wide impact.

8. Fifty-first-generation turbine cars were given to the public to road test in 1962–1964 by Chrysler. They traveled more than 1 million miles with an operational downtime of 4%. By 1977, the engine had reached the fourth generation and could achieve performance, economy and pollution-reduction goals to satisfy US vehicle standards (Lehto, 2010). Although successful, the program ran out of funds and was terminated.

7 Recommendations, Decisions and Judgments by the Managerial Accountant With the Managerial Accountant's Compass

The managerial accountant makes a variety of recommendations, decisions and judgments applying a range of methods and processes specific to managerial accounting using financial and non-financial information in planning and control. Where the managerial accountant is not the decision maker, they prepare a recommendation. A recommendation describes the preferred course of action accompanied by a rationale. A decision is the outcome from the process of formulating options (alternatives), evaluating them and choosing between them (Baron, 2008). A decision involves judgment if there is evaluation of evidence (Baron, 2008) or the need to estimate, infer or predict the character of unknown events (Hastie & Dawes, 2001). A decision also involves the commitment of resources. There are many processes for making decisions available to the managerial accountant. Some are specialized methods and processes that provide a specific answer to given problems (e.g., discounted cash flow). Some consider more than one option and all possible consequences including chance event outcomes, resource costs and utility (e.g., decision tree). There is a need for decisions to be integrated with the role and responsibilities of the managerial accountant because poor decisions have a major impact on the organization.

The role and responsibilities of the managerial accountant are concerned with revenue and expenses, and this has seven implications for decision making, and each of them is considered. First, the impact of decisions is financial. Second, the process often requires preliminary problem solving and using creativity to perceive the world differently, make connections between seemingly unrelated phenomena, discover hidden patterns and generate practical solutions. Third, the decision making should be situated in an extended stepwise process, which begins with problem identification and concludes after implementation. Fourth, the decision process is affected by cognitive bias and the consequences of using heuristics. Fifth the process is affected by constraints and risks. Sixth a decision requires approval and managing of its implementation, which may also have behavioral consequences. Finally, the many ways of making judgments about success are considered. Thus, decisions as well as the process are not simple. The managerial accountant needs to be aware of these implications and consider each when making a decision. Most decisions have a financial impact.

7.1 Financial Impact of Recommendations, Decisions and Judgments

The financial impact of recommendations, decisions and judgments on managerial accounting is its financial outcomes. The outcomes from decisions are apparent but aggregated in the Statement of Financial Position (Balance Sheet), the Income (Profit and Loss) Statement,[1] the Statement of Cash Flows, and the Statement of Changes in Equity. The names used depend upon the jurisdiction. However, the Income (Profit and Loss) Statement in its classified (or multi-step) form[2] for internal use, is the focus of most managerial accountant's activities, so it is used as the focus for this discussion of decisions. Since the Profit and Loss (Income) Statement is produced for each period, the traditional time horizons of short term and long term are used. This is set out in Table 7–1, which uses the format of a fully classified (or multi-step) Income (Profit and Loss) Statement, that is, it provides subtotals to make it easier for readers. To avoid the table becoming unwieldy, only major decisions are included, earlier decisions in it are not repeated horizontally or vertically, and headings are used to show aggregate or roll-up decisions and information. Information is the essential input to most decisions, so the likely information sought or available is also identified. The examples of financial and qualitative information are drawn from the discussion in Chapter 4 on information.

Inspecting Table 7–1 results in two observations. In the multi-step income statement, the impact of decisions can be judged at four critical stages: gross profit, operating profit, pretax profit and after tax. Second, there is overlap between decisions and information. On the decision side, some are interdependent and may form a phased sequence. For example, changing to a sustainable package may affect delivery arrangements and warranty coverage. Also, new decisions may reverse or override existing decisions. For example, the failure of the growth strategy may result in retrenchments. On the information-side, some information accompanying an earlier decision may require updating. For example, the current contractual arrangements with suppliers that provide for volume discount. Equally, some information may require drill-down to determine the contributing factors. For example, whether changes to operating expenses are due to revenue or cost of goods sold, or both. Also, some information may be fragmented and require assembly or calculation to be usable. For example, total cost of advertising and branding across traditional and social media. Finally, an assessment of the deficiencies of available information may require problem solving or creativity by the managerial accountant.

Table 7–1 Short- and long-term decisions and information using the format of a fully classified Profit and Loss (Income) Statement for internal use.

Section if Fully Classified	Decision Subject Matter		Examples of Information
	Short Term	Long Term	
Operating revenue Sales revenue	• Products/services • Forecast sales • Pricing product/service • Profit margin • Order size • Territories occupied • Credit terms offered • Doubtful debts follow-up	• Market share • Growth (projected and actual) • New products/services • Price inflation or deflation • Trends with sales • Channels to market • Return on capital invested • Bad debt	• List prices • Costs of obtaining sales • Variances • Economic, political and social environment • Demand • Competitor intelligence • Product margin • Profit margin or compared with the amount of money invested by calculating return on capital employed • Billing
Cost of goods sold[3]	• Raw materials • Production schedule • Capacity • Productivity • Cost behavior • Overheads • Inventory stock level • Inventory turnover • Inventory unsaleable	• Innovation of product or process • Product mix • Preferred suppliers • Discounts and rebates for volume purchases • Inventory replenishment • Inventory storage	• Costs of purchasing • Carrying costs • Cost of quality • Cost of returns and write downs • Portfolio of products or services • Availability of products or services • Quality standards • Industry reputation • Frequency and effect of returns and write downs

Section if Fully Classified	Decision Subject Matter		Examples of Information
	Short Term	Long Term	
Cost of goods sold (*continued*)	• Warranty coverage • Guarantee provided and accepted	• Supplier selection • Interest rate and amount • Volume • Product/service mix • Outsource/In-house supply • Risk	
Gross profit	Budgeted and actual	Forecast and trends	• History and forecast • Gross margin
Operating expenses	• Total cost of expenses (actual) • Proportion to sales • Trend • Reasons for incurring and changes	• Expected rate of growth • Relationship to given estimated sales volume • Cash flow requirements	• Total expenses: Year-to-date, year-on-year, seasonal/monthly • Control and compliance with policies and processes
Selling expenses	• Total selling expenses (actual and budget) • Total selling expenses trend	• Selling costs trend • Responses to competitor selling arrangements and performance • Ecommerce	• Expenses by territory and organizational subunit (e.g., branch) • Variances (summary and detail) • Customer surveys • Competitor actions and their impact
Sales salaries and commissions expense	• Number of sales employees • Basis (permanent, part-time/casual) • Salary rates • Expected performance • Contractual obligations for terminating employees	• Sourcing in-house or outsource • Employ family members • Salary increases including increments • Staffing for expected growth or contraction • Profile of knowledge, skills and abilities	• Cost of working conditions • Costs revealed by benchmarks by external consultants • Conditions required by industrial awards • Job descriptions of knowledge, skills and abilities in sales

(*Continued*)

Table 7-1 (Continued)

Section if Fully Classified	Decision Subject Matter		Examples of Information
	Short Term	Long Term	
Sales salaries and commissions expense (continued)	• Commission rates • Number of employees on commission • Basis (permanent, part-time/casual) • Targets, incentives & rewards	• Rate and commission paid through brokers or associations • Dependence of sales on commissions • Likelihood of new channels eliminating commissions or requiring commissions	• Costs of existing and competitor rates for new and incumbent sales employees • Existing and projected sales targets
Advertising expense	• Expenditure (actual and budget) • Frequency • Placement • Effectiveness	• Product placement and other promotions • Sponsorship deals (organization and individual ambassador) • Linkage to new products/services	• Costs of advertising, promotion and sponsorship • Customer perception of brand and products/services • Advertising channels and schedules
Freight out expense	• Number of consignments • Cost reduction opportunities • Preferred suppliers • Customer returns and non-deliveries	• New forms of packaging and consignment • Connection with advertising	• Costs of packaging and handling • Sustainability of methods of packaging • Adequacy of protection of the product, service and tools used
Sales premises rent expense	• Suitability of current location • Rent or buy • Need for larger, different premises	• Market and competitor rates • Prestige from naming rights • Demographic and socioeconomic factors affecting location	• Cost of occupying premises • Cost of quitting premises • Contact and arrangements for tenure

Section if Fully Classified	Decision Subject Matter		Examples of Information
	Short Term	Long Term	
Depreciation sales equipment expense	• Purchase plan • Cash flow benefits • Period purchased • Eligible rate	• Fixed asset capital budget for new and replacement items • Cash flow (funded by operations, other income or financed by loan)	• Total cost of purchase over life • Period of purchase • Eligible rate • Taxation rate • Available cash or loan to fund
Administrative expenses	• Acceptability of total administrative expenses actual and budget • Total administrative expenses trend	• Acceptability of administrative expenses trend • Responses to competitor administrative arrangements	• Administrative expenses and variances • Competitor actions and their impact
Office salaries expense	• Office staff salary rates • Number of office staff • Grades or levels of office staff	• Market (industry) rates • Competitor rates • Opportunities for elimination, automation and outsourcing	• Expenses including benefits and overheads • Changing market and competitor rates • Costs and variances • Changing market and competitor rates • Job design changes
Utilities expense	• Cost reduction opportunities from discounts and rebates • Changed work practices	• Trend in expense • Savings negotiable with supplier • Savings from more efficient consumption	• Contract arrangements, service charges, rates and period of commitment
Office premises expense	See, 'Selling expenses'	See, 'Selling expenses'	See, 'Selling expenses'
Depreciation on office equipment expense	See, 'Selling expenses'	See, 'Selling expenses'	See, 'Selling expenses'

(Continued)

Table 7-1 (Continued)

Section if Fully Classified	Decision Subject Matter		Examples of Information
	Short Term	Long Term	
Insurance expense	• Preferred supplier • Type and extent of coverage and excess • Cost, discounts and rebates	• Trends	• Costs • Claims history • Suppliers
Financial expenses	(For organizations not in the financial industry)		
Interest expenses	• Borrowing and repayment conditions	• Reductions in interest rate • Impact on profit • Repayment of principal	• Cash flow • Type of borrowings (bonds, loans, convertible debt or lines of credit) • Amount of principal • Rates and term offered
Discount allowed	• Cost • Reasons for allowance	• Impact on profit	• Discounts negotiated • Terms of discount • Life of discount
Profit before income tax	• Profit amount • Profit margin • Profitability ratios	• Forecasts, trends and targets • Competitor comparison	• Organizational unit and segment reporting • Loan covenants
Income tax expense	• Provisional tax payable	• Impact of tax losses	• Acceptable tax minimization advice
Profit after tax	• See 'Profit', above	• See 'Profit', above	• See 'Profit', above

7.2   Importance of Problem Solving and Creativity

Frequently, a decision is preceded by problem solving. Problem solving is a non-routine activity oriented toward changing an undesirable state of affairs (Robertson, 2017). Much of the problem solving by the managerial accountant is directed at determining the characteristics of a problem to establish whether it is solvable or has to be managed. Often problem solving becomes a shadow activity. A shadow activity is one which must be completed to complete the original task. Effort in a shadow activity can be both underestimated by the managerial accountant, and not recognized by non-accounting managers. As a result, the managerial accountant may take shortcuts, which detrimentally affect the final decision. Therefore, any process description of decision making should separate problem solving as an activity in its own right. Problem solving also entails creativity. It is facilitated by imposing constraints (limitations to resources, including time) or a vision of an alternate reality (Kozbelt, Beghetto & Runco, 2010). To produce information, the managerial accountant frequently has to use creativity to overcome incomplete information search and allow analysis as well as formulate options. Creativity also requires time and freedom from stress so the managerial accountant needs the decision process to provide opportunities for creativity to be invoked (This is an issue of self-care discussed in Chapter 10.) The issue of creativity in accounting often is misconstrued as using financial engineering to apply accounting methods that remain legal, while bordering on fraud.[4] In contrast, Speckbacher (2017) suggests creativity needs to be understood as part of management control that has a role in shaping, framing and defining the problems that require decisions. The decision process therefore is extended to incorporate problem solving and creativity.

7.3   Extended Stepwise Decision Process (Problem Identification to Implementation)

Most descriptions of management or business decision making processes have too few steps because they view decisions as similar, ordinary, discrete and quickly executed steps. It is not clear whether this is because textbooks do the same or whether there is some intrinsic appeal to steps such as setting goal, collecting data, considering options and making the decision. However, it is clear this simplicity has three adverse consequences. It avoids the complexity of needing to build understanding of the problem. It does not allow time to build commitment to a course of action. It does not recognize that the managerial accountant deals with such a broad field of decisions that this process is incomplete. The extended stepwise decision process is proposed to address these shortcomings. A major advantage is its ability to handle non-programed decisions. Programed decisions are standard decisions that always follow the same routine; once established, they can be codified into an easy-to-follow sequence. Non-programmed or unstructured decisions are non-standard and non-routine, so each decision is different from prior decisions, despite apparent similarities. Another advantage of the extended stepwise decision process is its applicability to decisions with a variety of characteristics and circumstances including:

- Structured or unstructured[5]
- Short or long-term horizon
- Routine and uncertain elements
- Strategic or tactical
- Immediate or deferrable
- Controls and feedback to trigger further decisions, and monitor and report on their status

Table 7–2 proposes an extended stepwise decision process. It incorporates the preliminary tasks such as problem solving and allows for creativity. It highlights some processes as iterative, such as clarifying goals and developing the criteria for making the decision. It allows for the ranking of options to be reviewed and considers implementation. While the extended stepwise decision process is not guaranteed to eliminate the effect of heuristics, cognitive biases or the behavioral consequences of decisions, it can mitigate them by replacing the immediate decision with a process that ensures due consideration. Although the setout of Table 7–2 is linear, there is scope for iterations, extended review and looping back where new information changes what has been settled in previous steps. The completion of a phase in the table identifies a review checkpoint.

The issue always confronting the managerial accountant is that any given problem with given information can yield many different results and thus give managers choices to select the course of action they prefer. So not only does the extended stepwise decision process need to incorporate additional steps, but it also needs to emphasize the last step in each phase is an automatic review of the conclusions from the preceding phase. This ensures there is thorough scrutiny and opportunities to question information and any intermediate conclusions and anticipates the effect of heuristics and biases. Thus, commitment is provisional and subject to review allowing for sunk costs to be recognized. As noted in Table 7–2, cognitive heuristics and biases operate at all times and thus require attention.

Table 7-2 Extended stepwise decision process highlighting the scope for cognitive bias and the review checkpoints.

Phase	Task Step	Task[6]	Commentary or Subtasks	Scope for Cognitive Bias
Decision domain	1	Identify decision maker	• Determine whether individual, representative or committee. • Determine where finalization and ratification rests.	In selecting the individual, composing the team or delegating the committee
Problem analysis	2	Problem recognition	• Specifically describe the symptoms of the problem or opportunity. • State whether the problem is fully or only partly manifested. • Identify whether the matter urgent, important or both.	In recognizing the phenomena as a problem, as well as overlooking risk
	3	Problem formulation	• State the problem in terms of root causes and prior attempts at resolution.[7] • Identify any uncertainties. • Estimate contingency and risk.	Perceiving the kind of problem, its character and the success of the candidate remedy
Data collection	4	Make predictions about the future to determine the impact of the problem.	• Consider influences external to the organization. • Consider influences internal to the organization.	Overlooking contributing factors Under- or over- weighting those factors
	5	Obtain information[8] allowing for delays in availability and time for checking.	• Although some information is available, some information may continue to be uncertain or unavailable. • Specify assumptions and reconsider contingency and risk.	Determining where to search Determining when to stop searching

(Continued)

Table 7-2 (Continued)

Phase	Task Step	Task	Commentary or Subtasks	Scope for Cognitive Bias
Creatively establish and evaluate options	6	Identify and devise as many reasonable options as possible.[9]	• Start with the basic options: 'do it', or 'don't do it'. • Use creativity to identify additional options and structure them into different classes. • Identify options that are equally attractive.	Determining what is a relevant option Determining how many options ought to be formulated (particularly suppressing search for additional options)
	7	Create logical evaluation criteria before commencing any evaluation considering characteristics, performance and implementation.	• Weigh the options. • Review the relative weights. • Examples of criteria to rank options: Decision Matrix, a SWOT[10] Analysis as template or 2 x 2 matrix	Determining what criterion to include and how they should be weighted Determining how to handle information that does not fit the criterion
Determine approach	8	Eliminate all the options that are low ranked.	• If two or more options are high ranked, re-examine their evaluation. • Check inputs and make changes.	Eliminating information that does not fit the criteria Creating additional criterion that is poor Modifying the criteria
	9	Review all the details of the remaining high- ranked close options.	• Amend criteria if rankings are anomalous	Overlooking information that might now be eligible for—inclusion Changing the criteria to favor an option
	10	Select the preferred option (the highest ranked option).	• Review the reasonableness of the final choice. • Consult with others.	Adding a late additional criterion. Selecting features of the information to support the choice.
Implementation	11	Detail the implementation plan from the criteria and implemented; reconsider the (rejected) options; and allocate resources.	• Review decision history. • Review feasibility. • Review risks or sacrifices. • Review tangible costs. • Review tangible benefits. • Review broader long-term consequences. • Explain the decision to those involved and affected.	Overlook consequences of the process, announcement or implementation conditions.

Phase	Task Step	Task	Commentary or Subtasks	Scope for Cognitive Bias
Implementation (*continued*)	12	Determine the method of implementation (sequenced, staged, parallel or simultaneous).	• Reconfirm commitments. • Prioritize stages. • Obtain resources. • Ensure clear accountabilities.[11]	Under- or over-state the time, effort, quality and risk.
Monitor and evaluate	13	Follow up.	• Ensure the implementation 'sticks'. • Realize benefits on which the decision was based.	Use new criteria or find additional favorable features.
	14	Evaluate decision or project processes and performance (lessons learned for future organizational decision making).	• Document the lessons to be learned. • Independently identify any benefit overestimation and cost underestimation.	Demand for a report that is positive or negative. Conceal embarrassing information.
	15	Conclude or terminate the implementation	• Transfer into routine operations.	Overlook consequences of making the arrangements permanent.

7.4   Process Effects and Consequences: Heuristics and Cognitive Bias

Surfacing the biases that invariably creep into the reasoning of any individual or group is important during decision making. Since the judgment of even highly experienced, superbly competent managers can be fallible, it is necessary to be aware of the use of heuristics and to counter the operation of cognitive biases. Signs of cognitive bias include overweighting one piece of information, or making faulty comparisons to another business case. Decision making uses heuristics or a 'rule of thumb' to solve a problem faster than would be accomplished used routine methods (Kahneman, 2012). The most prevalent heuristic is satisficing,[12] which is searching available options until an acceptability threshold is met (Simon, 1956). That is, most but not all needs are met. This uses the assumption of bounded rationality or limited choice, because when individuals make decisions, their rationality is limited by the tractability of the decision problem, the cognitive limitations of their minds, and the time available to make the decision (Gigerenzer & Seltern, 2002). Satisficing contrasts with optimizing is also known as maximizing utility or satisfaction (Stirling, 2003).[13] Another common heuristic is the Pareto principle, law of the vital few, principle of factor sparsity or, more commonly, the 80–20 rule. It claims that the 'vital few' produce most of the results.[14] For example, 80% of sales are ordered by 20% of the clients. Cognitive biases are a systematic pattern of deviating from rational judgment by making illogical inferences about situations and other people (Kahneman, 2012). Figure 7–1 traces three interrelated cognitive biases (over-confidence, framing and confirmation) and then differentiates whether it is applied to historical or future information noting there is a common overlap in the social bias. One bias is common to both prospective and retrospective groups. It is attribution bias or the fundamental attribution error, which Kahneman (2012) calls the correspondence bias.[15] These biases all govern the preference for selecting and attending to information. However, Kahneman does not suggest how to overcome them.

One possible response to avoid being biased is to conduct a pre-mortem. Its objective is to formally raise uncertainties (Campbell, Whitehead & Finkelstein, 2009). However, they do not protect against self-interest, which can be unconscious. A supplementary check is the four tests in Table 7–3, which should lead to stronger governance. However, they too are not infallible protectors against cognitive bias. A simple test overlooked by Kahneman (2012) is seeking additional information from experienced practitioners in the form of dialog and dissent. This is traditionally known as the 'devil's advocate' with the refinement that multiple persons are used to address the tendency to conformity and moderate any pathological conflict or competition among advisers (George, 1972). Thus, overcoming cognitive biases requires considerable attention at all stages of the process.

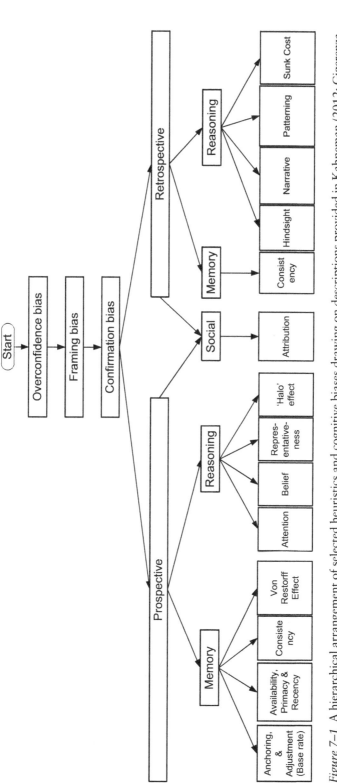

Figure 7-1 A hierarchical arrangement of selected heuristics and cognitive biases drawing on descriptions provided in Kahneman (2012; Gigerenza, Todd & ABC Research Group, 1999).

Table 7–3 Tests that should lead to stronger governance, obtaining additional information or experience, or encouraging more dialog through challenges.

Test	Key Question	Commentary
Familiarity	Is this decision identical or similar to any others we frequently or recently made?	Identify and examine the major uncertainties associated with the decision. Determine the knowledge and experience of those associated with the decision.
Feedback	Was feedback in past decisions filtered or unreliable?	Objective assessment is difficult where information is incomplete. Filtering information may protect managers or senior managers from bad news.
Measure emotions	How similar are our emotions on this decision to those we have experienced in related decisions?	Emotions affect judgment. Emotions may be rekindled from similar or earlier situations. Emotions may be affected by social relationships or manipulated by sales skilled persons.
Independence	Is this decision likely to be influenced by any inappropriate personal interests or attachments?	Personal interests and attachments can be concealed where an option receives high agreement, appears obvious or is convenient.

One reason that Kahneman (2012) is pessimistic that cognitive biases can be overcome is that he believes cognitive processes can circumvent most checks including considering whether to seek opinions from others. Therefore, the managerial accountant should show leadership in these situations in two ways. First by giving examples of the business consequences of heuristics and cognitive biases. Second by introducing the problem early in the extended stepwise decision process. This can be done in conjunction with considering constraints and risks.

7.5   Constraints and Risks to the Decision-Making Process

Most decision process descriptions emphasize using goals to guide decision making rather than understanding constraints and risks. It is through the latter that oversimplified assumptions become apparent, inappropriately subdivided stages and arrangements have their issues surfaced, the need for creative solutions becomes apparent, and additional investigation is found necessary. Dervin (1998) shows that giving attention to constraints and risks highlights the benefit of an exploratory probe, and sense-making, which allows a quick reaction once results become apparent. The managerial accountant is aware that the early stages of the decision process are an opportunity to show that uncertainty cannot be eliminated. There are four common causes of uncertainty. The first is that complete information cannot always be obtained, often owing to cost or time constraints. Thus, some uncertainty remains and the managerial accountant will need to find ways to make sure that initial estimates are treated as preliminary, ensure there is a clear expectation by all parties that they will be revised and refined during later stages, and that all factors will be re-examined. The use of contingency and risk estimation should therefore be introduced early in the decision process.

Another source of uncertainty arises from placing undue reliance on financial information. Considering qualitative factors will often reveal additional risks or place greater weight on known risks. The managerial accountant is acutely aware that decisions on feasibility require justification on economic, operational and technical factors; of those, the operational factors should be weighted most highly.[16] In addition, implementation timeframes may need to be extended. More intensive consultation process may be required when legitimate qualitative concerns are raised by managers and employees. Or, testing and migration may be under-scoped.

The third source of uncertainty lies in the gaming[17] behavior of people. There are people who bluff, use tactics to omit or slant information to their benefit, consciously use schemes involving deception, and try to anticipate what the other person, organization unit or organization will do and develop tactical responses accordingly. The extent to which the employment of gaming behavior and the particular behavior that will be chosen cannot be predicted contributes to uncertainty.

The final source of uncertainty is the outsourced decision. Direct outsourcing occurs when it is referred to another organization. Indirect outsourcing occurs when it is referred to a committee, a consultant or deferred as non-urgent. Outsourcing may appear to shift risk to the provider of the outsourced service, but they can readily shift it back by complaining about a lack of information or inadequate information. While a specialist or a committee may outsource the decision to hasten it, or give imprimatur to it, in most cases, operational managers will become responsible during implementation. During implementation, the managerial accountant may discover untoward aspects not previously considered and thus may be the bearer of bad news.

For all these reasons of uncertainty, the managerial accountant will spend time making sense of a situation before deciding on a course of action and avoid relying on knowledge of 'how we always do it' or what she or he has previously done, and reflect on its context. This ensures that the managerial accountant recognizes that risk does not manifest itself from some exogenous contingent event, but rather is driven by the behaviors and decisions of people. Constraints and risk should then be part of any approval.

7.6   Approval, Implementation and Its Behavioral Consequences

An approval decision may be a stand-alone (single) decision or a cluster of several. Care is required in the latter since studies of government procurement show that a number of small, yet rational decisions cumulatively produce an outcome that is either suboptimal or undesirable. In the dynamic environment of an organization, this can occur because a series of small decisions adversely changes the context of subsequent choices (Kahn, 1966). Since there is usually more than one right or acceptable answer, sometimes the approved option should be irreversibly abandoned. So, prior to implementation, the extended decision process requires review of the approval in light of its decision history, its broader long-term consequences and feasibility.

Implementation should begin with a review of the rejected options in case circumstances have changed favoring one of them. This is prudent because the final step in Table 7–2 (Step 14) requires an evaluation to improve the quality of the decision, and it may then indicate implementation was unwise. Implementation begins with an adjustment to the approval characteristics (funding, time, quality) needed to make it work. The managerial accountant will always seek to have all approval decisions encompass an implementation plan so that the resource arrangements are clear. Where a separate approval is necessary, the managerial accountant will ensure it is fully detailed to avoid becoming hostage to an incomplete or ambiguous implementation resources and priorities. Where the implementation plan includes a timetable, it needs to be validated and associated with a change plan determined as feasible. In all cases, the aim is to identify shortcomings or suggest improvements before implementation commences. Whatever the decision, human behavior changes unpredictably in response to the decision. The managerial accountant will exercise considerable judgment and care in considering behavioral consequences of decisions. Four behavioral consequences can be apparent.

The first behavioral consequence arises from the meaning interpreted by managers (and employees) about information provided to them. Cost control is exercised by and through people. Nothing much has changed since Dickey (1960) observed that where production cost standards are established and imposed on production managers and employees, this results in low morale, loss of cost consciousness and productivity resistance. The managerial accountant may also be the unwitting recipient of exhortations from senior managers that have behavioral accounting consequence. Often senior managers refer to control or responsibility, when what they mean is control over costs or responsibility to ensure organizational survival. For example, the organizational objective of maximizing profits by minimizing costs is often manifested in control systems. In providing managers with performance information that contains what is perceived as either shortcomings or implied threats to established arrangements, the managerial accountant can unthinkingly define their role as extracting from each manager the greatest contribution to achieving organization goals. Non-accounting managers and employees may then perceive they have less freedom to make decisions, that is, less autonomy as well as less stability and security. In these circumstances, the managerial accountant will be particularly concerned to (a) provide feedback that is constructive and appropriate, (b) contribute to a structured environment, and (c) overcome functional fixation with accounting reports,[18] which then affects their interpretation.

The second behavioral consequence is dysfunctional decision making. It is decisions that deviate from what is normal or ideally expected. There are many areas in which dysfunctional decisions in planning or policy have a major impact on the organization including:

- Budgeting (where the creation of budgetary slack[19] occurs)
- Transfer pricing (if market prices are falling then it may fall toward the corporate or group's marginal cost)
- Return on Investment (where a new project at a lower ROI than earlier projects is likely to be rejected)
- Quantitative measurement of performance[20] (Ridgeway, 1956), particularly where single criterion indexes, multiple criteria indices or a composite criteria index is used (where there are attempts, some successful, to manipulate or 'game' the index)
- Performance evaluation for key result indicators[21] (where artificial trade-offs are made between them or all efforts are directed solely at exceeding the one which provides the greatest financial reward).

Some understandable reasons for this include: transferring one rating of a feature to other features;[22] considering the short term over long term; not considering all possible options including the 'do nothing' option; favoring a particular option on the basis of a single outstanding characteristic (for example, evaluating suppliers based on their organization size or current customer base); ignoring lines of control (reporting arrangements); substituting short-term personal goals for organizational goals (for example, position titles for career opportunities) and filtering the information communicated to avoid reducing the confidence of management in the manager. The managerial accountant will be concerned to avoid becoming a critic rather than trusted advisor to non-accounting managers and will try to overcome manager attitudes that range from mildly hostile to outright distrustful. One way of doing this is to rekindle interest in the systems to identify where there is a lack of understanding, discover weaknesses being ignored or reach agreement on how systems can be improved to provide better information and decision support.

The final behavioral consequence arises from perceived management disinterest or self-interest. Frequently managers (and employees) conclude that senior managers do not care about their burdensome workload or working circumstances because nothing is done to improve conditions. The managerial accountant will be concerned to always show they are sensitive to this situation. Some managers and employees respond with a 'tick the box' approach to compliance.[23] This results in activities that satisfy bureaucratic expediency and avoids them drawing unfavorable attention to themselves or their organizational subunit. Some will take a 9–5 approach.[24] Others include a changed perception (e.g., 'them and us'), trying to create a favorable impression in the eyes of superiors (e.g., 'I beat the budget') or avoid criticism (e.g., by becoming risk adverse). The managerial accountant will take this one-by-one with non-accounting managers and may need to carefully and delicately champion for change, while avoiding being shot for being the messenger of bad news[25] that will eventually become apparent. The final aspect of the extended stepwise decision process is judging success.

7.7   Judging Success Subjectively and Against Realized Benefits

Success is judged subjectively whether or not there are any criteria. If there is no agreed criteria, managers and employees give their own opinion at different points in time, and often more than once. When a criterion is used, it can be applied in different ways. Consistent with the discussion in section 7.1, the managerial accountant uses a financial measure such as increased profit. But this is qualified in three respects. First, if there is little competition in the market then profits are not as impressive as profits made in a competitive market. Second, the amount of profit is relative to size and competitors in the same industry. Third, an organization may prioritize other objectives, for example, to improve cash flow, increase margins, improve product quality, boost customer service, raise market share, reduce costs by retrenching employees, or sell-off or outsource unprofitable functions. In all cases, the point in time when success is judged may occur before benefits are realized. However, this uses quantitative information, and there is also qualitative information. Drawing on earlier comments, three examples are discussed that show that judgments about success can be qualitative factors.

First, the actual process to which the decision refers may be misperceived. It may appear unstructured, ad hoc or easy. This is often the case if those making the judgment are outside the working group or have limited participation (e.g., at times of trouble). Or, it may arise from the decision maker seeking to reduce an unstructured decision into structured, routine sub-decisions (Mintzberg, Raisinghani & Theoret, 1976).

Second, the agreed option may prompt thinking that produces serendipitous attractive new options favored in hindsight. While Chambers (1965: 16) in a classic analysis of inventory showed there is a 'superabundance of alternatives', this is not normally the case, and generally there is a starvation of options. Prudent decision making requires a large number of options[26] to be generated because it is essential to have a range of possibilities or approaches as they will have different consequences, and poor options are the precursor to a poor decision (Simon, 1979).

Third is recognition of vested interests. All managers have vested interests (Ahrens & Chapman, 2007). They include monetary performance rewards, non-monetary awards, power, status or prestige and their regard for other organizational units. These may not be assuaged by management control systems. More importantly, their vested interest may not be apparent.

Some authors suggest problems judging success can be overcome, but the abiding nature of this problem suggests it is not easy. Newell, Lagnado and Shanks, (2007) recommend accompanying the decision with the criteria to evaluate its success. Blenko, Mankins and Rogers (2010) suggest the substitution of effectiveness for success. The real problem seems to be that the criteria for success is multi-faceted, and more than one is used. Key questions in judging success include:

- Speed of decision making (a drawn out or delayed decision is considered procrastinating or waiting for the inevitable)
- Speed of execution (how quickly the project or activity is completed)
- Effort (the resources required, both budgeted and unbudgeted) with the goal of minimizing effort
- Impact on the target group (and whether they consider it favorably)
- Buyers' remorse (was the correct option selected)
- Disruptions, calamities and losses compared with expected risk

The managerial accountant will maintain collegiate relationships with non-accounting managers to discover the criteria they are using and whether subjective factors are intruding on their judgment. Another difficulty in judging success is there are numerous parties who use different criteria, so there is always likely to be debate about a success. The managerial accountant can provide guidance where managers are beginning to define success against their preferred criterion. The managerial accountant can either point to these difficulties or offer a fresh examination if necessary, reconsidering the range of options.[27]

Contrasted with subjective judgments on success is realization of benefits. This depends upon the basis for the decision, amendments approved at different stages, and the assumptions and detail in analyses. For this reason, the realization of benefits should be signaled as part of approval and incorporated in future budgets (Oliver & Walker, 2006).

If implementation reveals difficulties realizing benefits, the original decision parameters for benefits and costs can be re-analyzed to determine whether there was an overestimation of benefits, underestimation of costs, or both. Realization of benefits is the major planned outcome, and failure to properly plan and evaluate it is tantamount to accepting the outcomes were not realistic but indicative or an ambit claim. Where this occurs, any evaluation in the extended stepwise decision process (Step 14) should independently assess whether the decision reasoning was preconscious, unconscious or conscious (Janis, 1959). Failures to realize benefits can be excused by external factors or attributed to failings of the implementation team. Anticipating this, the managerial accountant will want to give close attention during the extended stepwise decision process to whether they are recognized in both formulating options and assigning weights in the criteria.

7.8   Conclusions for the Managerial Accountant's Compass for Decision Making

This chapter has made a major contribution to framing the managerial accountant's compass. Most organizational decisions are not isolated. They are part of a series of decisions, so the individual decision is influenced by prior decisions and the extent to which their implementation was completed. The extended stepwise decision process emphasizes that a successful decision is underpinned by problem analysis. Sometimes this involves creativity and awareness of changing circumstances. It continues through the implementation and the realization of claimed benefits. Although senior management judges' success at different times and makes their judgment known, so to do other managers and employees. The managerial accountant uses their collegiate relationships across the organization and the extended decision process to assist reach an optimal decision and then during implementation to obtain outcomes beneficial to the organization. Both feature ethical processes and ethical behavior.

The contributions to the managerial accountant's compass from this chapter contribute to its cardinal points. The financial outcomes underlying recommendations, decisions and judgments are expressed in the managerial accountant's compass goal, another cardinal point of the managerial accountant's compass. The extended stepwise decision process and implementation contribute to the methods one of the cardinal point of the managerial accountant's compass. Judging success and realizing benefits are also methods used by the managerial accountant. The consideration of risks and constraints during the extended stepwise decision process has a close relationship with boundaries and constraints in the managerial accountant's compass. The discussion of heuristics and cognitive bias are placed in the relationships with others cardinal point of the managerial accountant's compass. Together recommendations, decisions and judgments have contributed to the four cardinal points of the managerial accountant's compass.

With the review of role and responsibilities complete, the next part contains three chapters that introduce and discuss the managerial accountant's compass. It begins with an overview of the managerial accountant's compass and then discusses its perimeter known as the context in detail in Chapter 8.

Notes

1. Both for-profit and non-profit organizations seek financial outcomes. For profit organizations, they are profitability and growth (Capon, Farley & Hoenig, 1996). For non-profit organizations, they are cost minimization subject to maintaining liquidity and solvency (Wacht, 1984), if necessary through obtaining revenue from grants or donations.
2. It provides more detail than the traditional structure of revenue, selling, and general and administrative expenses. A classified income statement typically is organized into five blocks: (1) sales revenue and cost of goods sold/sales; (2) other operating revenue; (3) operating expenses; (4) other non-operating expenses, if applicable and (5) profit. The line items below these form budget categories and determine whether the expense item impacts gross profit, operating profit, or only net profit.
3. There are variations to terminology depending upon the industry. Cost of goods sold is the total cost of acquiring raw materials and turning them into finished goods, so it includes direct labor, direct materials and manufacturing overhead. For merchandising businesses, it includes inventory and is designated cost of sales (which may include services). For exclusively service delivery organizations, it is designated cost of services.
4. Griffiths (1987) was read by partners at Ernst and Whinney, and Arthur Young when they were separate companies. Jameson (1988) identifies the managerial accounting connection with this kind of creative accounting in his discussion of budgets and variances highlighting the anecdotal variance analysis, that is excuses.
5. A structured decision features goals, resources are availability, known processes and a well-defined context. These tend to be routine operational decisions. An unstructured decision has uncertain outcomes, unknown resources and unique context.
6. There is a strong likelihood that intermediate decisions as well as the final decision will be affected by cognitive biases and that the receipt of the decision will be accompanied by unintended consequences. Therefore, all tasks should be informed by these human or behavioral considerations or factors. The impact of cognitive biases is discussed in their own right in the following section.
7. A root cause is the initiating cause of either a condition, or a causal chain that when removed eliminates the untoward outcome or effect. While it may be a process that is missing, incomplete or not followed, quality management asks why at least five times to prevent finding a cause that is not the ultimate cause (Wilson, Dell, & Anderson, 1993; Ohno, 1988).
8. Roeder (2011) makes a connection between reading as a learned skill and the reduced capacity to concentrate on the mass of information received through internet searches and hyperlink connections. Information must be understood before it can become knowledge, so skimming and attending to fragments of information that seem most relevant is a counterproductive practice.

9. All decisions have at least two options: the proposed course of action and the implied retention of the status quo. Options offer different approaches for changing the initial condition into the desired condition, which can be restated as a goal. The number of options should be sufficient to provide the decision maker with a spectrum of choices in more than one dimension. If the minimum is taken as three dimensions, and there are two options, this suggests a minimum of six feasible options would be proposed for evaluation against predetermined criteria.

10. A SWOT analysis or SWOT matrix contains two sets of conclusions: (1) the internal or business characteristics assessed with strengths (advantage over competitors) and weaknesses (disadvantage relative to competitors); and (2) the external or environment characteristics assessed with opportunities (favorable situations for competitive advantage) and threats (potential negative effect on the business). The table below depicts the relationship visually.

Relationship to the organization	Helpful	Harmful
Internal	Strengths	Weaknesses
External	Opportunities	Threats

It is completed after analysis is conducted and is used as a summary. After completing the SWOT matrix, conclusions are drawn using a qualitative rating (high, medium or low). Although some authors like to use figures from a scale and multiply 'Importance' X ['Rating' or 'Probability'], this produces a misleading quantitative index on what is based on a subjective analysis.

11. A McKinsey review of 2,000 executives in 900 organizations found mediocre implementation, the most problematic aspect of organization change, while the hallmark of success was 2 years after a change effort ended the change itself endured (Johnston, Lefort & Tesvic, 2017).

12. It is a combination of 'satisfy' and 'suffice'. Simon (1956) used it to explain the behavior of decision makers who were unable to determine the optimal solution. This was caused by either computational intractability or a lack of information. He later rephrased it as "decision makers can satisfice either by finding optimum solutions for a simplified world, or by finding satisfactory solutions for a more realistic world" (Simon, 1979).

13. A Pareto solution (or Pareto efficiency) to a decision problem has the property that it cannot be improved with respect to any criterion without its performance worsening with regard to some other criterion. So, this is a test that the managerial accountant can use with regard to activities, employees or organizational units. It already has been used for evaluating economic systems and public policies.

14. Pareto's original observation was that about 80% of the effects come from 20% of the causes, but it is applied to relationships between inputs and outputs, as well as effort and results (Koch, 2017).

15. Attribution theory is the use of information by a perceiver to arrive at causal explanations for their observations of others, even where there is none (Heider, 1958). The attributed cause may be some enduring internal characteristic, (e.g., personality, motives or beliefs) or some situation or event outside a person's control.

16 Hidden in their 1968 computer utilization report from McKinsey Consulting Organization (1971: 104) were three tests of feasibility put as questions: Economic: Is there a greater monetary return than he costs to develop and implement it? Operational: After the system becomes operational will it be

successfully used? Technical: Can this application be developed or implemented with the available technology and budget?

17. Gaming is also known as abusing the system, bending the rules, cheating the system, milking the system, playing the system, testing the system for loopholes or working the system.

18. Functional fixation occurs where the person attaches a certain meaning to an object or idea and then is unable to perceive other possible meanings or uses as a result of a mental block against using the object in a new way (Duncker, 1945).

19. Budgetary slack is either the deliberate (a) underestimation of budgeted revenue or (b) overestimation of budgeted expenses for the period (and sometimes within the period as well). It gives the manager the best chance of reaching budget targets because if costs increase or there are revenue shortfalls, there is a cushion to avoid an unfavorable variance numbers. Budgetary slack often occurs where performance appraisals and bonuses are tied to the achievement of budgeted numbers.

20. Problems include directing attention away from an overall goal, arbitrary weighting, leading to contradictory managerial decisions, observable unintended consequences including tension, reduced morale and communication distortion.

21. These typically include profitability, market position, productivity, product leadership, employee/manager development, employee attitudes, morale and social responsibility.

22. Edward Thorndyke (1920) asked two commanding officers to evaluate their subordinates. He found that once their commander rated the initial factor highly it was likely that later factors would also be rated highly, and vice versa. He named this the 'halo effect'. Rosenzweig (2014) applied this to business. He concluded that when an organization is regarded positively, factors such as managerial style, organization culture and strategy are attributed as the crucial drivers that led to success. Conversely, when an organization is out of favor, the same factors are usually viewed negatively, regardless whether they led to the poor outcomes or not.

23. The more extreme form of tick-the-box is pencil whipping. It is completing a form or record, especially a checklist, without performing the implied work required or without obtaining the supporting information or evidence. It may extend to providing incomplete or falsified information. The cognitive bias halo effect may contribute to pencil whipping not being detected because the person has a favorable overall impression of the manager or employee, and this impression is transferred to the impression that work is being done satisfactorily.

24. This does not necessarily mean 'do as little as possible'. It may mean not developing loyalty (for example, having a 3-year employment horizon), saving energy for outside-the-organization social impacts or demanding some aspect of personal fulfillment from their jobs, and being willing to freelance (Ernest & Young, 2015).

25. In an extended study using conversation analysis, Maynard (2003) suggests that when giving bad news, it is best to (a) signal it in advance, (b) prime the recipient, (c) be prepared to chat further and (d) try to use empirical objective measures that have independent agreement.

26. Organizational decision making reaches different conclusions to consumer choice theory. Consumer and retailing theory suggests that an abundance of choice (a) may delay or prevent a sale (known as decision paralysis) and (b) may not contribute to satisfaction of the consumer because it can cause anxiety (Schwartz, 2004). Organizational decision theory, which has major

financial consequences and obligations of care to stakeholders, requires the generation of feasible options to obtain as many different perspectives as possible. In many cases there are trade-offs in terms of time taken to formulate them and the impossibility of obtaining knowledge of all options, or all consequences that follow from each option (Barnard & Simon, 1947). Often in practice, decision making is curtailed because the circumstances are unfamiliar, and there is urgency to resolve the situation. Both these are inimical to good decision making.

27. Examples of methods include brainstorming; reverse brainstorming where the opposite outcome from the desired outcome is the target; Crawford slip writing technique (Crawford & Demodovich, 1983; Crawford & Krone, 1984) where notes are made, using different perceptual positions (self, other, observer); concept fans that take steps backward (De Bono, 1992), metaphorical thinking (using comparisons); reframing matrix using several perspectives such as product, plan, people and potential (Morgan, 1993); radiant thinking or mind mapping (Buzan, 2005); and listing attributes and then identifying as many variations of the attribute as possible.

Part IV

Development of the Managerial Accountant's Compass

8 Managerial Accountant's Compass and Its Context

This chapter is the first of three that describe the rationale behind the managerial accountant's compass. It gives the managerial accountant a comprehensive framework that encompasses their role and responsibilities. It ensures the managerial accountant works toward their performance, planning targets by making their time more productive. It guides the use information to address managerial accounting practices, issues and challenges. It supports an extended decision process to actively understand a specific organization problem or opportunity. It is compatible with a range of managerial accounting theories and theories of human cognition and action. It accepts that discourse actively constructs, enacts and negotiates managerial accounting, and encourages the reflexive use of language. The discussion following both describes assumed knowledge of the managerial accountant and suggests avenues that the managerial accountant can constructively explore with non-accounting managers. As noted earlier, it features the use of questions to engender communication. The managerial accountant's compass promotes a sense of enquiry or discovery.

8.1 Rationale for the Structure of the Managerial Accountant's Compass

The genesis of the managerial accountant's compass lies in the distinction between processes and states (Joos, 1968; Kenny, 2003; Mourelatos, 1978). It is formalized as stocks and flows in economics (Fisher, 1896) and is used in management and accounting.[1] System dynamics, which is also concerned with resources and their use, prefers 'levels' and 'rates' respectively (Forrester, 1968). The managerial accountant's compass has an inner structure that corresponds to processes and states respectively. The inner framework of processes involves both inputs and outputs or, factors and responses respectively, and the use of the five is discussed in detail in Chapter 9.

The outer perimeter is the result of considering states or particular aspects of a larger systems. It captures historic, present and likely future external forces that can affect the work of the managerial accountant. In other words, it is the context over which the managerial accountant has little control but can monitor.

After the managerial accountant's compass was constructed, a check using first principles (Aristotle, 1996; Kant, 1999) was used to validate it (Barnes, 1993). 'First principles' means rethinking a problem from the ground up, using foundational propositions or assumptions that stand alone (Irwin, 1990). The concentric circles approach avoids introducing a hierarchy into the model, and this was consistent with avoiding the dualism of a macro- and micro-analysis. The ubiquity of goals and boundaries or constraints was clear from the literature on a range of managerial accounting topics. The managerial accountant provides advice and assistance, and this entails communication. Collegiate working relationships enable communication, and the most desirable form is nonviolent communication (Rosenberg, 2015). One of the most salient points in the major textbooks is that managerial accounting lacks the accounting standards of financial accounting, but they commend to readers some guidelines that cannot be further reduced or simplified. This suggests the desirability principles placed with goals. However, any guideline and any law can be broken so the behavior or conduct of an activity so decisions shape character and vice versa. That suggests the need for ethics, and with it, self-care. Otherwise judgment may not be considered in the long term. Although these are then taken as self-evident, Cartesian doubt suggests continuing skepticism so the provisional conclusions should be reconsidered, and this now occurs.

The discussion of theories, discourse, information, role and responsibilities, performance and decisions all established that doing anything in managerial accounting requires goals to be established. They also showed that there are limitations or restrictions, although this is not necessarily explicit, so boundaries are necessary to scope and constrain action. The managerial accountant has considerable freedom to select their preferred method because there is a wide range of established calculations, analyses and evaluations available, and boundaries and constraints also affect this selection so methods and models are identified. Methods are tools and techniques, many of which were discussed in Chapter 3. Models refer to the theories or analytical frameworks, many of which were discussed in Chapter 2. Methods and models do not stand alone. Their selection and implementation require guidance, and these can be conveniently labeled principles since they are basic guides to understanding and action. The earlier discussion of role and responsibilities encouraged the managerial accountant to form collegiate relationships with non-accounting managers as well as senior managers, in addition to their accounting pees. Thus, collegiate relationships with others are added to the managerial accountant's compass. These four elements are regarded as separate but united by a common good. The managerial accountant and their practices should be ethical, and integrating self-care[2] practices into the daily routine mitigates against poor judgment, so it is the fifth cardinal point at the center. Information and discourse are analogous to infrastructure and so are common to both. This established them and suggested the metaphor of the compass.

8.2 Visual Depiction of the Managerial Accountant's Compass

The managerial compass consists of five processes and four contextual states. It provides an analytical framework for the managerial accountant to bear in mind when fulfilling their role and responsibilities assisting non-accountant managers and employees. This set which comprises the inner framework of processes and outer perimeter of states is shown in Figure 8–1, using the metaphor of a compass with an external perimeter or frame.

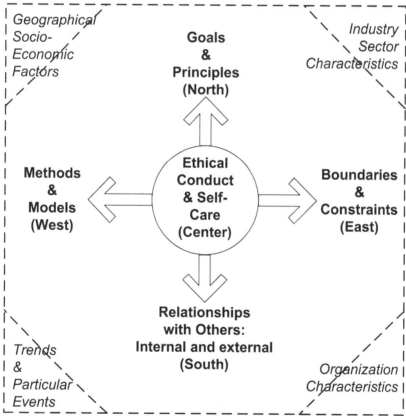

Note to Figure: Theories, information, analyses resulting in recommendations, decisions, and, judgements are selected and applied within the Managerial Accountant's Compass framework.

Figure 8–1 The managerial accountant's compass comprising the inner framework of processes with five cardinal points and the outer perimeter of states with four contextual factors.

Neither the inner set of processes nor the outer perimeter of states are privileged. In other words, the starting point can be either the compass or the context. The sequence of compass points or context corners can take any order. This recognizes individual differences in patterns of thinking as well as differences in the approach to sense-making.

8.3 Inner Framework of Processes: Five Cardinal Points of the Managerial Accountant's Compass

The managerial accountant's compass uses the analogy of the four cardinal directions or cardinal points (north, east, south and west), with east being in the clockwise direction of rotation from north. Dynastic Chinese culture and some other Central Asian cultures view the center as a fifth principal direction hence the managerial compass has five points. Centrally positioning ethical conduct and self-care ensure it is connected to all points, and this is why the other four compass points do not have their own connections.

The managerial accountant's compass has two planes: vertical and horizontal. In the vertical plane are goals (concerning the expected future and customer profitability), principles (the guides to consistent action), and relations with other people (non-accountant managers and employees). In the horizontal plane are the boundaries and constraints (including the conditions under which managerial accountant's work), and the methods and models. The fifth point is the center of the managerial compass. At the very center of the compass is the requirement to act ethically, when making decisions, and particularly when faced with an ethical dilemma, and this is affirmed with self-care. Together, they are a set of issues and considerations that the managerial accountant can address to determine whether their initial assessment is incomplete. The managerial accountant's compass applies equally whether financial or non-financial information[3] is being used by the managerial accountant. The outer perimeter of the managerial compass provides context with four external considerations.

8.4 Outer Perimeter of States: Context

The five compass points are surrounded by the outer perimeter to give the managerial accountant a context for the role and responsibilities. Taken in clockwise order, the four contextual factors move from the global to the personal. The four factors are (1) geographical factors, (2) industry characteristics, (3) organization characteristics, and (4) trends and particular events. Each is now discussed, suggesting points for attention by the managerial accountant to supply detail based on the circumstances of their own organization, and their role and responsibilities.

Geographical Socioeconomic Factors (Global, Domestic, and Regional or Community)

Geographical factors affect the socioeconomic circumstances of the industry, organization and individuals (Hofer, 1975; Porter, 1985). Their extent of impact may refer to global[4] (or international), domestic (national), and regional or community. This may be due to cyclical or structural factors. Cyclical factors relate to the demand side of the economy. They include expansion/recession, spending/saving, and employment/unemployment. Fiscal policies seek to stabilize the demand-side disturbances to the economy and are short term. They are measured with indicators of employment, industrial production, sales and personal income. Or they may be structural factors that do not change with the economic cycle and relate to the supply-side of the economy. Structural factors include laws, demographics, the relative size of major sectors, and skills, experiences and knowledge, and they require long-term policies. They can be measured with shifts in capital and labor, changes in resource availability and political change. For both, the managerial accountant has to determine their relative weight and the duration of the impact and their implications for their industry and organization.

Industry Sector Characteristics

Industry characteristics affect risk and return (performance). There are eight commonly identified industry characteristics that the managerial accountant should use to contextualize their work:

1. Industry group within an economic sector
2. Market structure
3. Industry size
4. Industry trends
5. Industry success factors
6. Industry competition
7. Industry government regulation
8. Technological advancement and automation at the industry level

The aim is to ensure that industry characteristics are not overlooked, so the managerial accountant can consider whether the changes are likely from its underlying economic structure.

> **Industry group within an economic sector:** An economic sector is a large segment of the economy (e.g., primary, secondary and tertiary, although there are other breakdowns[5]) in which organizations share the same or a related product or service (Wolfe, 1955). An industry is a specific grouping of organizations with highly

similar business activities. Industries are usually further sub-categorized into various, more specific groupings to enable meaningful comparison. So, the managerial accountant will consider what attracts investors to the sector and subgroup, and what is important to them.

Market structure: This is the organization of the market and its consequences. There are four types of market structure (Chamberlin, 1933) as shown in Table 8–1. Many decisions of the managerial accountant in an organization are shaped by the type of market structure as it influences products, volume, extent of technology innovation and adoption, geographic spread and regulation.

Table 8–1 Market structure and its implications for the managerial accountant's compass.

Market Structure	Characteristics	Implications for the Managerial Accountant's Compass
Pure competition	Many competing organizations selling identical products or services.	Since the products are similar and it is easy to start up, there is considerable information about the product and competitors.
Monopolistic competition	Many small organizations selling slightly differentiated products or services	Since there are many competing organizations, competition is high.
Oligopoly	A small number of organizations are responsible for most sales.	The actions of one organization (for example, a price cut or an aggressive advertising campaign) significantly affect actions of its rivals.
Monopoly	A single seller for a product. The product has no close substitutes.	Since there is little or no competition, there is frequently government oversight or government granted production rights in which controls apply.

Economists usually represent market structure in terms of the seller, buyer and consequences as shown in Table 8–2. The managerial accountant can consider information availability, pricing changes and the tendency for government intervention.

Table 8–2 Market structure for seller and buyers for one, two few and many traders and its consequences for industry behavior.

Number of traders	One	Two	Few	Many
Competition	*Imperfect*			
Seller	Pure monopoly* or monopoly	Duopoly	Oligopoly	Perfect
Buyer	Monopsony (monopolistic competition)	–	Oligopsony	
Possible consequences	Lack of substitute and price discrimination even where there is government regulation	Collusion even where there is government regulation	Collusion (strategic interaction by the cartel) even where there is government regulation	Possibly perfect information, homogeneous products, perfect property rights, no effect on third parties, and lack of economies of scale or network effects

* Where no close substitutes for the product are available

Industry size: It is traditionally divided into large, medium and small, although small and medium may be amalgamated as small-to-medium enterprises (SME). It may be related to market structure (e.g., an oligopoly is the industry). The managerial accountant will determine whether there are 'flagship' organizations that provide strategic leadership and direction to suppliers, customers and operate as a coordinated network (frequently in competition with similar networks) as this can affect joint ventures, market sharing, technology transfer and supplier development (Rugman & D'Cruz, 1997).

Industry trends: This includes the behavior of consumer, new product development, outsourcing, and industry-wide training or certification. Some industry trends are apparent from a five forces analysis (Porter, 1985). The managerial accountant will be aware of industry directions for consumers, and adoption of technology as this can identify early adopters (Moore, 2014).

Industry success factors: These are the features and actions that an industry needs to possess if it is to be successful. It is unclear whether clustering for vertical and horizontal integration is viable owing to their tendency to become monopolies. The managerial accountant can make their own assessment using their preferred theories and understanding of strategy.

Industry competition: This is evident from increasing profits, market share and sales volume by varying the elements of the marketing mix: price, product, distribution and promotion. Again, the managerial accountant can make their own assessment (e.g., by integrating different sources of external information).

Industry government regulation: This is the right of local, state or federal regulators to control industry behavior. It may use price setting mechanisms, regulate the quantity or quality of products and services produced, or provide consumer protection. Or, it may permit self-regulation through codes administered by trade associations. Unprecedented products and services are often unregulated owing to little awareness of the hazards they pose (e.g., loss of privacy), or little effort to investigate their dangers.[6]

Technological advancement and automation at the industry level:[7] This may be adoption of technology,[8] or its advancements for processes,[9] its embodiment in products and services, or automation of equipment or processes in operations (e.g., warehousing), as well as administration. The consequences may include low levels of social interaction, changes to the empowerment of technical personnel and outsourcing. Although a technology may start in an organization, an industry may increase its reliability and efficiency.[10] The managerial accountant should be familiar with the architecture to offer recommendations about operations and strategy.[11] In addition, they will be aware which systems are preferred for decision making to assess the accuracy and completeness of their information.

Organization Characteristics

Four major organization characteristics are discussed: performance, stage in life cycle, execution of strategy and financial position. These are selected on the basis of their inclusion in macro and micro discussions of organizations including high-performance organizations (e.g., Capon, Farley & Hoenig, 1996; Ittner & Larcker, 2006; Richard, Devinney, Yip & Johnson, 2009). The aim is to achieve broad coverage, so the managerial accountant has a broad base of information that is likely to include weak signals, which may indicate emerging issues.

Organization Performance

Performance[12] is considered with nine characteristics that should be known to the managerial accountant. They are

1. Organization history in terms of origin, people and evolution
2. Corporate financial backing

3. Organization size
4. Organization structure
5. Organization culture
6. Organization policies
7. Organization creativity and innovation
8. Organization risk profile
9. Organization reputation

Each is briefly discussed to identify the kinds of information the managerial accountant could search from documents or obtain from conversations, which would provide context for their work. No causal claims are made, nor is the extent of risk assessed. That is left up to the managerial accountant.

> **Organization history:** This concerns its origin (e.g., Ferruccio Lamborghini founded his automobile company because his personal complaints to Enzo Ferrari were ignored), the part played by key people (e.g., the marketer and engineer combination of the Hon. C. S. Rolls and Charles Royce, respectively), its evolution (e.g., product or services offered) and location (e.g., Boeing moved from Seattle to Chicago) in the present day.
>
> **Corporate backing or parent:** The legal entity that ultimately owns and controls the organization allowing them to control management and determine whether trading continues. It may indicate the extent of resources available and likelihood to continue as a growing concern.
>
> **Organization size:** This differs from the industry nomenclature and usually is stated as the number of employees or the average annual revenue. Its size can make it vulnerable to events outside of it. The size may be measured in various ways, for example, according to net profit, total assets, total sales revenue, total number of employees, geographic spread or tax paid. Organization size may affect reputation and the capability to fund innovation or use new or unproven technology.
>
> **Organization structure:** This is the formal establishment of position titles, duties, and authority to pursue strategies and goals combined with the filling of them with employees and contractors and assessment of performance. The five generic organization configurations proposed by Mintzberg (1979, 2009) are used in Table 8–3 to differentiate common characteristics from Ketchen, Jr., Thomas & Snow (1993), Kotter (1978), Lawrence & Lorsch (1967) and Miles & Snow (1978). These are coordination (supervision, standardization of work processes, standardization of outputs), level of skill and training, and job design (division of labor, unit grouping, behavior formalization and performance

Table 8–3 Organization configurations based on the identifying characteristics of coordination (supervision, standardization of work processes, standardization of outputs), skills and training, design of jobs (division of labor, unit grouping, behavior formalization and performance control), and assessing its benefits and disadvantages.

Ideal or Pure Configuration	Scope	Management	Skill level & Training	Job Design		Behavior Formalization	Performance Control	Assessment		
	Goal	Coordination		Job Specialization (Division of Labor)	Unit Grouping			Benefit	Disadvantage	Example
Simple structure	Founder's preference	Direct supervision	Unskilled	Task specific	Usually functional	Observation	Direct instruction	Easy to recruit	Employee turnover	Café
Machine organization	Efficiency (greatest quantitative bang for the quantitative buck)	Standardized processes in detail Standardized outputs	Employees need only basic skills and training	Highly specialized tasks	Work as individual employees	Rules, policies job descriptions Formal communication	Measurement of mass production processes and outputs	Easy to train employees	Employees are often bored or stifled	McDonald's fast food chain
Professional Organization	Proficiency	Standardized skills Autonomous resisting influence of colleagues and administrators	Employees are highly skilled and trained usually outside the organization with some internal training	Broad tasks corresponding to skills and qualifications	Work independently and in some teams	Follow routines Use functional specialties Oriented to clients	Standing committees and task forces	Employees carrying out own processes according to the predetermined protocols	Employee loyalty is to their profession	Hospital

Ideal or Pure Configuration	Scope	Management	Job Design				Performance Control	Assessment		
	Goal	Coordination	Skill level & Training	Job Specialization (Division of Labor)	Unit Grouping	Behavior Formalization		Benefit	Disadvantage	Example
Entrepreneurial Organization (replaces divisionalized)	Obedience to a single leader	Standardized outputs	Some but expertise is paramount	Allocation of tasks as goals	Loose coupling of units	Head office sets targets.	Set and monitor performance standards	Market oriented and focused despite size	Diversity suffer in complex or dynamic environment.	Putin's Russia
Project organization (previously innovative organization, and adhocracy)	Creation of product or service	Mutual adjustment and selective decentralization	Employees are highly skilled and trained, usually outside the organization.	Uses expertise from experience, training or qualifications	Employees work in teams.	Work carried out on behalf of a client	Some inefficiency and slack permitted	Allows creative solutions to be customized	Little distinction between planning and execution of work	Film making Advertising

control). The managerial accountant can compare this ideal model with the arrangements they observe, to assess whether there are any potential weaknesses that affect their role as well as organizational viability.

Organization culture: In includes the shared values, legends, rituals, beliefs, meanings, values, norms and language which govern how employees behave, which may differ in its subculture (Kotter & Heskett, 1992; Schein, 1992). It is partly expressed in codes of conduct and standards of service. It may also be visible in how employees dress, perform their jobs and interact with customers. Other influences on behavior are senior management and employee peers. There may be a discrepancy between espoused culture and practiced culture. The managerial accountant may need to explore this for themselves since culture is developed through tradition, history and structure, so it is impossible to find many that prevail codified (e.g., Wieder, 1974).

Organization policies: These include principles, rules and guidelines formulated or adopted by an organization consistent with its long-term goals and communicated in a form that is widely accessible. Organization policies as guiding principle used to set direction are often differentiated from processes or steps to accomplish routine activities. The managerial accountant will clarify the policies created for organizational governance, customer service (including complaints), for pricing of products and services, for accounting and for external compliance (e.g., taxation, trade practices).

Organization creativity and innovation: Creativity is unleashing the potential of the mind to conceive new ideas, and putting those ideas to work by making an idea viable through identifying an unrecognized and unmet need. Innovation changes the consumer's wants by creating new ones, extinguishing old ones and creating new ways of satisfying customers. Some are incremental improvements in products/services, business methods and customer services. For these, the managerial accountant asks, "Would we still do this if we weren't already doing it?" Drucker (1980) encourages the purposeful abandonment of current products/services and arrangements. Radical innovations involve finding an entirely new way to do things. As such, they are often risky and difficult to implement. The managerial accountant can provide information outside the core organizational routines to simplify, improve, enable and deliver the innovation (Govindarajan & Trimble, 2010).

Organization risk profile:[13] The willingness to take risks and preparedness against threats over the uncertainty of lost value. Instead of trying to identify individual risks directly, risk can be

Table 8–4 Ranking individual risk factors in two dimensions (relative importance and level of control) for customers, its products and services, and processes.

| | | Level of Control Over Risk | |
		High Control	Low Control
Relative Importance of Risk	*High likelihood*	Ambiguity in customer needs Organization relies on the customer. Products or services have high customer consumption.	Customer relationships based on cost or no long-term commitment Difficulties in quickly changing processes Products or services conform to external standards
	Low likelihood	Customer partnering Custom products and services Knowledge, skills and abilities can recognize and respond to the threats Examples from other organizational subunits	Unreliable information processes and systems Commodity products or services Unforeseeable threats omitted from contingency plans or planning scenarios

approached by considering importance and control. The Keil, Cule, Lyytinen and Schmidt (1998) software project approach has been reformulated in Table 8–4 to accounting by considering customers, products and services, and processes using a two-dimensional grid. The managerial account can assess how non-accounting managers perceive and react to risk.

Organization reputation: The opinions held by stakeholders and others as a result of evaluating the ambiguous information they receive from the organization, the media and other monitors of the organization (Fombrun & Shanley, 1990). The core of reputation are specific categories including product quality, corporate governance, employee relations, intellectual capital, financial performance, and handling environmental and social issues (Eccles, Newquist & Schatz, 2007). The managerial accountant can consider whether there is anything they are involved with, which can expose the organization to reputational risk and avoid having to participate in crisis management to handle those already affecting reputation.

The nine areas for organizational performance relate to performance provide a wide coverage of the organization characteristics associated with performance but need to be supplemented with understanding the stage in organization's life cycle.

Organization Stage in Organization Life Cycle

An organization passes though distinct stages over periods of time (Oliver, 2012).[14] Table 8–5 outlines the stages. Although organizational life cycles are shortening, from 60 years in the 1920s, to 1–15 years this is not shown.[15] Not every organization will pass through each stage; nor is it necessary for the stages to be experienced in the sequence shown in the life cycle.[16] The organizational life cycle is independent of economic life cycles (alternating phases of economic growth and decline associated with gross domestic product) which have their own periodicity (e.g., Juglar fixed-investment cycle of 7 to 11 years identified by Schumpeter, 1954). The managerial accountant who understands where their organization is on the life cycle may be able to foresee upcoming life cycle challenges and to allow timely decisions and judgments.

Table 8–5 Stage of life cycle and implications for managerial accountant's compass.

Stage of Organization in Life Cycle	Distinguishing Features	Implications for the Managerial Accountant's Compass
Startup	Covers inception or acquisition from the initial idea until the general purpose financial statements are produced for the first year	Establishing the organization as a full- or part-time operation requires a different set of skills, analyses and evaluation criteria than running it
Growth	Includes the initial growth and any secondary expansion. Initial growth is focused on the defined customer base and establishing a market presence. Secondary expansion is establishing new markets and distribution channels.	Concerns with improving profitability may introduce issues for ethical organizational behavior and culture, as well as difficulties in managing growth.
Maturity	As the organization experiences the end of growth, there may be some sales and revenue may be static, or they may be reduced. This may not be apparent if there is inflation.	Responding to reduced or stable revenue, profitability, or erosion of market share requires strategic changes and may lead to cost reduction or cost cutting.[17]
Decline[18]	The organization must either cease its business or accept a takeover.[19] A successful turnaround may return the business to a growth or maturity stage.	Decline may involve new stakeholders, as well as changes to the conduct and oversight of business activities.

Many models of organization life cycles have been proposed. However, attempts to associate measures of effectiveness with them have proven less robust over time (Quinn & Cameron, 1983). However, all models appear to agree that there are distinct differences between early and mature stages and execution of strategy.

Organization Execution of Its Strategy

Strategy is ambiguous[20] so the managerial accountant can make enquiries about the following organization strategy characteristics to build rapport with non-accounting managers and explore any inconsistencies as well as reassess their information needs. There are 12 strategy characteristics that can be found in execution:

1. Vision
2. Mission
3. Product or service groups
4. Product or service mix
5. Capacity utilization
6. Distribution channels
7. Markets
8. Market share concentration
9. Resources and capabilities
10. Opportunities
11. Supply–chain
12. Competitor

> **Vision:** A statement on what the desired future optimal state, to make clear what the organization needs to achieve.
>
> **Mission:** A definition of the present state or purpose of an organization by outlining the specific sector in which it operates, describing what is done, how it is done, to whom it is directed (market and client) and what value is brought.
>
> **Product or service groups:** Products or services can be considered individually (as line items) or as collections (product groups) or as variations to a specific product that appeal to different customers (product range). A product or a service is an item purchased and consumed that has tangible and intangible features that satisfy the customer (Drucker, 1974). This allows the managerial accountant to consider product mix and market segmentation.
>
> **Product or service mix:** The range of products or services offered to customers and the relationships between them. The number and their proportions may be limited by production or stocking constraints.
>
> **Capacity utilization:** A measurement of the extent to which the practical output levels are met or used.[21] It is frequently expressed

as the percentage of total capacity that is actually being achieved in a given period.

Distribution channels: The businesses or intermediaries (agents and brokers) through which products or services pass, until they reach the end consumer (Drucker, 1974). The managerial accountant will take into account the different costs and revenues of distribution channels.

Markets: The medium that allows buyers and sellers of a specific product or service to interact in order to facilitate an exchange. It implies an area and possibly other systems (e.g., hire), institutions (e.g., volunteer), processes (e.g., barter), social relations (e.g., extended family) and infrastructures (e.g., subsidies), which accomplish an exchange.

Market share concentration: The proportion an organization has of a specified market. Concentration ratio measures the market share (expressed as a percentage) of the four largest organizations in an industry.[22] Governments consider whether takeovers and mergers affect concentration.

Resources and capabilities: The economic or productive factors required to accomplish an activity or achieve desired outcome. Basic resources are land, labor, and capital and actions. Capabilities are measures of abilities to provide benefits. Resources identified as part of the resource-based view of the firm may lead to competitive advantage. Resources and capabilities may be scarce, overvalued or unappreciated.

Opportunities: Occasions or situations that contain circumstances open to exploitation with uncertain outcomes, requiring commitment of resources and involving exposure to risk. Opportunities have to be recognized and are time bound.

Supply-chain:[23] The entire system of organizations, people, processes, information, and resources involved in the production and distribution of a commodity and providing it to the customer. They may be loosely or closely coupled.

Competitor: An organization with the potential to offer a similar product or service, act without warning to change the appeal of its products and services reasonably or unreasonably, or retaliate to threats to reduce its market share. An agile competitor can quickly change its strategy.

The managerial accountant together with the organization's non-accounting managers contributes to executing strategy. Execution requires judgment and attention as customer and shareholder value can be both created and destroyed. In understanding organization characteristics, the managerial accountant will consider whether information is available on these characteristics and is up-to-date. Bearing in mind the earlier discussion on discourse, the managerial accountant may prefer to introduce new information in ways that avoid disrupting the meanings that non-accounting managers attach to their actions (e.g., as a risk assessment, an innovation that adds value or providing information about trends).

Organization Financial Position

The organization financial position is a snapshot of its current sales revenue (and other income), profit (or surplus revenue) and retained earnings. Additional information may include working capital and capital investment (or capital budget).

For capital budgeting purposes, an organization uses two forms of financing to purchase the assets employed or used in the business: debt (borrowed money) and cash (equity), or a combination of both. For debt, the cost of the debt is the interest rate charged calculated on an after-tax rate for the net cost of debt. For equity, it is the implicit cost to allow for return on equity. Generally, to arrive at a total organization value, a weighting is applied to the cost of capital which is then used as the required rate of return to discount cash flows. The managerial accountant will be aware that financing requires cash flow, and this is dependent upon efficient and effective operations.

Organization was examined from four perspectives: performance, stage in life cycle, execution of strategy and financial position. They give the managerial accountant useful information about the organization. Some of that information is dynamic, so understandings obtained should always be rechecked before being carried over to a current situation.

Trends and Particular Events

Trends and particular events often impact the vision, mission, brand, and competitive position of the organization as well as the credibility of its management. Usually, they are easy to recognize but difficult to harness. Trends and particular events may themselves not be innovations and may distract from plans and activities that are innovative. The managerial accountant considers how trends and particular events can be successfully exploited so time is not wasted, any investment is not squandered, morale is improved, and external relationships are solidified.

Trends and Megatrends

Trends refer to change or development. Trends can be general, averages or a direction-specific development, or change in condition, output or process, and the determination whether it is a fad or a fashion (Brindle & Stearns, 2001). Some are megatrends: a profound trajectory of social, economic, environmental or technological change (Hajkowicz, 2015).

Although trends and megatrends are important in their own right, they also cross influence each other. Various authors have identified different numbers of megatrends. Naisbitt (1984) identified ten. Hajkowicz (2015) suggested seven. Ernest and Young (2015) identified six megatrends. A composite of them results in four trends used to highlight issues that affect the role and responsibilities of the managerial accountant:

1.   The global marketplace becomes more integrated.
2.   Digital expansion improves services but affects privacy.
3.   Urbanization continues disadvantaging regions.
4.   Health and health care are reimagined.

> **The global marketplace becomes more integrated:** This trend is supported by financial system linkages, resilient supply chains, favorable exchange rates, trade agreements, favorable demographics and willing consumers prepared to accept entrepreneurship. There are also stronger nationalistic, religious and ethnic movements around the world.
>
> **Digital expansion improves services but affects privacy:** The capture of vast amounts of information using new communication and delivery media will transform existing products and create new markets. This brings new competition and introduces ethical issues for the stewardship of the information that can be collected.
>
> **Urbanization continues disadvantaging regions:** The number and scale of cities continues to grow. This requires planning to attract sustained investment in infrastructure, utilities and housing. In regions, food production competes with new technologies that can access oil, gas and minerals on agricultural land. Environmental policies are applied inconsistently and often do not favor agriculture.
>
> **Health and health care is reimagined:** Changing demographics, rising incomes in rapid-growth markets and chronic-diseases attract organizations outside health care. Promoting healthy behaviors and self-care is sporadic.

Megatrends have paradoxical and dialectical aspects (Naisbitt, 1984). For example, while 'high touch' (i.e., human involvement) is valued, the increased dependency on technology is reducing their presence in customer interactions. The managerial accountant can overlay the megatrends on their organization, and organizations they may wish to work for in the future to consider their consequences[24] as it is unclear exactly how quickly the changes will occur.

Particular events

Particular events (both natural and caused by humans) emphasize unusual, unplanned incidents or episodes that have an influence beyond their immediate triggering circumstances. For example, the global financial crisis of 2007–2008 continues to have many repercussions outside the financial sector as its dimensions are analyzed. Obvious concerns are the presence of undisclosed conflicts of interest, and the failure of regulators to both prevent questionable trading practices and recognize the looming crisis and avert it. There are also compensation structures that encourage short-term deals which created bubbles in the real estate and stock market. Ball (2009) considers that risky positions supported with extraordinary leverage will inevitably succumb to the efficient market hypothesis (Fama, 1970). The managerial accountant therefore needs to consider both the consequences of poor regulation and the possibility of rare events that are outside the contingency or disaster plan of an organization. For example, disruptions to the sale of products and services, unexpected reductions to consumer spending power, restrictions on travel and communications, or dramatic price increase. Transformative businesses can take advantage of these trends and events.

8.5 Summary of Contextual Factors to the Managerial Compass

In summary, to evaluate context, the managerial accountant has four matters to consider. There are the geographical factors that have three levels: global, national and regional. There are the influencing factors of the industry. They include the industry group within an economic sector, market structure, industry size, industry trends, industry success factors, industry competition, industry government regulation, and technological advancement and automation at the industry level. There are the immediate factors of the organization. Its performance characteristics include its history, corporate backing or parent, size, structure, culture, policies, creativity and innovation, and risk profile. These are supplemented with studies of the stage in the organization life cycle, its financial position, and its execution of strategy. There are the trends and particular or one-off events. Trends and one-off events can differentially affect industries and organizations (e.g., prices, competition and regulation). The factors that comprise context give the managerial accountant a checklist for investigating whether their analyses and recommendations overlook any salient influences. If these are overlooked or misunderstood, the managerial accountant cannot fulfill their role and responsibilities.

Notes

1. Some problems in the distinction between stocks and flows are identified by Clower (1959) and Harrison (1980). In accounting, profit or income is represented as a flow. In economics, stock amounts include money, financial assets, liabilities, wealth, real means of production, capital, inventories and labor, while, flow magnitudes include income, spending, saving, debt repayment, fixed investment, inventory investment and labor utilization. Thus, capital

is a stock that produces a periodic income, which is a flow. The presence of these terms in psychology has other unconnected uses with cognition (e.g., Meehl, 1992).

2. Self-care refers to activities undertaken with the intention of enhancing energy, restoring health and manage stress. They ought to be part of a plan to maintain professionalism and avoid preventable illnesses and injuries, which is discussed in chapter 10.

3. Financial information takes the form of numbers as a monetary amount. It may be a profit statement, a job cost, a price, a budget amount, a variance or an actual amount. Non-financial information may either be numbers (such as the number of hours a machine is used) or take the form or words, symbols or diagrams. For this reason, many managerial accountants prefer to distinguish between quantitative information (that uses numbers) and qualitative information that is concerned with characteristics or properties. For example, a decision to outsource may consider the importance of employee morale and loyalty. The use of qualitative factors may also arise because quantitative data are not available, and estimates by experts vary (Oliver, 2012).

4. Globalization is the term used to describe the removal of borders for the international expansion of markets. Globalization has occurred with the adoption of the Gregorian calendar and since land and mercantile trade expanded from Europe. While cultural, political, technological and economic domains of countries expand beyond their own national boundary through creating transnational corporations (businesses with a base in one country but conducting operations in a number of other countries), the rate of globalization has been increased through agreement on standards, improved technologies and the lifting of trade restrictions.

5. To further confuse the classification, the terms 'sector' and 'industry' are often used interchangeably. Improvements in technology require less labor, and they move to the tertiary sector (Clark, 1940).

6. Issues include the very high standards of proof that are required to prove danger and the apparent unquestioning adoption by consumers. The presumption that new chemicals and technologies are safe until proven otherwise is a fundamental problem. Many new chemicals were introduced because they promised benefits but were later shown to cause great harm (e.g., some neurotoxicants, asbestos, thalidomide, diethylstilbestrol and the chlorofluorocarbons; Grandjean & Landrigan, 2014).

7. In a study of the decline of the pre-eminent cotton industry, Lazonick (1983: 232) uses the distinction between the manager of neoclassical theory who, "to use modern language, optimizes subject to 'given' constraints and the entrepreneur who alters these constraints, thus creating new profitable opportunities". That is, managerial activity is different to entrepreneurial activity; so feasible technological choices and profitable opportunities may be constrained across the industry (Schumpeter, 1947).

8. Technology is the industrial use of scientific discoveries. There is no guarantee they will be successfully implemented (e.g., superconductivity of electricity with zero resistance has been known since 1991 but has not been commercialized), or that the superior technology will become established in the marketplaces (e.g., for video the VHS system replaced the superior quality Sony Beta recording).

9. Accounting software packages have replaced manual (i.e., handwritten) journals and ledgers, creating a central repository of accounting information. Also, manual worksheets completed with pencil and corrected using an eraser have been replaced by spreadsheet productivity applications, which allow calculations to be automatically completed, numbers to be changed and new

numbers derived using formulas. These changes allow decisions to be made earlier in some cases.

10. One or more organizations may independently be pursuing an innovation to maximize sales before competitors can offer a similar or superior copy, but then see the advantages of pooling knowledge. This may occur through a joint venture (e.g., Concorde), sale to an organization with related capabilities or the result of catastrophe (e.g., after Comet crashes British jet, and aircraft technology was shared with US manufacturers, notably Boeing.

11. Some organizations mistakenly install an integrated system such as an enterprise resource planning system believing that it will standardize operations and eliminate many subsidiary and shadow systems. Generally, their lack of attention to the design of the new system and migration between old and new systems results in a myriad of existing systems (for their features, or for their reliability), although management may not become aware of this for some time. There have been some cases where purchasing and sales information captured and transferred to the general ledger for business financial and non-financial reporting resolved discrepancies between reports produced by systems containing different data. However, more information does not produce better decisions. The expression 'garbage-in, garbage-out' is a reminder that where managers and employees blindly rely on reports produced by automated systems, they are likely to make substandard decisions.

12. Measures of performance include net profit, total assets, total sales, total revenue, tax paid, number of employees or number of branches.

13. Uncertainty is a potential, unpredictable and uncontrollable outcome. Risk involves damage, injury, liability, loss or any other negative occurrence that is caused by external or internal vulnerabilities that may be avoided through pre-emptive action.

14. The business life cycle is distinguished from the economic cycle. The economic cycle is the periodic but irregular rise and fall of economic activity, measured by fluctuations in real gross domestic product and other macroeconomic variables. Both the business life cycle and the economic cycle are irregular and unpredictable. While the economic cycle may affect the business cycle, other factors such as owner competence, product or service viability and competition affect the cycle experienced by a particular business. Peaks and troughs in the economic cycle may not coincide with the profitability of a particular business.

15. Adizes (1988) describes a more detailed version of stages in the life cycle based around predictability and flexibility (with analogies). His book is full of aphorisms including, 'too many priorities means no priorities' (p. 34) and 'What kind of people are left in a [threatening] environment? Administrators' (p. 78). Part 2 deals with culture as leadership. More generally, Adizes' sees interrelationships (p. 130–131) between performance (what), administration (how), entrepreneurship (when hides why) and integration (who and with whom). The energy of power (ability to reward and punish), authority (the capability to say yes or no) and influence are associated with implementing decisions.

16. Some organizations are designed for the short-term. For example, quasi government authority setup to host Olympic competitions. Moreover, methods that bring success in a particular stage may not be successful in later stages. The organizations may be run from home, from a secretarial service or from a formal office.

17. The first author of Coyne, Coyne and Coyne (2010) is a former McKinsey associate and executive assistant to the Deputy Secretary of the Treasury. He proposes systematic methods to reduce costs assuming (a) that some cost cutting has already occurred and that there are no obvious areas or items

that could be cut, and (b) massive savings from high-risk actions would not be countenanced.

18. An organization may experience a one-off internal or external event that disrupts revenue. For example, an external disruption would be the cessation of supply of electricity. For example, an internal disruption would be an employee strike. One-off events lead to the loss of revenue but generally are not responsible for decline unless risk has been improperly assessed. For example, insurance cover for the organization has not been obtained or kept up-to-date.

19. A comprehensive review of takeovers in Australia between 2010 and 2015 (Damien & James, 2016), found 42.9% of hostile bids came from a foreign bidder and just 11.4% were bids from private equity; only 8.6% of hostile bids attracted rival offers. The average share price premium offered started at 37.2% and reached 53%.

20. Mintzberg (1987) provides five definitions of strategy: (1) plan or consciously intended course of action; (2) ploy or a specific maneuver intended to outwit an adversary; (3) pattern or realized strategy irrespective of the plan; (4) position or a mediating force between an organization and the environment and (5) perspective or view of the world shared by members of an organization. Thus, an organization has a deliberate strategy and an emergent strategy.

21. Capacity measurement should be regarded as a strategic direction and not as a means to evaluate operational performance (Brausch & Taylor, 1997). This will prevent to operation managers from attempting to increase production to reduce unfavorable capacity volume variances resulting in the possible harmful effects of increasing inventory that becomes obsolescent, damaged or surplus to demand. A contribution margin report can be useful. Since all definitions of capacity except theoretical capacity are based on the output that embed waste, downtime and idle capacity into the everyday operations of the factory, there is impetus to maximize capacity, but this overlooks the ultimate goal of producing better, faster and cheaper products (McNair, 1994). Debruine and Sopariwala (1994) advocate using practical capacity because it is the maximum levels at which each plant (factory), shift, cell or work-island can operate efficiently, and thereby uncovers the cost of unused resources. It differentiates the cost of resources available from the cost of resources actually used for a particular purpose. Gantt (1994) highlighted erroneous decisions that can follow when production is reduced (e.g., when the economy is in a recession and production levels drop). More accurate cost structures are necessary to show the cost of inefficiency or the cost of not producing at capacity. Methods that allocate all the production overhead costs to the output regardless of volume creates inflated costs, provides managers with incorrect information, and subsequently facilitates incorrect decisions.

22. Another indicator of firm size, the Herfindahl–Hirschman Index, is a commonly accepted an indicator of the amount of competition among organizations in an industry.

23. Supply chain management encompasses the planning and management of all activities involved in sourcing and procurement, conversion and all logistics management activities. This requires coordination and collaboration between channel partners, which include suppliers, intermediaries, third-party service providers and customers (Karaian, 2014). In essence, supply chain management integrates supply and demand management within and across organizations (Council of Supply Chain Management Professionals, Supply chain management definitions and glossary, 2013).

24. For example, Alvin Toffler popularized the view that the economies would shift from manufacturing and mass production to a computerized and

information-based model using contemporary trends and headlines. He concluded that 'future shock' (1965) was the product of growing feeling of anxiety brought on by the bewildering and ever-accelerating pace at which life was changing. F. M. Esfandiary (also known as FM-2030) proposed that people will eventually become wholly made of synthetic parts, so humans would become 'post-biological organisms' and his predictions included a so-called Santa Claus machine that would produce three-dimensional objects in the manner of copying machines, teleconferencing, telemedicine and teleshopping (1977). 'Nano-technology' was coined by the Tokyo Science University Professor Norio Taniguchi in 1974 to describe the precision manufacture of materials with nanometer tolerances, and Eric Drexler (2007) popularized the potential of molecular nanotechnology. Ray Kurzweil created optical character and speech recognition systems and music synthesizers capable of accurately duplicating the sounds of real instruments. More recently, he explored health and medical learning and is employed to bring natural language understanding to Google. Hans Moravec (1998) is known for his work on robotics, artificial intelligence and generalizing Moore's law to technologies predating the integrated circuit, and extrapolating it to predict super-intelligence. These futurists have all seen transformation as a nonlinear phenomenon. In contrast, some commentators believe that cultural rather than ideological differences will affect economies. For example, Huntington suggests there are nine major civilizations concurrently seeking to exert their sovereign identity (1996) which occurs while there is internal instability from rival praetorian groups (2006).

9 Four Cardinal Points of the Managerial Accountant's Compass

This chapter is the second of three that discuss the managerial accountant's compass. It details the four cardinal points of the compass introduced in Chapter 8 and depicted in Figure 8–1. The four cardinal points are north (goals and principles), south (methods and models), east (boundaries and constraints) and west (collegiate relationship with other managers and employees), and they guide the managerial accountant in exercising their role and responsibilities. Chapter 10 discusses the center cardinal point, that of ethical conduct, which includes self-care for the managerial accountant. As with the previous chapter, the discussion both describes assumed knowledge of the managerial accountant, uses questions to guide attention and suggests avenues that the managerial accountant can constructively explore with non-accounting managers.

9.1 North: Goals and Principles for Organization Success

Earlier chapters showed the prevalence of goals and principles in managerial accounting. They are placed together because they provide foundational guidelines for the role and responsibilities of the managerial accountant. Each is examined in relation to theories to assist, and consequences for, the managerial accountant.

9.1.1 Goals

Goal-oriented theories show the dual nature of goals. They are personal, but they specify expected organizational outcomes. Three theories give insight into motivation and behavior. Locke (1968) claims a relationship between goals and performance. Later, this was elaborated to suggest that goals should have five characteristics: clarity, challenge, complexity, commitment and feedback (Locke & Latham, 1990).[1] Expectancy theory (Vroom & Yetton, 1985) showed that individuals are motivated by goals if there is a desirable reward, which can be achieved through their effort. Management by objectives (Drucker, 1954) uses goals, renamed objectives, to measure organizational effectiveness for short-term and long-term outcomes. For accounting, Flamholtz (1996) shows it contributes to understanding, predicting and controlling the goal-directed behavior of others. So, goals are more than observable and measurable ends to be achieved within specified time frame. They represent an organization's plans and anticipate the demands from its customers. Some organizations set profitability or growth goals. According to Drucker (1974),[2] profitability is an outcome of a successful business, not a goal in its own right. In any case, profitability overlooks service (customer service satisfaction or customer retention) and social outcomes.

Based on the earlier discussion which established that the managerial accountant provides information that can improve decision making, three goals[3] can be identified which are directed at this outcome:

1. Advice: To support non-accounting managers make better decisions. These cover their strategic, tactical and operational activities. It spans the functions of planning, organizing, directing (or coordinating or leading) and controlling;[4]
2. Motivation: To influence non-accounting managers so they achieve organization plans[5] and abide by codes of conduct. This may require devising suitable incentives and providing feedback.
3. Assessment of viability (of the organization and organizational unit): To select and measure the performance of processes or groups (but not individuals because this falls to their line supervisor). This includes assessing economy, effectiveness, competitive position and competitiveness, as well as identifying the potential for improvement.

These goals have long-, mid-, and short-term time horizons with milestones as there is a relationship between them. Goals are connected with principles because they allow goals to be evaluated in their own right and supplement any specific criteria used to judge whether goals are met.

9.1.2 *Principles*

Although financial accounting has established principles[6] (Gordon, 1964), managerial accountants have no such agreed list. Principles are a foundation for reasoning and action that has general applicability (Harré, 1970). However, principles have to be adapted to the particular situation and its context. Twelve principles are proposed, listed in order from broad to narrow. They are drawn from discussion in earlier chapters and the literature cited for each principle. The principle opens with a brief statement and is then elaborated, supported with an example. Each principle concludes with guidance on its application. The principles are independent from each other. Before discussing each principle, they are summarized below:

1. Information and decisions change human behavior, so the behavioral consequences of a decision should be anticipated.
2. The existence of a market with economic exchange that coordinates economic transactions should be recognized.
3. All pertinent information to the issue/s in question must be sought.
4. Use four criteria for information: quantitative measurements (typically financial results or cost information), qualitative factors (e.g., constituents or gradings), strategic criteria and risk.
5. Pursue simplicity, particularly in the design and implementation of systems to produce accounting information.
6. Intended use guides the analysis and the interpretation of results.
7. Prefer a conservative estimate.
8. State a range of different outcomes as best case, the expected case and the worst case.
9. Use both financial and non-financial information in any recommendation, decision or judgement.
10. Always work from total costing to unit costing.
11. Value or usefulness of a product or service is ultimately judged by the customer and is shown by their consumption of it.
12. Benefits must exceed expenses or costs.

Principle #1: Information and decisions change human behavior, so the behavioral consequences of a decision should be anticipated. A decision based on sound economic or technical grounds that is consistent with the goals of the organization may encounter implementation difficulties if the employees believe it diminishes their self-worth as a human being or threatens them. Typically, the behavioral consequences of decisions are particularly likely to be serious where rewards and pay are affected. This also can occur when planning for change.

Changes in human behavior manifest themselves as silent resistance (e.g., taking personal advantage of the available resources to obtain payment or, consciously allowing unplanned consequences to develop). The major mistakes that can occur in following this principle include downplaying the reaction of an individual employee or employees as a group. This may result from underestimating the affront taken by employees, or the tipping effect of a particular decision. Another is delivering criticisms of performance (underperformance) which the recipient does not accept as fair.

Principle #2: Recognize the existence of a market with economic exchange that coordinates economic transactions. Typically, a freely moving market that experiences corrective downturns is the best decision-making device for signaling how resources should be allocated if they are priced. There are markets in information, products and services. A market may have transaction-costs and asymmetrical knowledge (Akerlof, 1970).

Although market implies the forces of demand and supply operate, it can be more broadly used to the meeting of interested parties under a variety of systems, institutions, processes, social relations and infrastructures. The ability to recognize a market provides a new perspective on the parties. The major mistakes that can occur in following this principle are assuming that there is no market, or overlooking the costs of coordination and administration.

Principle #3: All pertinent information to the issue/s in question must be sought. Observation, interviews and sampling are all suitable methods for obtaining information. Typically, there is a trade-off between performing routine analyses and conducting supplementary analyses to ensure that the most accurate and relevant information is presented to the decision maker. It may lead to reconsidering assumptions that formed the basis of the original dataset, as well as specifying the assumptions associated with any new analyses or computations.[7]

The managerial accountant must use judgment in obtaining information and may be limited by time to collect or analyze information. The major mistakes that can occur in following this principle include considering information which is peripheral or misleading, allowing costs, and time to outweigh the benefits of accurate information, and delaying a decision until all possible information can be collated. This may then result in the use of out-of-date information and a decision that is no longer timely.

Principle #4: Use four criteria for information: quantitative measurements (typically financial results or cost information), qualitative factors (e.g., constituents or gradings), strategic criteria and, risk. Typical qualitative factors are aimed at aspects of an organization are difficult or impossible to quantify such as (a) effect on employee morale; (b) impact on schedules, or deadlines; (c) consequences for relationships with and commitments to suppliers; (d) effect on current and prospective customers; and (e) long-term future effect on profitability.

The use of four criteria guides information seeking and analysis. Although immediate and medium-term financial benefits are important in terms of cash flow they may not be realistic or may be subject to risk. In these decision-making situations, qualitative aspects may reveal inadequate analysis or unexpected downsides. The major mistakes that can occur in following this principle include allowing heuristics and cognitive biases (Kahneman, 2012) to select the factors to which attention is given. A related concern is overweighting some factors.

Principle #5: Pursue simplicity[8] to produce accounting information. Simplicity refers to the deliberate effort to produce a solution that has the fewest possible variables and requires the minimum resources to maintain. Typically, many organizations have high costs and are experiencing reduced profitability, so any proposed arrangements should consume as few resources as possible. While this has similarities with Occam's razor,[9] the emphasis here is on producing value for the organization.

Simplicity is desirable in calculations, analyses, and in the design and implementation of systems. In calculations, it includes providing steps that show intermediate workings. In analyses, it is focusing on the major factors that have an impact. In systems, it is separating the routine from the exceptional. The major mistakes that can occur in following this principle is preferring a solution that seeks to use the maximum amount of information and relying on computing power to capture and process the information. More complex understanding begins with elegantly simple foundations.

Principle #6: Intended use guides the analysis and the interpretation of results. That is, analyses and answers undertaken for one purpose should not be transferred and applied to other purposes without first establishing whether they are identical. Since there are many different concepts, classifications and analyses, it is tempting to try and re-use or re-purpose available information. Moreover, as is clear from the discussion of discourse in Chapter 2, there are ambiguities as well as personal interests at work. Typical examples of the use of this principle are making cost calculations and avoiding reliance on previously calculated and available figures for revenues and expenses.

Since there are many valid options to calculate and analyze, all can produce fair, accurate and defensible measures. The major mistakes that can occur in following this principle include poor task definition and assuming that calculations for one period are unaffected by events and trends and retain their functionality in later periods.

Principle #7: Prefer a conservative estimate.[10] When measuring or approximating the quantity, degree or worth of something, avoid excess. It is reasonable to estimate where calculating precise numbers is too time-consuming or too difficult, or there may be disputes over the precise number. Typically, estimates are appropriate for indirect costs where an imperfect cost allocation base[11] is used owing to difficulties in collecting accurate costs, or the fact that costs would exceed benefits of accurate collection.

The quality of an estimate stems primarily from how closely it represents or predicts reality. So, estimates require care, and where time is involved, middle timescales (days and weeks) are best for conceptualizing accomplishments. The major mistakes that can occur in following this principle include giving a single estimate without an adequate basis or being unwilling to admit an estimate is imperfect and subject to change.

Principle #8: State a range of different outcomes as best case, the expected case and the worst case. Typically, these correspond to three results reported: an optimistic level, the expected or present level, and the minimum level. Although this is common when information has any uncertainty in a sensitivity or a 'what-if'[12] analysis, the advantages are numerous. The major advantage is that a figure is given context, and alternatives are provided.

It is usual to identify the variables that contribute to the range. This can then help simplify the model, test its robustness, or explore relationships between input and output variables. Identifying variables may also guide the choice or method of analysis. The major mistakes that can occur in following this principle is using numbers or factors for the worst and best case, which do not indicate the true interval between best and worst, or skew the interval so the expected value is biased.

Principle #9: Use both financial and non-financial information in any recommendation, decision or judgment. The information does not have to be combined, and it may not necessarily triangulate. Non-financial information may be measurements, categories which may or may not have gradations, or separate reports (e.g., social, environmental and human rights information). Typical examples include weighting the financial advantage of outsourcing against qualitative characteristics, which may suggest caution. As a check, quantitative information can also be expressed qualitatively (e.g., by rating or ranking).

Using financial and non-financial information can require additional effort to search for it, as well as, determine how to balance it. The major mistakes that can occur in following this principle include privileging financial information or selecting poor quality non-financial information. A related mistake is mixing lead and lag information instead of balancing both forward and historical information.

Principle #10: Always work from total costing to unit costing. While calculating an average cost or unit cost with respect to the level of activity allows a total cost to be better understood, unit costs must be used cautiously. Typically, any decision should be based on calculating total costs, not extrapolating from unit costs. The reason for calculating unit costs after total costs are available is that unit costs are a function of the total activity. That is, any unit cost depends upon a particular input or output level (depending what is being calculated).

This principle should not be confused with unit level costs in the cost hierarchy of unit, batch, product and facility level costs. The major mistake that occurs in following this principle is over-reliance on unit costs. This may have two drastic consequences. The first is the temptation to use unit costs from an earlier period because they are readily available. They may be inaccurate owing to unperceived changes in prices or process arrangements. The second is that reductions in volume leads to reduced revenue. This may result in insufficient cash flow to pay debts as and when they fall due.

Principle #11: Value or usefulness of a product or service is ultimately judged by the customer and is shown by their consumption of it. The price paid and the experience of customer with the product or service determines its value to the customer. Typically, value is manifested by repeat purchases by the customer, not purchasing a competitor product when the preferred product is out-of-stock or confidence in its features or performance.

The operation of value is shown when a product or service with similar features becomes available or the price is increased. The major mistakes that can occur in following this principle include substituting personal opinions on value, being unsystematic in discovering the value of a product or service to the customer, or failing to recognize shifts in value from the customer suddenly having to do without it.

Principle #12: Benefits must exceed expenses or costs. Their measurement should fall within the same organizational unit, so a unit cannot claim benefits by shifting its expenses elsewhere. This principle is not to be confused with 'buying the cheapest',[13] or, avoiding incurring costs. It implies that all pertinent costs and benefits are diligently established even if other policies are used to override the principle.[14] Typical examples of the use of this principle are whether it is more economical to make a product or component in-house rather than buy it in and whether the short-term gains from an organization reducing costs will be offset by any future revenue losses in the medium and long term.

This principle is used when considering matters such as how to improve operational efficiency as well in for broad organizational strategic decisions. The only exception to this principle is in the areas of compliance where costs may be incurred to avoid the opprobrium of legal proceedings and reputation being tarnished. The major mistakes that can occur in following this principle include failing to make clear that benefits depend upon goals and values, omitting items (costs and benefits), misclassifying costs and benefits, comparing costs and benefits over different periods, miscounting, inflating, or discounting the quantum of a cost or benefit, and overlooking implementation consequences including risks.

The 12 principles above provide the managerial accountant with a fairly coherent set guide on working with information, framing analyses and making decisions. Of course, the managerial accountant has to select the principles to apply, but if in doubt, the managerial accountant can apply each one-by-one to the particular problem or opportunity they are studying.

9.2   East: Boundaries and Constraints for Scoping

Earlier chapters showed the prevalence of boundaries and constraints in managerial accounting, particularly Chapter 7. They are placed together because they are interrelated and affect organizations as well as the role and responsibilities of the managerial accountant. Boundaries occur where inputs and outputs occur, which separate the system from its environment (Miller & Rice, 1967). Constraints are limitations or restriction to action. Boundaries and constraints scope information seeking, analysis, the disclosure in preparing recommendations, and decisions, as well as passing judgments.

9.2.1 Boundaries

A 'boundary' is used for tangible limits. It takes effect at the extremes as a result of a definite limitation. A 'constraint' is used for intangible limits, so it can prevent further change or use. The managerial accountant operates with two boundaries (Broadbent, 2011). The first boundary is the external boundary, that is, beyond the organization. It limits both the scope of the managerial accountant's information gathering and information disclosure. For example, if the managerial accountant takes a 'supply chain' perspective, then they will begin to negotiate with other organizations to have a proper understanding of expenses and revenues.

The second boundary is internal. If the organization has a separate financial accountant role, then the managerial accountant relies on information and intelligence from financial accounting to help them influence organizational processes and provide active guidance to managers and employees. Since there are many differences, Table 9–1 presents the key differences between managerial and financial accounting roles as domain boundaries.

Table 9–1 Domain boundaries of managerial accounting with financial accounting highlighting key differences.

Domain	Type of Accounting Role	
	Managerial	Financial
Purpose	Decision making	Communicate financial position to external users
Primary users	Internal managers including Board of Directors	External users: equity investors, lenders and other creditors (if applicable, supplier, employee, customer)
Other user	Allowed access by Board or CEO	Analyst, regulator, customers suppliers, trade unions
Level of the user	All in organization (CEO to employee)	Proficient user Other user with low or negligible knowledge and experience
Type of information	Specific	Generalized to overall organization and segments (e.g., financial statement)
Focus/Emphasis	Future oriented	Past oriented
Frequency of reporting	Monthly or more frequently	Typically, every 6 months and annually, unless there is a market disclosure need
Precision	Estimates	Objective, accurate and reliable
Time span	Current to very long-term horizon	Historical period, e. g., annual
Constraints and rules for decisions	Do not have to follow Generally Accepted Accounting Principles (GAAP)	GAAP compliant CPA audited
Consequences of recommendations and decisions	Directly designed to influence employee behavior	Usually one of a number of inputs to any decision

The division of accounting into financial and managerial results in different roles and responsibilities. Financial accounting focuses largely on financial information and compliance and audit requirements, reporting on what has been achieved within specific time periods, and communicates this to a primarily external audience who are unfamiliar with the operations of the organization. It provides information on end results. In contrast, managerial accounting serves primarily internal organizational needs. Although it still uses information, it obtains that information from the systems that support end results and other systems that contain details of how those results were accomplished. The managerial accountant therefore always is aware that the ultimate destination of some of their information is financial statements.

Managerial accounting is also distinguished from related disciplines and business functions. The discipline of finance is concerned with discounted cash flows for capital budgeting. However, it uses aggregate monetary values for the capital budget as the input to most of its calculations. The managerial accountant is concerned with proposals for components of that aggregate amount and accounting for each approved project within the capital budget. The discipline of marketing is concerned with pricing products or services based on marketing and sales considerations. It may produce its own information where it considers the information available from existing information systems is unsatisfactory (Foster & Gupta, 1994). The managerial accountant is concerned with preparing the revenue and expense related analyses for products or services as individual product (or service) lines, or at the product (or service) group level. These other business functions rely on the managerial accountant to provide information and examine proposals, but the boundaries may be blurred depending upon the expertise within these other business functions and their organizational power.

9.2.2   *Constraints*

The managerial accountant operates with constraints.[15] Some of the constraints are dependent upon the stage of the organization and its strategic organizational unit in the business life cycle. For example, an organization in start-up stage, or cessation/turnaround stage, has limited funds, and this will constrain spending on infrastructure and human resources. There are also constraints relating to the information selected for analysis or made available to non-accounting managers and employees. Where the headcount in the organization is constrained or where systems are slow to process and finalize information, it may be necessary to work with limited information or make estimates. The managerial accountant will use their judgment to determine the effect on accuracy and delaying decisions. Other constraints are specific to the board and senior managers of the organization. For example, senior management may have predispositions toward products/services, markets and territories, or competitors. The managerial accountant must discover and consider these constraints, as using this information differentiates managerial accountants in the same industry, or even in the same organization.

9.3 South: Methods and Models for Managerial Accounting Analyses

Earlier chapters highlighted the range and importance of methods and models in managerial accounting. They are placed together because the expressions techniques and tools understate the skill of the managerial accountant in selecting and applying them to reveal, validate and provide non-accounting managers with a practical understanding of information about managerial accounting particular to their organization. As Demski (2010) points out, it is easy to make a correct calculation when given the algorithm, but selecting the correct algorithm is an art in itself. Methods comprise concepts, analytical frameworks, formulas, processes and formats. Examples of concepts are indirect costs, contribution margin and resources. Examples of analytical frameworks are broad average costing, inventory management, budgeting and allocating resources to portfolios. Examples of formulas are those for breakeven and the various variances. Examples of methods include normal costing, lean accounting and benefit realization. Examples of formats are the reports used for the various methods and processes. Models are used for estimation, prediction, calibration and optimization. Models can be quantitative, semi-quantitative (producing approximate results rather than exact or absolute results), or qualitative and hybrid (combing both qualitative and quantitative) aspects.

9.3.1 Methods

Methods are considered from the dual points of view of focus and resource utilization. Focus refers to whether the goal is operations, strategy or both. Resource utilization refers to whether the goal is planning and control, or performance. By placing them in a matrix, as depicted in Figure 9–1, it produces four systematic methods that the Managerial Accountant uses:

- Making cost and management of costs visible
- Improving the performance of an organization
- Ensuring control, compliance and accountability, or governance over organizational resources
- Strategies to create and capture value in Strategic Business Units[16] (SBUs).

These four methods may not be balanced across the managerial accountant's roles and responsibilities as the time and effort spent on them is

Focus

	Operations	Strategy
Planning & Control **Resource Utilisation**	**Make the behaviour and management of costs visible** - Traditional (Product) and non-traditional costing - Management of costs including project reporting	**Evaluating performance (Compliance and accountability, or, governance)** - Internal dimensions of - Effectiveness - Efficiency - Economy
Performance	**Improve performance of the organisation** - Improving processes - Improving decisions - Improving outcomes	**Strategic creation and capturing of value in Strategic Business Units** - Adaptability - Customer focus - Balance innovation and compliance

Figure 9–1 Dual view of methods: Focus (operations or strategy) and resource utilization (planning/control and performance).

affected by their level (entry, intermediate, senior) and the characteristics discussed as the context of the managerial accountant's compass. Based on discussion from earlier chapters, for each of the four methods, common options are suggested, key questions are proposed and issues likely to arise that require decisions are identified.

Methods of Making Costs Visible

To make costs visible, the managerial accountant is concerned with the assignment and behavior of costs. Most managers are aware of the importance of costs, since any reduction will directly and immediately improve the 'bottom line'.[17] Comprehending the cost structure is crucial for success in strategic positioning. Discussion of costs is likely to create vigorous debate among non-accounting managers. There are two reasons for this. First, non-accounting managers do not appreciate that when managerial accountants assemble costs, it is with a specific purpose and recipient in mind. For example, the cost of a particular product is not the same for the factory manager and the marketing manager. Second, the cost itself may be calculated using a number of different methods depending upon what information is available. For example, if there is detailed information on how employees and managers spend their time, the costs will be traceable and can be made direct costs instead of indirect costs. There is no single correct answer in analyzing and calculating costs although there is always a correct answer given the measurements used in any particular calculation. This does not mean that costs are the sole criteria, but decisions are always made with an awareness of costs and how they can be managed. Many non-accounting managers regard costs as certain and complete numbers. The managerial accountant will always point out that numbers are one of two components, the quantitative and the qualitative, and that the numbers contain some estimates, often associated with standards or aggregations, unless the information is collected from the lowest and definitive level.

The three options for making costs visible are

- Using traditional or broad average costing for jobs and processes to uniformly distribute costs. This assumes that products or services are alike in their consumption of resources after considering the behavior of costs and the assignment of costs to cost objects[18] and their cost drivers.[19] It requires reliable allocation methods and income reporting.
- Refining costs to overcome unwitting or deliberate cross-subsidization, that is, over-costing some products or services and under-costing others. Typically, the focus is on overhead costs using homogeneous cost pools or activities to consider how services use consumables and capacity-related resources differently, or how different consumers use services. However, the number of direct cost categories may also be reconsidered based on improved tracing of costs.
- Managing the re-allocation of costs, including the difficult but important support and common costs (Wells, 2006) to ensure full costing and better transfer pricing.

The key questions for making costs visible include:

- What outcomes are being accomplished with resources?
- How well are the costs of resources allocated?
- What kind of costing system is appropriate? This will explore the selection of broad average costing, cost refinement with additional cost categories and cost pools, or activity-based costing.
- How adequate is our costing system? This will explore whether opportunity costs from capacity under-utilization are considered.
- How can cost information be improved? This will explore how cost information can be used for the management of costs not just the calculation of costs.

- How does the costing system relate to budgets? This will explore whether budget or predetermined (standard) costs are used.
- Is the costing system comprehensive? This will explore whether all costs are counted, including common and support costs, whether allowances are made for manufacturing and selling markups, and the impact of rebates.

Some issues for decision making that arise with making costs visible are the following:

- Agreeing a report (worksheet, schedule or statement) format that communicates adequately to non-accounting managers
- Managing direct costs by understanding the relative importance of labor and materials
- The consequences of operating a multi-product business (with a product mix) that uses different resources
- Overcoming the problems of determining indirect costs
- Assessing the importance of external factors

The managerial accountant will always place costing in the light of better understanding the expenses related to products and services.

Methods of Improving the Performance of Organizational Resources

To improve the performance of an organization, the managerial accountant will be concerned with customer expectations and working capital. This usually entails taking a short-term view. The reason is that reduced profitability affects the viability of the organization, and the sense of urgency requires an immediate improvement in profitability. However, decisions taken to attain short-term objectives may have unfavorable repercussions. For this reason, all quantitative analyses should be accompanied by consideration of long-term consequences and qualitative factors.

The broad options for improving the performance of an organization are

- Cost volume profit[20] calculations, which establish the relationship between costs, selling price and income using a stated set of assumptions regarding fixed costs and variable costs
- Inventory management to allow uninterrupted production, sales and/ or customer-service levels at the minimum cost
- Management of costs,[21] that is, providing managers with reliable information to manage the use of resources (actual and budgeted) that will enable them to increase value to customers and achieve organizational objectives

The key questions for improving the performance of organizational resources include the following:

- Are processes/activities efficient? (In terms of cost, quality and time)
- What is the breakeven for products?
- What is the impact of volume on costs?
- Is there sufficient process and product and service innovation/creativity?
- Do processes ensure quality and add value that are both recognized by the customer?
- Is there careful inventory management? This applies to the traditional view of inventory (holding safety stock, then re-ordering) or options such as JIT (raw materials for production) and/or JIT for sales (with finished goods).
- Is working capital minimized?
- How are managers motivated? This should consider both the short-term achievements and the long-term consequences.

Some issues for decision making that arise with improving the performance are

- Resolving conflict between different aspects of profitability (customers, prices of products and services, inventory and risk)
- Anticipating the behavioral accounting consequences of measuring performance
- Ensuring managers and employees behave ethically and receive training to ensure they are aware of the difficulties they will encounter in behaving ethically
- Assessing the importance of external factors

The managerial accountant will place improving performance in the light of being ready to respond to competitor initiatives and changing customer expectations.

Methods of Evaluating Performance to Ensure Control,
Compliance and Accountability or Governance Over
Organizational Resources

To ensure control, compliance and accountability or governance over organizational resources, the managerial accountant will be concerned with a framework to monitor, evaluate and report on performance in the organization. An early framework (COSO, 2013) proposed viewing controls as preventive, detective and corrective, and highlighted the importance of information within the organization. But controls should be considered more than processes.[22] They include corporate culture, systems, structure, policies and task descriptions. More recently, it is taken to include the relationships between an organization's management, its board, its shareholders, other stakeholders, the structure through which the objectives of the organization are set, and the means of attaining those objectives and monitoring performance are determined (OECD, 2004). This gives the managerial accountant wide scope for evaluating performance.

The broad options for evaluating the performance of organizational resources are

- Budgeting to quantify sales volumes and revenues, resource quantities, costs and expenses, assets, liabilities and cash flows for products and services, organizational units and organizations.
- Applying controls and producing variances. Controls are policies and processes implemented by an organization to help ensure the validity and accuracy of its financial statements. A variance is a difference between a budgeted, planned or standard cost or revenue, and the actual amount incurred or sold.
- Project reporting is advising management in the four areas: (1) progress against milestones; (2) costs incurred; (3) quality of the deliverables; and (4) highlighting exposures of a project. Project reporting also involves understanding the risk-taking proclivities of individuals, the organization culture and its cultural background.

Key questions for control, compliance, governance and accountability are

- How well are resources and processes protected?[23] Protection will cover prevention including policy, detection including audit and correction of untoward situations.
- How much adherence to rules and values occurs? This begins with tone at the top,[24] which refers to the ethical atmosphere in the workplace established by its board of directors, audit committee, and senior management (that is, the organization's leadership). It also considers whether a rogue manager or employee can operate undetected and whether there is a work-safe environment, irrespective of the financial position of the organization.
- How accountable are managers and employees? This includes having documented up-to-date processes, a specific budget that excludes non-controllable costs, providing informative reports and project reporting.
- How are managers given indications of unsatisfactory performance and poor decisions? They should have critical success factors (see Chapter 6), receive variances using the flexed budget for comparison with standardized costs, and be supported by a learning organization[25] where diagnostic and evaluative methodological tools help to identify, promote and evaluate the quality of learning processes inside

organizations, both as individuals and collectively (Easterby-Smith & Araujo, 1999) so employees are flexible, adaptive and productive.

- How frequently are projects reviewed for non-beneficial constraints that affect accountability? A project approved on expected financial return may fail to realize some or all benefits. It is too late when the project is near completion to attempt to control costs and ensure timely delivery at agreed quality.

Some issues for decision making that arise with evaluating the performance of an organization are

- The effectiveness of the controls and accountability in terms of prevention, detection and correction of unacceptable behavior. Organizations may place too much emphasis on budgets.[26] Budgets and budgeting in its present form, using modern budgeting disciplines, is recent (Ackoff, 1969). Attention is needed to complementary forms of accountability.
- The adequacy of governance in place at the board and senior management levels and its mechanisms for overcoming conflict among them. The budgeting process is inherently a source of potential conflict because managers have strong incentives for projecting the lowest possible 'positive' and the highest possible 'negative', results but senior management seeks the reverse. This conflict can be mitigated by rational policies, goodwill on both sides and implementation with formal budgetary reviews at reasonable intervals, and realistic adjustments based on actual events.
- The stated commitment and actual behavior to comply with any industry code of conduct, organization supplements to the code and government legislation
- The extent to which external resources are used to augment the organization are properly controlled and managed

The managerial accountant will always place evaluating performance in the light of ensuring alignment between goals and behavior, and compliance, so accountability obligations to external authorities and the public are satisfied.

Methods for the Strategic Creation and Capture of Value in Strategic Business Units[27]

The broad options for creating and capturing value[28] from the allocation and the augmentation of resources are

- Fitting the external corporate strategy[29] to the social environment and industry competition

- Identifying, leveraging, developing, deploying, and measuring capabilities and core competencies so each Strategic Business Unit (SBU) transforms its resources
- Allocating resources to portfolios and projects (capital budgeting)
- Pricing products and services to set a selling price taking into consideration costs, the customer's perceived value of the product, and competitor action in the marketplace.

Key questions for creating and capturing value from the strategic allocation and augmentation of organizational resources are

- What value does the SBU generate for the organization? This can be at the level of the price paid at purchase for the product (or service), or the worth of the organization stake (e.g., if the stake is shares, then the value is the dividend).
- What capabilities are required to successfully perform unique processes are important to the SBU? This considers whether it can develop the capabilities in the short term.
- How does the SBU adapt and evolve in changing times? This involves accomplishing its goals, executing its strategy, mitigating risk and reconfiguring its resources.
- Has the SBU competitive position improved against competitors? The SBU must be clear on its basis for attracting and keeping customers.
- What changes in the marketplace is the SBU able to withstand? The SBU will plan its prices for the short term and long term, recognize how new competitors will enter the market, anticipate price discounting by price leaders and prepare for unexpected government regulatory changes.
- Is long-term competitiveness of the SBU in its industry attained? The SUB will compare itself with market leader product life cycles and be able to fund a product refresh or replacement program.

Some issues for decision making that arise with creating and capturing value are:

- Difficulties in establishing what is meant by value. Value is an ambiguous term for the managerial accountant because it is used to describe two different phenomena: the worth of (1) products/ services and the (2) organization. They are frequently confused. When considered as products/services (meaning as parts and wholes they have worth), value can mean exchange value or use value. Exchange value is the price paid (or quotation which is invoiced) at time of sale (which may include some bargaining). Use value is the worth is subjectively assessed by customers at any time based on the features of the product or service (which were endowed by the designers and production processes). A customer can value anything! Value as an organization means a stake in the organization that has worth. It can be measured as earnings (e.g., profit reported), earnings available for distribution (e.g., as dividends), share price of a public company (but may include some sentiment or effects in macro economy) or future access to investment capital at favorable rates to fund operations.

- Establishing how value is created across the organization. Value creation is revenue earned from customers willing to purchase a product or service. It is affected by competition and competitive advantage. Value capture is the profit associated with providing a product or service. It is associated with what constitutes the industry and how it is likely to evolve. They involve the customer's economics and making use of innovations (Germany & Muralidharan, 2001). The creation and capture of value requires both broad and detailed analyses. Attention to operating expenses, training and customer service can produce policy changes (e.g., Paynter, 1947: 390–393). A more recent, but time-consuming analysis, uses a value chain (Porter, 1985). From a cost point of view, it is essential to understand the entire value chain in which the organization participates; this requires the assiduous efforts of the managerial accountant (Shank & Govindrajan, 1991, 1992). Once completed, many strategic questions such as the scope of operations, the linkages with suppliers and customers, and the cost-causing factors (also known as cost drivers) can be considered. As there are interconnected relationships among the activities in the value chain, the managerial accountant needs to examine all the cost relationships[30] (Hergert & Morris, 1989) from the point of view of the entire organization, because they do not have a single functional responsibility (as does the sales or production manager). The managerial accountant will also consider whether there are constraints (Goldratt, 1990) at the linkages between organization functions that prevent the organization reaching from reaching a higher-level of achievement and need to be alleviated in a cost-effective manner.
- Establishing strong linkages between strategy, industrial design of products and services, and performance measurement. Particularly where strategy is emergent, the organization is knowledge intensive and there is a dynamic environment, the design needs to be multi-faceted (Nixon, 2006). Thus opportunities for value creation may be overlooked.

The managerial accountant will always place the strategic creation and capture of value in the light of organization prosperity and survival.

Details of the methods used by the managerial accountant are outlined in Figure 9–2, the managerial accountant's toolkit. It delineates four
kinds of decisions and the desirability of having both a short-term and
long-term viewpoint. These are outlined with regard to the managerial
decisions by topic, issue, process and tool. Consistent with the managerial
accountant's compass, it also shows that ethical behavior applies to all
the themes and topics.

In summary, the four methods recognize there are short-term imperatives and long-term aims to balance the criteria for making decisions. The
four methods should not be viewed independently as they are interrelated.
One means of recognizing this is through considering the selling price of a
product. In addition, to product and period costs there is the margin for
the product and the margin on period costs. These may also be affected by
a rebate.[31] Figure 9–3 provides a visual breakdown of the major elements.

Although Figure 9–3 purports to account for all the factors contributing
to price, it should be noted that it is still incomplete. For example, the
existence of rebates may distort the period costs as currently they can be
earned without any corresponding sales being made. One common means
of bringing these together is to build a model.

9.3.2   *Financial Models*

Methods can lead to the design and operation of models which have a
financial orientation. The aim of constructing any model is to explore or
understand real world.[32] So a financial model is a simplified, subjective,
selective and algorithmic representation of financial reality. It is simplified
because it does not contain all possible characteristics and interrelationships that exist. It is subjective because the builder of the model determines
what is relevant and important for its purpose. It is selective because the
model builder is concerned with excluding or combining some inputs
and reformulating processes. It is a representation of reality because it
separates the logical (functions) from physical (actually implemented
structure, system) aspects. It is an algorithmic representation of reality
because it performs a function[33] such as calculating a relationship (e.g.,
positive, negative, inverse, linear), forecast or extrapolation, or describing an outcome. For these reasons, the model is an abstraction and an
approximation of reality, and it contains assumptions.

Model building depends on four assumptions. First that the phenomena being modeled does not change while the model is built, or once it
is in use.[34] Where the model builder is a third party, development should
include checkpoints to assess whether the planned design remains acceptable. Second, it assumes that the manager authorizing the model building
can specify their requirements, and they remain constant over the period
of model building and use.[35] Third, the type of model may be misinter-
preted. An optimization model, also known as maximization of utility,

Ethical code (principles and standards) requires you to (1) behave ethically (2) encourage others to behave ethically; and (3) seek advice from an advisor or from a professional association for ethical dilemmas or lapses.

To provide financial and non-financial information for resource transformation decisions and making judgements (recognise, augment, allocate, deploy, leverage, develop, measure, value, accountability and control organisational resources)

Method	Make Costs Visible (Multiple classification)			Improve Performance of Resources			Evaluate Performance (with Compliance & Governance)			Create & Capture Value Strategy			
Method	Broad Average Product Costs	Refining Costs (Direct & Overhead)	Cost Re-allocation (Support & Common)	Manage-ment of Costs	Cost Volume Profit	Inventory Management	Budgets & Budgeting	Controls & Variances	Project Reporting (Capital Inv)	SBU External Strategy	SBU Internal Strategy	Capital Investments & Allocate Resources to Portfolios	Price Setting & Product Mix
Issue / Conditions, Limitations, Assumptions	• Actual Costs • Normal Costs • Cost Behaviour • Inventory Costing	• Product Profitability • Customer profitability • Product Mix • Criteria for Implementing ABC	• Net Profit affected by allocation of Support Department Costs, Common Costs & Revenue from "Bundled" Products	• Cost categories managed • Method of Inventory Costing • Human (Behavioural) Aspects of Managing Costs	• Marginal Analysis of Changes in Costs and Volumes; • Cost Behaviour • CVP Assumptions	• Costs associated with goods for sale • Just-In-Time • Inventory Costing	• Master Budget • Flexible Budget • Standard Costs • Human Aspects of Budgeting	• Flexing the Static Budget (Flexible Budget) • Decomposition of differences between Actual and Budget figures into Levels (1, 2, and 3) of Variances • Levers of Control especially Interactive versus Diagnostic	• Portfolio of projects • Independent vs mutually exclusive projects • Selection and appraisal • Human (Behavioural) aspects of projects	• Strategy (Plan Vs Result) • Strategic Business Unit (SBU) • Macro & Micro Environ-ment	• Strategic Business Unit (SBU) • Internal Environment • Tangible / Intangible resources • Human & Govern-ment regulation	• Accounting versus Finance Perspective • Method of Capital Budgeting • Relevant Costs • Qualitative Considerations • Human Behavioural Aspects (goal conguence)	• Market-Based Pricing • Method of Cost Plus Pricing • Competitor actions • Govern-ment regulation
Process Guide	Stages in Job Order Costing & Estimating a Cost Function	Refining with pools and categories or by activities	Allocate Costs (of Revenues)	Differentiate costs. Period from Inventoriable	Equation, Contribut-ion Margin, Graph Methods	EOQ Decision Model	Steps to Prepare Schedules; Articulated Budget	Price (Spending) and Efficiency (Rate) Variance Decomposition	Iteration of Project Documentat-ion	Strategic Analysis, Choice & Realisation		Stages of Capital Investment	Time Horizon Pricing
Analytical Framework	• Cost object • Cost allocation base and measure • Direct cost categories (e.g., DM, DL) • Cost pools for indirect costs (Overheads) • Behaviour/Fcn (Variable, Fixed, Mixed, Curvi-linear) • Regression or Hi:Lo cost drivers & cost functions	• Cost drivers • Separate Departmental Rate versus Single Activity rates • Overallocated or Underallocated Usage (actual or budgeted) • Comparing Alternative Costing Systems • Other ABC Uses (e.g., Customer Profitability) • ABC variants e.g. Time-based ABC	• Direct, Step-Down, or Reciprocal allocation of support costs based on (actual or budgeted) Usage • Stand-alone or incremental cost allocation of common costs • Define cost allocation methods and allowable costs in contracts	• Treatment of Fixed Costs in Variable (or Direct) Costing, Throughput (Super Variable) or Contribution Margin, & Absorption Costing • Denomin-ator & Numerator in Costs • Managing unused processing capacity • Different types of costs	• Contribut-ion Margin • Break-Even Point (BEP $, %, and units) • Contribut-ion Margin ($ and units) • Contribut-ion Margin Ratio • CM versus Gross Margin • Numerator in Costs • Operating Leverage • Margin of Safety	• EOQ • Re-order point • Safety stock • Absorption costing Vs Variable costing for inventory • Ordering costs • Carrying costs • Variable & throughput costing • Absorption costing & Capacity • MRP/ERP, Lean accounting • JIT	• Standard Costs • Articulated Budget • Operating Budget Schedules • Financial Budget Schedules (Capital expenditure, Cash, Balance Sheet, Cash Flows) • Kaizen Budgeting	• Level 3 variances: • DM Price V. • DM Efficiency V. • DL Price V. • DL Efficiency V. • Variable (Mfg.) Overhead Spending V. • Variable (Mfg.) Ovenh'd Efficiency V. • Fixed (Mfg.) Overhead Spending V. • Fixed Overhead Spending V. • Product Volume V. • Operating Income V. • Selling (or Sales) Price V. (L2) • Sales Volume (or Quantity) V. (L3): • Market Share V. • Market Size V.	• Project preliminaries (develop schedule of resources, costs, timings, & contingencies by stage) • Governance over progress, reporting, variations in scope, quality, progress, and judging outputs • Timely communication and benefit realisation • Ensuring risk management and benefit realisation • Post project audit • Valuing the resulting asset	• PESTEL • Five Forces • Generic Strategies • Strategic evaluation (DuPont) • Operating Income variance evaluation • Strategic analysis of operating income (growth/ market, price recovery, productivity)	• PE/RTH • Resource Conversion Hierarchy (Resources, Capabilities, Core Competen-cies) • Evaluation of capabilities (Value Chain), Growth-Share Matrix, and Core Competen-cies (DART)	*Accepted methods:* • DCF (NPV and IRR) with Opportunity Cost of Investment • Comparison of NPV and IRR • Relevant Costs, Cash Flows • Improve individual flows • *Disputed methods:* • AARR • ROI • *Hybrid method:* • Payback (Uniform and Non-Uniform) • Qualitative Evaluation	• Target price Cost-plus price • Target Rate of Return on Investment • Pricing Influences (Customers, Competitors, Costs) • Customer Perceived Value • Value Engineering • Price Discriminat-ion • Variable Cost Pricing
Financial Reports	• Product and period cost report (Total and/or Unit) • Prime cost, Conversion cost • Mfg costs • Non-Mfg costs (Overhead)	• Activity report (Total and/or Unit) • Fully classified income statement	• Cost re-allocation schedule • Fully classified income statement	• Quality cost report • Operating Statement	• Contribution margin income statement	• COG manufactur-ed • COGS statement	• Budgeted income statement • Budgeted balance sheet	• Contribution margin income statement	• Project performance report	• Operating income statement	• Operating income statement	• Operating income statement	• Quality cost report • Operating income statement

Figure 9–2 The managerial accountant's basic toolkit grouped by the four methods and emphasizing the variety of analytical frameworks, processes and reports that share consistent concepts and classifications.

Total Selling Price (Wholesale or Retail)

Determined by using Target Selling Price or Cost Plus Markup

Cost Behaviour	Cost Assignment — Total Cost — Product Cost — Direct / Prime Costs		Product Cost — Indirect / Conversion Costs / Manufacturing Overhead*	Period (Discretionary Costs) — Direct / Sales	Period — Indirect / General	Period — Indirect / Administration	Cost re-allocation — From Support To operations	Rebates** — Type	Margin (to calculate percentage of total income is profit)
				An alternative to SG&A is the Activity Cost Hierarchy (it identifies: Unit-level costs, Batch-level costs, Product-sustaining level costs, and, Facility-sustaining level costs)					Gross Manufacturing Margin / Sales Margin (Gross Profit Margin)
Variable	• Direct Manufacturing Materials (DMM)*	• Direct Manufacturing Labour (DML)*	• Indirect materials for machine maintenance • Materials movement • Machine testing and certification • Quality assurance • Product design salaries, stationery and premises • Purchasing salaries, stationery and premises • Utilities usage for machines (Power, Gas, Water)	• Sales commissions • Packaging for delivery • Storage of finished goods • Distribution to wholesaler and/ or retailer	• Utilities usage (Power, gas, Water) • Cleaning	• Administrative travel		Types include: (a) Inventory related including: (i) A volume target is reached; (ii) A target percentage increase or growth in either quantity or purchase amount for a specific item triggers the rebate; (b) Non-inventory related including: (i) A contribution to promotional costs e.g., catalogues; (ii) A contribution to advertising expenses; (iii) Received in exchange for services rendered in the course of the entity's ordinary activities	
Fixed over the relevant range	• A labour cost may be fixed if it can be directly traced in an economically feasible way (e.g. Factory Shift Supervisor always in charge of one particular product, the cost object)		• Salaries: Factory supervision • Forklift lease & maintenance • Rent or Loan: Factory premises • Factory rent • Cleaning of factory • Land tax and rates • Factory insurance • Utilities connection (Power, gas, Water) • Non-cash: Machine depreciation	• Sales and marketing salaries • Sales and marketing travel • Sales and marketing training • Sales and marketing stationery and equipment • Advertising • Sales training • Non-cash: Bad debt expense • Non-cash: Depreciation (Fitout)	• Utilities connection (Power, gas, Water) • Land tax and rates • Land and buildings services (e.g. garbage collection) • Non-cash: Depreciation (Vehicles)	• Office of CEO salaries • Administrative salaries (Information Technology, Accounting, Human Resources) • Administrative training • Administrative equipment (lease, loan, or buy) • Admin buildings insurance • Admin training			

Cost Behaviour

The aim is to convert fixed costs to variable where practicable to avoid under-utilisation of resources (e.g., by replacing salary with hourly rates and by replacing availability with usage).

This is not a definitive list. The items above are examples.

* Assumes the sector is manufacturing

** A part of the purchase price is returned by the seller to the buyer when a specified quantity or value of products or services have been purchased within a specified period. Rebate is recognised when related target is met and recorded in the income statement (as a reduction of cost of sales in a presentation of expenses by function

Figure 9–3 Classifying costs by behavior and function showing support cost re-allocation and margins.

may be irrelevant. If a satisficing model is adequate, the design must provide for it because some models are unable to find the second-best solution or the set of acceptable solutions.[36] Finally, it assumes that assumptions uncovered are adequately documented to avoid misapprehension about the model.[37] The managerial accountant should encourage modeling to begin informally with discussion and pencil and paper (Hanks & Belliston, 1990; Nelms, 1981) to surface assumptions and identify the need for computations, charting/graphs, and simple database in the model (Morris, 1987). This encroaches on the criteria for a good model.

The essential criteria of a good quantitative or qualitative, broad or specific model includes accuracy, clarity, flexibility, granularity, efficiency and auditability (Avon, 2013; Blackwood, 2014; Bodmer, 2014; Constantine & Lockwood, 1999; Ho & Lee, 2004; Hogg, 1994). This is not an exhaustive list but allows the managerial accountant to promote models that are consistent with the information attributes discussed in Chapter 2. Table 9–2 summarizes the common issues, serious shortcomings and desirable controls for models using this criterion.

One consequence of an appreciation of the criteria for good models will be that the managerial no longer condones 'quick and dirty' model building because it has a high probability of undetected errors (Panko, 1998).

The managerial accountant can propose to non-accounting managers these criteria or obtain an equivalent set from IT if they find the majority of models are developed in an ad hoc and poorly controlled manner. Non-accounting managers may not be aware what quality is desirable. Since it may also be a symptom of inadequate funding of development, or poor existing systems, the managerial accountant may also want to explore software development planning in IT.

Many of these issues arise because the model is not viewed as having a life cycle (Oliver, 2012). In brief, it begins with analysis[38] and specification of requirements,[39] followed by preliminary then detailed design. Before the model becomes operational, it should be tested with a suite of representative information by a user familiar with the existing outputs. After implementation, arrangements must be made to maintain it. There are two implications of the life cycle view for the managerial accountant. They are ensuring the model is periodically reviewed to ensure it meets the criteria outlined above and that there is funding (time, money and labor) to make these checks and keep them up-to-date. This is connected with the specificity and scope of the model.

The final decision facing the managerial accountant is whether to endorse building a model specific to the issue at hand or a generic model than can be used for similar problems.[40] A specific model can be worksheet based. The managerial accountant can show leadership using their familiarity with spreadsheets by proposing an economical model[41] (that is, rapid completion without further work). Some models are available

Table 9–2 Criteria for models matched with common issues, serious shortcomings and desirable controls for models for broad and specific models.

Criteria	Issue	Shortcomings	Controls
Accuracy	• Correct inputs • Correct results	• Lack of in-built error detection and protection • Inadequate training of users • Poor design • Lack of error reducing features	• Cross checking, usually within the model • Transparency of formulas or transformations • Industry specific • Statutory compliance
Clarity	• Understanding the functions of the model intended by its builder(s) • Interpretation of the functions by those who use it	• Use of values without explanation • Use of formulaic content without justification	• Clear, complete documentation (internal & external) • Standardized and consistent approach to design to ease usability
Flexibility	• Ease of adaption to changing aspects of a problem • Ease of adaption to an increased volume of information	• Rigidity of design • Nesting of functions	• Anticipate future uses • Variations to the model
Granularity	• Detail in the model • Affects scope and functionality	• Likelihood of errors • Limitations of only using aggregate information	• Integrity checks • Consistency between details (periods, level of detail and decisions)
Efficiency	• Human capacity to easily locate and inspect critical portions • Machine streamlining of task processing	• Unplanned design • Rapid development • Unplanned enhancement	• Modular design • Extensive testing • Cost of ongoing support and downtime
Auditability	• Support in planning and decision making has wider business impact	• May not have been designed for use in basic business functions (e.g., accounting, payroll)	• Validation of input information • Full audit trail (to source documents and archiving) • Change controls especially over design of specific internal, operations • Security over the model and its stored information

or can be constructed, which produces an acceptable solution which expresses the decision. This allows the action taken to be compared with the solution from the model. Where models can be constructed but do not produce clear solutions, they can use heuristics or report the range of alternatives. This allows comparison of the alternative solutions. Where adequate models cannot be immediately constructed, or the importance of the decision does not justify the cost of a full model, a partial model may be adequate if sufficient input information can be agreed and a process can produce output that can serve as inputs for human decision making if there are no better methods for conducting the analysis.[42] It may lead to better understanding of the context and limitations of the model and use of existing alternatives. By seeing the specific model, the managerial accountant will be able to suggest whether there is scope for it to perform any generic functions. This may entail considering whether it can use a particular theory or contain elements from many theories and be either empirical, that is, verifiable by observation or experience, or be constituted entirely by logic.

The managerial account has a major advantage in their facility with the combination of methods and models. Their understanding of models and wide experience building and using them can give them insights into the model-building process that will be valued by non-accounting managers. For example, the integrated three-statement model includes the various functions of an organization work together to show how decisions impact its overall performance.[43] When this is combined with their understanding of information, managerial accounting theories, and use concepts and classifications, they can also build collegiate relationships.

9.4 West: Collegiate Relationships With Other Managers and Employees With Demonstrated Competencies

The managerial accountant has unique relationships within and external to the organization that they need to manage. The concept of a relational self as part of social activity was identified by Mead (1934). A more recent approach (Anderson & Chen, 2002) extended this view of identity into work roles picking up earlier observations on unfamiliar organizational settings (Louis, 1980; Reichers, 1987). For the managerial accountant, four collegiate relationships are identified[44] and discussed. The collegiate relationships are with senior management, with non-accounting managers, with non-accounting employees, and with other accountants, both internal and external. Collegiate relationships are earned through competencies. Three distinct competencies are discussed, all which make use of discourse and information previously examined in Chapters 3 and 4, respectively.

9.4.1 *Collegiate Relationships With Senior Managers*

Collegiate relationships with senior managers and the board of directors arise from the managerial accountant performing analyses and providing interpretations of those analyses. They examine the availability and utilization of financial and non-financial resources in operations and in implementing strategy both supporting recommendations for decisions and evaluation of outcomes from decisions. This work may be requested by senior managers as routine or ad hoc advice and assistance, although the managerial accountant will be expected to be proactive if they are part of the senior executive decision-making group or provide input to it.

9.4.2 *Collegiate Relationships With Non-Accounting Managers*

The majority of collegiate relationships the managerial accountant establishes and maintains are with non-accountant managers. As noted in earlier chapters, the managerial accountant provides leadership and facilitates an internal consulting role for themselves as a trusted advisor (Maister et al., 2001). This is the collegiate relationship that the managerial accountant should spend most of their time cultivating as it where they can have the broadest impact. It can take the form of formal partnering on major tasks (whether or not openly declared), being reciprocal informants for formal and informal information gathering, or being an informal mutual sounding board for ideas. This enables the managerial accountant to resolve issues in the use and interpretation of financial and non-financial information, as well as improve the quality of information and reports used by non-accounting managers. In some cases, this may overlap financial accounting where the information is ultimately reported in either general purpose financial reports as a financial statement, disclosure notes, commentary, or a special purpose financial report requested by an equity investor or lender.

9.4.3 *Collegiate Relationships With Non-Accounting Employees*

The managerial accountant will establish a few collegiate relationships with non-accounting employees. Although the managerial accountant will work though the supervisor of the employees, there will be occasions when they are given permission by the non-accounting line manager to contact employees directly, or line employees may approach them directly for advice and assistance. The collegiate relationship may involve obtaining or verifying transaction detail, as part of an investigation seeking answers to queries, clarifying accounting information contained in reports and interpreting information in accounting reports. Of course, for practical purposes, the manager of the employees may encourage the managerial accountant to communicate directly with the employees, and this may be given as an open invitation. Where this occurs, the managerial accountant will ensure that the manager of the employees is kept up-to-date to demonstrate their practical understanding that the employees are resources that the manager needs to manage and deploy on activities that are of the value to the organization. In addition, there may be instances where the managerial accountant inspects operations in conjunction with the line manager (and perhaps internal audit) to verify the effectiveness of controls where problems have been found.

9.4.4 Collegiate Relationships with Other Accountants (Internal and External)

The managerial accountant will have collegiate relationships with other financial and managerial accountants. The majority of relationships will be within the organization, but where necessary, they will extend to external accountants. Examples include suppliers, customers, and consultants. These collegiate relationships are both professional and developmental. They are a source of advice and assistance, as well as information about the activities of the organization based on the work they are doing. They can inform the managerial accountant on what is occurring in the organization, which may identify what information is available for analyses and what resources can support their managerial accounting work.

9.4.5 Competencies in Collegial Relationships

All these collegiate relationships have three distinct competencies (Simon, Guetzkow, Kozmetsky & Tyndall, 1954) for both operations and strategy. The first is partnering with and advising managers.[45] This is a broad competency because it occurs during the stages of planning, organizing, directing or leading, and controlling, and motivating all managers toward organization goals. While strategy development is most common in partnering, which entails assessing the organization's competitive position, thus ensuring the organization's long-term competitiveness in its industry, this competency may begin with advising on routine operations. It answers the question "How do non-accounting managers regard the managerial accountant?" The second is technical expertise,[46] that is, the knowledge, skills and abilities to perform tasks.[47] For the managerial accountant it is properly identifying, measuring, analyzing, interpreting and communicating information. Its scope is also broad: organizational units, programs, managers, teams, individual employees, and projects, whether in-sourced and outsourced. It answers the question "How well are non-accountants informed about accounting matters?" The third is score keeping, which refers to confirming historical information for internal and external users. This includes preparation of management accounts, ensuring compliance with regulations and maintaining acceptable standards of corporate governance. As a significant amount of this work is now automated, there are stewardship obligations over the integrity of information. It answers the question, "How are we doing?" In all three competencies, the managerial accountant obtains the appropriate financial and non-financial information and presents it as ready for non-accounting managers to make operational and strategic decisions about using organization's resources. The three competencies are summarized in Table 9–3. It shows that managerial accountants do not simply perform

Table 9–3 Competencies for collegiate relationships with senior managers, non-accounting managers, employees and other accountants with key questions and activities.

		Competency		
		Partnering and Advising	*Technical Expertise*	*Score Keeping*
	Key question	How do non-accounting managers regard the managerial accountant?	How well are non-accounting managers informed about accounting matters?	How are we doing?
	Key activities	Planning, organizing, directing, controlling and motivating	Identification, measurement, analysis, interpretation and communication of information	Accumulation of historical information for external and internal users
	Automation	Low	Low	High
Collegiate relationship	Senior managers and the board (usually includes non-accountants)	Regulatory compliance and maintain governance standards	Strategy planning and evaluation	–
	Managers (non-accounting)	Prepare specific purpose reports	Organize, leadership and control	–
	Operational employees (line or staff)[48]	–	Elicit information	Elicit information
	Accountants	Strategy evaluation	Cost calculation	Maintain and prepare accounts Compliance Stewardship

analyses and recommend decisions. They actively facilitate decisions by senior management, non-accounting managers and organizational group-ings (e.g., committees) to formulate and apply the resulting plans and controls that continue throughout implementation.

From inspection of Table 9–3, it can be concluded that most of these collegiate relationships are with non-accountants. As a result, any infor-mation provided will need to be targeted to their needs and thoughtfully communicated. This will entail avoiding accounting jargon, avoiding the promotion of fads and counterproductive bandwagon effects[49] (Rohlfs, 2003), defining any accounting terms and expressions that are unavoid-able, giving reasons for the chosen method of analysis together with any assumptions and expressing any limitations in the information.

The managerial accountant will be aware of space limitations for their report. Consequently, their report should be accompanied by a com-mentary that discusses anything omitted from the report as well as any working files (e.g., spreadsheet). Methods that were rejected will also be identified together with the assumptions they would require. The formula, equation, relevant template or proforma that is being used will be pre-sented first, in full. The values that have been selected for, and substituted in the formula, will be clearly shown, ideally in the model. The model will display the actual analysis will be detailed in full showing, so all intermediate steps can be followed. Unless it is clear from the model or the report, any result or solution will be qualified in terms of the problem or the information used in the calculation in the commentary. Similarly, the report should contain the interpretation of the result in terms of the problem with reference to the methods and models utilized and explain the implications of any analysis or recommendation to the business func-tion and the organization. In addition, any previous similar analyses that have been performed should be in the report highlighting differences in results or conclusions drawn.

A consequence of establishing collegiate relationships with non-accoun-tants is the need to build and sustain it. Initially, non-accounting managers may be suspicious of the knowledge, expertise and motives of the manage-rial accountant and feel threatened in their dealings with the managerial accountant. The managerial accountant may also not appreciate the day-to-day effort by non-accountants in their myriad of operational responsi-bilities. This includes dealing with the idiosyncrasies and temperaments of employees and customers (whether internal or external). This can often be a distraction and interruption when the managerial accountant is trying to obtain or provide information. The managerial accountant needs to allocate time to establishing and managing their collegiate relationships with non-accountants as it can be time-consuming and necessitate a diplo-matic approach if the collegiate relationship is to be sustained and produc-tive. There may be social occasions to develop relationships and explore common ground. Since the managerial accountant has a diverse range of collegiate relationships across the organization, they need to be aware of individual differences and show empathy in their collegiate relationships.

9.5   Summary of the Managerial Accountant's Compass Cardinal Points

This chapter introduced the four cardinal points of the managerial accountant's compass. Goals and principles (north point) focus the managerial accountant on what is to be achieved. Boundaries and constraints (east point) provide limitations. Methods and models (west point) allow the managerial accountant to provide a concise understanding of controls, future behavior, and anticipate the consequences of change. Collegiate relationships with others (south point) are a reminder of the social character of work and importance of interaction for advising and partnering. There is no usage sequence because the managerial accountant can commence with any of the points and work through them in any order. The next chapter examines the last cardinal point: the center, which is a high standard of ethics, as it pervades everything the managerial accountant does, and self-care.

Notes

1. This is sometimes expressed with the acronym SMART which is defined in several variations as S—Specific, Significant or Stretching; M—Measurable, Meaningful or Motivational; A—Agreed, Attainable, Achievable, Acceptable or Action Oriented; R—Realistic, Relevant, Reasonable, Rewarding or Results Oriented; and T—Time based, Time bound, Timely, Tangible or Trackable.
2. Drucker (1974) states that he developed his book *Management* out of his seminars and teaching, so in that sense it has been field tested. At the time he took a controversial stand on many management practices including focusing on performance and not feelings, avoiding safety through mediocrity and the lack of integrity when following orders, managing your manager and being a successful knowledge worker. It also contains one of my all-time favorite quotes 'when I describe a hardware firm in the mid-west, you can be certain it is not hardware and not in the mid-west'!
3. There are other ways the goals could be depicted, for example, as issues faced by particular organizational units that require resolution in a priority sequence, by considering revenue and costs of organizational segments in terms of profitability, or by grouping products or services according to their position in the product or service life cycle indicating the action to be taken. The three goals listed emphasize the range of managerial accounting.
4. Control is wider than accounting controls that deal with methods and processes for authorizing transactions, monitoring disbursements, safeguarding assets, to ensure the accuracy and validity of all accounting records. It is promoting and protecting effective and efficient operational practices so that information is reliable, organization policies are followed, and there is conformance to government legislation and regulations. Pfister (2009) refers to the former as focused and the later as comprehensive.

5. This raises the topic of goal congruence and behavioral aspects of behavior discussed in the section titled Behavioral Accounting, or influences over behavior and decisions in managerial accounting.

6. They include: (1) revenue recognition (revenue occurs at time of sale); (2) expense recognition (expense is recognized when goods or services are received from another entity; (3) valuation at cost (use historical cost subject to exceptions); (4) objectivity (factual verifiable data is preferred to subjective measurement of value); (5) economic entity (owner and proprietorship are separate); (6) monetary unit (items with non-financial or non-monetary information are not recorded); (7) time period (activity is reported in distinct time periods; (8) full disclosure (information is disclosed in the financial statement or its notes; (9) materiality principle (insignificant amounts are not reported); (10) conservatism (the lower income or asset value is reported); (11) consistency (similar processes should be used year after year; (12) going concern (entity will continue to operate indefinitely). These abstracted principles are incorporated in some accounting frameworks and standards. However, they are oriented to financial statements describing past events, and not the future, which is the concern of managerial accountants.

7. Managerial accountants will be on their guard for problem over-simplification. The tendency of corporate planners to assume away complexity, reducing reality to convenient factors, often polar opposite caricatures, is likely to leave the implementers of the strategy with insurmountable problems that even a consultant would be unable to resolve.

8. The formulation of this principle arises from discussions with Mark McCoy on the desirability of including a criterion separate to the matter under consideration which allows viable options to be compared by determining which requires the fewest beliefs and avoids adding ad hoc factors to create a favorable scenario.

9. Occam's razor recommends that the solution with the fewest assumptions should be preferred.

10. Conservative means that an estimate will err on the side of caution by neither overestimating revenue nor underestimating expenses. The rationale for this is that the business environment can change quickly, so managers should understand how sales revenue, costs and profit may change.

11. A cost allocation base is a factor that links indirect costs with a cost object in a systematic way. For example, the usage of a machine may also indicate the frequency of its maintenance. In manufacturing, common cost allocation bases are both financial (e.g., direct labor cost) and non-financial (e.g., machine hours, units produced, direct labor hours and direct materials usage).

12. A sensitivity analysis takes a 'what if' analysis a step further and systematically attempts to either discover important inputs and connections, or assess the uncertainty of each input and connection. Sensitivity analysis is not a risk analysis method because it cannot incorporate uncertainty into decision making. It also differs from scenario analysis, which uses different scenarios.

13. Where contracts are involved, this can be expressed as accepting the prima facie lowest cost tender.

14. Use of policies such as gender equality or diversity may be used to sidestep this principle of merit decision making.

15. Constraints are used to refer to conditions as well as to bottlenecks. In this sense, constraints may not be capable of removal but may need to be managed.

16. A SBU is not necessarily the same as an organizational unit. An SBU is usually a larger specialized division within large organization.

17. The only other action that results in an immediate improvement to the bottom line is where an organization is able to obtain revenue from a supplier in the guise of marketing or promotional payments. For an example of the process, see Packer (2014).

18. Cost objects can be anything for which a cost is measured. The most common cost object is a product line item or a service line item. Other cost objects include activities, product groups, organizational units or the organization as a whole.

19. A cost driver is something that affects the level of costs incurred. Common cost drivers are labor hours and machine usage hours (usually stated as machine hours).

20. For pedagogical reasons, this topic is used as an entrée to managerial accounting. The reasons include: (a) It is a self-contained topic that (b) introduces the terminology of cost behavior (direct and indirect costs) and cost assignment (fixed costs over the relevant range, variable costs, and mixed costs), and (c) uses contribution margin to replace gross margin. These are key concepts for students unfamiliar with managerial accounting and problems and solutions in cost–volume–profit problems help understanding and demonstrate their use.

21. It is essential to differentiate between product (or service) costing information and the management of costs. Product costing seeks accurate costing through detailed direct cost categories and a greater number of indirect cost activities. Cost management is concerned with (a) activities that are a significant proportion of total costs, (b) activities that have clear cause-effect relationship with the cost object, and (c) activities that are reliable lead estimators for forecasts.

22. Simons (1994) identifies three new control systems that allow strategic change: (1) belief systems that communicate core values and provide inspiration and direction, (2) boundary systems that frame the strategic domain and define the limits of freedom, and (3) interactive systems that provide flexibility in adapting to competitive environments and encourage organizational learning. More importantly diagnostic measurement systems are gamed in order to achieve incentive goals that do not meet the end organizations goals with dysfunctional side effects (pp. 81–83). Examples include (a) measuring the wrong variables, (b) building slack into targets, (c) gaming the system to increase the numbers measuring productivity, (d) smoothing the timing and flow of data without changing the underlying transactions being measured, (e) biasing or transmitting only data that will be perceived to be favorable, (f) illegal acts that violate organizational laws.

23. In many cases, only internal employees will have sufficient understanding of processes to identify account balance misstatement. The CFO may obstruct fraud detection as occurred in the case of WorldCom (Cooper, 2008). It was Cooper, the internal auditor at WorldCom, who uncovered an USD11 billion fraud. She shows that (a) telecommunications line costs were capitalized by calling them 'prepaid capacity' (decreasing expenses and increasing profits) on the balance sheet (increasing assets); (b) it was done with hundreds of entries to a variety of accounts in order to confuse anyone who might later look at them; and (c) the audit committee chair and members were not an independent group of individuals to whom an employee can voice concerns and be taken seriously. Sadly, the role of internal auditors did not change with Sarbanes-Oxley, which only deals with external auditors and CEO/CFO responsibilities. The internal audit function needs to report both functionally

and administratively to the audit committee, and internal auditors need wider powers to test transactions, particularly where systems are fragmented, or numerous small systems are pieced together (whether or not the result of acquisitions, and the merging of many small organizations).

24. The corporate failures following the global financial crisis have identified some examples of poor tone at the top. For example, they include premature sign-off of accounts, loosening internal controls, seeking profits ahead of ethics, privileging selected stakeholders, using compliance with the law as a defense, having unresolved conflicts of interest, peer pressure, and ignoring public expectations of what constitutes ethical behavior by executives in public organizations (Schaubroeck, Avolio, Lord, Dimotakis, Hannah et al., 2012; Pickerd, Summers & Wood, 2015).

25. A learning organization differs from organizational learning. Organizational learning analyses the processes involved in individual and collective learning inside organizations (Tsang, 1997). A learning organization is a system capable of bringing about its own continuing transformation (Schön, 1973); later developments focused on feedback to detect and correct error, single-loop learning chosen goals, values, plans and rules are operationalized, and double- loop learning where an organization's underlying norms, policies and objectives are modified.

26. Modern formal budgets not only limit expenditures; they also predict income, profits and returns on investment a year ahead. They take into account historical patterns and real-world events. Typically, budgets are developed bottom up to meet top-down business goals for profit or return.

27. The strategic management term 'strategic business unit' refers to a semi-autonomous independent unit that operates separately, but it is an important part of the parent organization.

28. Creation of value is distinguished from capturing value because the history of business is replete with organizations that have succeeded in the first and failed in the second. For example, the graphical user interface devised by Xerox was exploited by first by Apple and then by Microsoft. Creating value involves identifying value opportunities. This can be done by identifying valuable problems. These are problems, which if successfully solved, will yield high value knowledge which can generate significant value for the organization. Capturing value is the extraction of value. However, some CEO's and majority shareholders exploit extractable value. The managerial accountant will want to consider whether pursuit of an exploitive strategy will cause a large reduction in the true economic net worth of the organization rather than create greater value over the long-term.

29. For many organizations, strategy has been simply a matter of positioning itself to take advantage of the economic momentum in its market. Key contributors to momentum are (a) the underlying growth of the economy, (b) the rate of inflation, (c) the level of income and (d) spending power of consumers.

30. Cost relationships may exist between (a) costs and production volume, (b) costs and profit, (c) costs and sales, (d) costs and periods, (e) costs and overheads, and (f) costs and quality. Cost relationships can also be found among the activities in the value chain.

31. A rebate is the return of part of a payment for a product or service after purchase is finalized by a seller to a buyer. The rebate may be calculated ad valorum on the gross value of sales or apply to selected products or apply at a particular rate only for a selected period. Currently under accounting standards, a rebate received may be reported as profit without being matched to the sale of the corresponding product.

32. A model should not be equated with a theory. A model represents hypotheses derived from theories. Sometimes the same model is applicable to different theories and then good design should distinguish between rival theories. Often the managerial accountant is interested in causal theories. Taking the four methods, examples are cost drivers for understanding costs, performance determinants for process improvement and motivation, behavior for governance, compliance and control, and value for strategy. Other causal theories may involve price determinants or information or decision impact on the behavior of managers and employees. The managerial accountant will therefore want to test the same theory in more than one way rather than repeatedly test it the same way. One difficulty with a model is that it can have more than one interpretation. When working with a model, the managerial accountant will want to be sure of (a) the fit of the model, (b) the theory is stated sufficiently specifically to determine a specific interpretation of the model, and (c) it tests the theory. An error in any of these will leading to ambiguity and/ or miscommunication with others who rely on the model.

33. Rivett (1980) updates an earlier attempt that classified models in seven basic structures that are separated from any particular method by differentiating between models where feedback affects the condition of the system and those which do not. So, of the several structures lack feedback: queuing (problems), allocation (problems), scheduling and routing, replacement and maintenance, some search problems, and competition where there is a slow reaction. There are three where feedback may occur: inventory problems, some search problems, and competition where there is quick reaction. The classification allows reference to relevant past situations and may direct attention to a standard analysis. In concluding his appraisal of model structures, Rivett (1980: 61–63) describes the key questions to be asked at the start of model building.

34. Examples of the kind of changes that violate this assumption include new objectives, adopting new polices, replacing senior managers, changes in the business environment and a series of small decisions that have a cumulative effect.

35. The influence of personal moods, emotions and emotional climate as well as whims, peccadillos can nullify powers of discrimination in matters such as costs, revenues, projects, value and utility (Rivett, 1980).

36. It is unlikely that the modeler will have time to (a) determine the set of minimum characteristics that will be acceptable to the organization and (b) determine both the best and worst acceptable solution and compare them to ascertain the need to be concerned with the issue in the first place. The issues of management exist in the minds of managers and their advisors, so getting a clear statement of the problem from them is vital. Rivett (1962) comments that where management has full knowledge of it objective and its performance, it is difficult to get more than 5% improvement in performance, even by using the most sophisticated mathematical and statistical analyses. He recommends that issues in this area are best left to managers to make intelligent improvements to a complex situation by trial and error. The greatest gains are achieved by measuring something for the first time or working in a new way that redefines objectives or removes constraints.

37. The documenting of an assumption answers three questions: (1) Why was an assumption needed? (2) What were the criteria used? (3) What was the decision? A standard design groups similar information into zones: the documentation zone (containing, title, purpose, filename, date prepared, date last revised); the input data zone, processing with formulas zone; and output or reports zone (Harrison & Yu, 1990; Thommes, 1992). These authors also recommend documenting any macros used.

38. Analysis often uses the basic data processing (IPO) model comprising the sequence: inputs (raw data used to depict the problem or scenario being modeled); outputs (data resulting from calculations or other transformations); and processing (computations to produce the output for example, formulas, functions, sorts, queries).

39. Analysis involves defining the questions to be answered, the time period of the model and its importance to the organization. Then detailed analysis will involve specifying the goal, constraints, inputs, current state, and any relationships with other data, variables and systems. The output also needs to be specified, and how and by whom result(s) will be evaluated.

40. Rivett (1980) suggests that the standard features of a model can be divided into macro features such as the effect of inflation, depreciation which is a form of saving and cost of capital (as an interest rate, a return to shareholders, or rate of return generated by other investments of the organization), and detail features including capacity utilization (for the short and long-term), valuation of assets, treatment of future revenue and costing parts of the whole (e.g., overheads, marginal costs, marginal revenues, marginal profitability).

41. Examples of economic design involve planning to (1) allow ease of expansion (inserting columns and rows); (2) layout to avoid ambiguity and unstated assumptions; and (3) adopting a standard design for the majority of spreadsheets (Rothery, 1990). Inserting rows and columns is easy if the spreadsheet steps down using a diagonal of rectangles (Richardson, 1996).

42. Ackoff and Churchman (1955) and Churchman (1961) claim that the choice between different methods is not an accounting problem. Apart from the change of perspective from needs of external users (e.g., audit and tax) to needs of managers within the organization, there is the issue of opportunity cost, elasticity and purpose. Purpose has already been discussed as one of the principles of the managerial accountant's compass.

43. The three statements (income statement, balance sheet and cash flow statement) are dynamically linked and provide a foundation for advanced financial modeling including discounted cash flow and projections (Tjia, 2018).

44. Using ethnomethodology these could be investigated in the workplace using membership categorization (Lepper, 2000) to determine how boundaries in collegiate relationships are established and maintained as part of social processes. Here the categories here are used to guide the managerial accountant toward the important social groupings in the organization who deserve attention.

45. This is referred to by Simon et al. (1954) as influencing. Again, advising and partnering seems to be a more apt description.

46. Simon et al. (1954) prefer the expression 'attention directing', but this presupposes the manager, in this case the managerial accountant, can gain attention. In some organizations accountants are dismissed and demeaned with the explicit label of 'bean counter'. However, there is no denying their technical expertise in both selecting the method and conducting the analysis. This differs from the problem solving that Simon et al. (1954) describe because the managerial accountant does not necessarily determine the best way to deal with the issue.

47. Technical expertise is also referred to as hard skills that an individual possesses. They contrast with soft skills, which are character and personality traits. Technical expertise may not reach the level of subject matter expert, that is, an authority in a particular area or topic.

48. The distinction between 'line' and 'staff' originated with the military as a way of separating the personnel who directly advance the organization in the achievement of its objectives (line) and those who indirectly contribute

to the accomplishment of these objectives in a role of counsel, service or advice. Applying these definitions to an organization, production and sales are examples of the former, while accounting, human resources, legal services and information technology are examples of the latter.

49. A bandwagon effect is a benefit that consumers enjoy as a result of others using the same product or service. The benefit may be direct in terms of agreeing on standards. There is also a secondary benefit that is overlooked by Rohlfs', namely, the social cohesion from shared experience. The latter often gives senior managers and board members topics to copy as well as discuss.

10 Ethical Conduct With Self-Care as the Fifth Point of the Managerial Accountant's Compass

This chapter is the third and last of the chapters that discuss the managerial accountant's compass. It details the fifth cardinal point of the compass introduced in Chapter 8 and depicted in Figure 8–1, which is ethics and self-care. Ethics is the values that people choose to live by and is of major, continuing concern to accountants and stakeholders of organizations.[1] Self-care is attitudes and behaviors that contribute to the maintenance of well-being, personal health, promote human development and a work–life balance. Self-care is allied to ethics because inattention to it can result in poor ethical decisions and behavior without regard for reputation. The combination of ethics and self-care completes the cardinal points that guide the managerial accountant in their role and responsibilities. As with the previous chapters, the discussion both describes the assumed knowledge of the managerial accountant, uses questions to guide attention and suggests avenues that the managerial accountant can constructively explore in their relationships with other managers and employees.

10.1 Ethical Theories Underpinning the Ethical Code

From the history and philosophy of ethics, it is possible to identify three main ethical theories. Virtue ethics is centered on the character of the individual. It was proposed by Aristotle (2002) and reinvigorated by MacIntyre (2007). The second theory is consequentialist ethics (Anscombe, 1958), which is concerned with beneficial outcomes from behavior. It was proposed by the utilitarian Bentham (1996) who advocated specific actions that produce the best consequence (act consequentialism). It was then supplemented by Mill (1871) who proposed utilitarianism as a moral rule to consider what produces the best consequence (rule consequentialism). Finally, there is obligation ethics, which emphasizes duty. It was advocated by Kant (1999) who proposed morally proper behavior regardless of the consequences (categorical imperative). Although the theories are distinct, in practice, there is a tendency to combine them.[2] That is, to consider both virtue and consequences. Against this background is business ethics that is concerned with the practices of individuals and groups within an organization that reflect or undermine its stated core values. Since most organizations are for-profit, profit-maximizing behavior has to be reconciled with noneconomic concerns. Whether the organization can serve society as advocated by Berle and Means (1968) remains unclear because ethics concerns behavior outside governmental regulation, and some organizations have shown themselves to be insensitive to communities they serve. Nevertheless, professions and organizations impose ethical codes on their members and employees respectively.

10.2   Ethical Code in Managerial Accounting: Ideals, Application and Implications

Generally, for information to be useful it should be prepared by ethical accountants based on ethical accounting practices. Each accounting professional association throughout the world has its own ethical code. Most ethical codes for managerial accountants amalgamate the three ethical theories. They demand individuals do more than conform to the letter of the code, so it is concerned with virtuous behavior. They obligate the managerial accountant to encourage other managerial accountants to observe the code, so it also embodies obligation or duty. They are concerned for the reputation of the profession, so this is consequentialist theory.

Selecting an Ethical Code

A simple, yet well thought-out ethical code was recently produced by the IMA (Institute of Management Accountants, 2017) as *The Statement of Ethical Professional Practice*, but hereafter referred to as the ethical code. There was an earlier version in 2005 consisting of just principles and standards. It is reproduced in many textbooks, for example, Horngren et al. (2015) and Hilton and Platt (2014) that are sold around the world as international editions, so the ethical code has exposure far beyond its originating professional membership. The IMA (2017) statement consists of principles, standards and resolving ethical issues.[3] Although they do not use the words ethical code, together the principles and standards comprise an ethical code.[4] The principles provide a generalized framework of values within which an ethical dilemma may be analyzed. These exist for circumstances where the ethical standards are silent or ambivalent. Standards give clear directives on the behavior expected. The IMA ethical code has two major advantages. First, it is easy to remember because it is short and expressed simply yet strongly. Second, its two-level hierarchy enables it to be used in most situations. The IMA ethical code compares favorably to the ethical codes of other professions outside accounting. It stands alone without supplementary pronouncements unlike some other ethical codes. It expects managerial accountants to show an active commitment to upholding a high standard of ethical conduct. A feature of the ethical code is its statement that a member's failure to comply with it may result in disciplinary action.

The ethical code states: "Members of the IMA shall behave ethically". This encompasses:

Principles of Ethical Conduct

A commitment to ethical professional practice includes four overarching principles that express values and standards that guide conduct. The four moral principles of ethical conduct are

1. Honesty [truthfulness]
2. Fairness [impartiality]
3. Objectivity [unaffected by personal feelings or opinions]
4. Responsibility [accountable for behavior]

While each of these words is used with its ordinary meaning in the English language shown in [square brackets], in managerial accounting, their meaning carries dual a reference. They apply to the managerial accountant's own behavior, but also to the information that the managerial accountant creates and disseminates. They also state an obligation to comply with and uphold the four ethical standards.

Standards of Ethical Conduct

The four professional standards of ethical conduct are

1. Competence
2. Confidentiality
3. Integrity
4. Credibility

Each standard is elaborated with three further points, except for integrity and credibility, each of which have four points. The statement is available as a two-sided wallet size PDF from their website.

Dual applicability

The statement obligates IMA members to encourage others in their organization to adhere to all four principles.

Resolving Ethical Issues

The statement advises members that encounter ethical issues to actively resolve them considering their protection against retaliation and all risks. It reminds members they may need to consider disaffiliating from the organization.

Evaluating the IMA Ethical Code

Six themes run through *The Statement of Ethical Professional Practice* (Institute of Management Accountants, 2017) with the relevant standards are shown in (parentheses) after the theme. Competence can be challenged at any time so maintaining and enhancing knowledge and skills goes beyond holding qualifications and keeping-up-to-date (Competence). The second treats behavior as complying and unprejudiced and implies a self-regulated approach (Competence; Integrity). The third is to properly manage information which encompasses its metadata, content quality, as well as the people, processes and technologies associated with its production, use and storage (Competence; Confidentiality; Credibility). The fourth is to avoid conflict of interest whether perceivable or real and whether or not there is the possibility of exploitation in a professional or official capacity to produce a personal or corporate benefit for a third party (Integrity). The fifth is to responsibly communicate potential or actual conflicts of interest, constraints or limitations in relation to behavior or judgments, which recognizes there are limits to confidentiality, and judgments are not to be subordinated to others; threats to objectivity must be managed (Credibility; Integrity). Finally, the managerial accountant should place the interests of the profession above personal interests (Integrity). The themes show there are six related attempts to protect stakeholders and the profession from unspecified but unacceptable behavior by managerial accountants. The managerial accountant is in a position of trust and a conflict of interest exists even if no unethical or improper act results as an appearance of impropriety can undermine that trust in the managerial accountant and the profession.

10.3   Analyzing Ethical Dilemmas for Managerial Accountants

An ethical dilemma is a choice the managerial accountant has to make between at least two possible moral choices which appear equally acceptable or hazardous. The choices may arise from conflict between actual elements of the ethical code or from consequences in following it. Often there is a shadow ethical dilemma: whether to act, or overlook, apparently minor ethical lapses. Since a minor ethical lapse may be a symptom of larger transgressions, it is prudent to take it up with the individual or group. It can be done in two steps, initially on a personal level, and subsequently with a codified confirmation.

An ethical dilemma is analyzed in four stages: indifference resulting in an ethical lapse, recognizing, planning and declaring a position, as shown in Table 10–1. Each stage has a corresponding action, and for each action there are checks or tests.

Table 10–1 Four stages of analyzing an ethical dilemma: indifference resulting in an ethical lapse, recognizing, planning and declaring a position.

Stage	Action	Checks or Tests
Indifference	Commit an ethical lapse.	1 By seeing nothing wrong with continuing with normal behavior 2 Avoiding the negative consequences and choosing a third less painful option (e.g., defer action, withdraw from the situation, use the need to maintain confidentiality to avoid action or believing a credulous answer to the question you asked)
Recognize the ethical dilemma.	Identify the conflict.	1 Determine how the managerial accountant is affected (Are they being asked to act unethically or to refrain from acting ethically?) 2 Identify the choice explicitly or implicitly suggested or by the other party(ies). (This may be continuing an unethical practice or not continuing.) 3 Identify other choices including clarify (what is being asked of them), explaining (the ethical implications), negotiating/persuading, escalating (to the next level of management), seeking external advice (accounting, legal) or quitting.
Plan the responses to the ethical dilemma.	Clarify what ethical principles or ethical standards are in conflict.	1 Evaluate the ethics of each choice, anticipate its consequences, and likely responses. For each choice, consider the short and long term. 2 Establish which ethical principle or ethical standard should dominate, that is, be followed. 3 Determine what sequence of actions to take to resolve the ethical dilemma for each of the possible responses that have been anticipated.
Declare a position on the ethical dilemma.	Determine the actions that will resolve the ethical dilemma.	1 Communicate with the other party(ies) to discover their ethical position, rationale. Encourage them to behave ethically. 2 Respond immediately to any further explicit unethical request. 3 Have regard to organizational protocols and procedures (e.g., anonymous reporting). 4 Record the incident and seek professional advice if it appears serious, ongoing or likely to escalate.

Indifference Because Acting Ethically Is Difficult and May Result in an Ethical Lapse

Indifference to ethical awareness can occur even where ethical codes exist for many reasons. One is indifference (Barnard, 1938). People tend to act co-operatively without questioning authority (La Boétie, 2007). They believe requests from their peers are genuine work requests. Another is that there are always people who will act in their own interest; some will encourage others to act unethically on their behalf. Finally, reasons may be provided which appear to have a reasonable rational (e.g., serving the interests of the organization, or attributing base motives to another individual). Recognition of the ethical dilemma therefore requires conscious effort.

Unfamiliarity with current protocols may make reporting unethical matters problematic. Internal policies may only accept a report of an ethical concern that conforms to format, timing, recipient and confidentiality. To avoid any attempt at a cover-up, employees may have to self-report each instance ethical lapse. External advisors on ethics usually require details and timely notification. It may be necessary to make contact by telephone, and if so, it is essential to ensure that the conversation is legally privileged. Awareness of these protocols ensures adequate preparation if faced with an unexpected ethical dilemma.

Indifference to the ethical dilemma or unethical behavior is an ethical lapse. Common examples include

- Immoral activities associated with work
- Questionable legal actions ('grey area')
- Disclosing confidential or misleading information to third parties
- Amending or engineering transaction, performance, and personal records and reports
- Making public statements which are contradicted in private information
- Accepting gifts in return for immediate or delayed favors

An ethical lapse may have two causes. One is overriding the ethical code with personal or group values or preferences. These include intuition, beliefs and interests that impose superior obligations from peers, family, and other individual or organizations. It can result in exchanging favors, making the most of a situation, using other moral principles (e.g., gratitude or self-improvement) or simply being opportunistic hoping not to be found out.

The other is justifying the unethical action with an indefensible excuse when asked to explain it. Josephson (1992) found nine excuses for unethical behavior:

- Self-deception. For example, "I can get away with it". Permanent concealment is unlikely because there is often a delay before events are discovered. Another expression is "Others are doing it". Many people do foolish things that they later truly regret.

- Self-indulgence. For example, the pursuit of personal desires whether or not hedonistic.
- Self-protection. For example, concealing apparent wrong-doing whether done by superiors or to cover-up potential embarrassment.
- Self-righteousness. For example, confidence that one's own beliefs are superior.
- Faulty reasoning associated with benefits or costs. For example, "I am only taking a small amount and that is not so bad".
- Seeking sympathy. For example, "I need money for my family".
- Dismissing the consequences. For example, "This is just a temporary job so I don't care about loss of reputation".
- Blaming others. For example, "My boss made me do it".
- The ambition to "beat the system". For example, "Their new electronic surveillance system hasn't been activated yet so anyone can still come through the backdoor".

Since this is a long list, it clearly shows that excuses for an ethical lapse are easily fabricated. They are known because others, who act independently and responsibly, reported the ethical lapse immediately or later. In some cases, friends and family can be affected. In other cases, it can change the perceptions of others so their attitudes and behavior change. Since the Nuremburg trials, the Superior Orders Defense ensures that an individual is not relieved from responsibility provided a moral choice was possible. Avoiding or breaking the rules of an organization or system can mean either exploiting loopholes, overcoming or bypassing the rules. Since this involves deceit, it becomes unethical. Given the principles and standards are so broad, it is also likely that unethical actions will bring the accounting profession into disrepute.

Frequently, an ethical lapse has unintended consequences. Often, they are unfair to others who are acting ethically and disadvantage others who may not know about the actions that affect them. There may also be unavoidable consequences which only become apparent much later. Some are quite serious as they that consequences far beyond the individual involved.

Recognize the Ethical Dilemma

An ethical dilemma affects the managerial accountant either directly because they are involved, or because they are aware others are acting unethically irrespective of its impact. They need to determine whether they are being asked to act unethically or to refrain from acting ethically. Although Table 10–1 differentiates between the unethical practice being ad hoc or continuing, it may not be possible to determine until later. Even when the managerial recognizes the ethical dilemma, there may be pressure to dismiss it from friends, peers or colleagues to ignore wrongdoing. Others may be observed to act unethically without being caught and even acknowledge their actions are unethical saying, "What are you going to do about it?"

Plan the Responses to an Ethical Dilemma

Planning the responses involves clarifying choices, and until this is completed, it is important to withhold the decision. Exploring the unethical request clarifies explicitly what the managerial accountant is being asked to do, and whether the requestor is aware they are requesting an unethical action. Once this is established further negotiation and persuasion can be pursued, to confirm the situation.

Because neither of the two options in an ethical dilemma will resolve the situation in an ethically acceptable fashion, there is a temptation to choose a third option that is far less painful. The third option avoids confronting the ethical dilemma by

- Deferring any action
- Withdrawing from the situation
- Using the need to maintain confidentiality[5]
- Believing a credulous answer to the question you asked

These appear more attractive than the choices from the ethical dilemma because both ethical dilemma choices bring an immediate negative result to the parties and provide no satisfactory outcome for the managerial accountant who has to make the choice. Any analysis must acknowledge that some loss is likely, but the reaction of the parties would depend upon the person, the circumstances, the eventualities, and the knowledge that the choice was guided by upholding the ethical code and not avoiding it, and this involves some regardless loss to self. That leads to declaring a position that avoids an ethical lapse; otherwise it returns to the first step and becomes a matter of indifference.

Declare a Position on the Ethical Dilemma

Resolving the ethical dilemma occurs when the managerial accountant declares their position and announces their decision. A discussion with the employee should discover their ethical position and establish whether their request is deliberate or poorly framed. If it was deliberate, the managerial accountant should always encourage the requestor to behave ethically. This may also clarify whether similar situations have occurred in the past and how they have been handled (whether ethically or unethically). It is desirable to immediately respond to any explicit, new unethical request. This can be either a rejection or delaying. Some circumstances are so extreme that making clear the request is rejected is essential to avoid being implicated in an untoward situation. Other circumstances allow a request for time to reflect on the request or situation. This is desirable when senior management needs to be involved or there is a need to clarify details. Not making a declaration or doing what is wrong is an ethical lapse. Some examples are provided to illustrate the analysis of ethical dilemmas.

10.4   Examples of Ethical Dilemmas Facing the Managerial Accountant

The handling of the following ethical dilemmas differs from textbook worked examples. They show the importance of planning the interaction and declaring a position as described in Table 10–1. Applying the ethical principles and standards requires effort in thinking about what they mean. The ethical code does not specify the circumstances that lead to ethical dilemmas. So, learning to behave ethically is more about understanding how to apply the code, rather than being able to recite it point by point. Three examples from business indicate the range of ethical dilemmas that the managerial accountant can face.

Scenario 10–1: Discovery of Unethical Behavior of a Peer

Scenario: You work in a large organization that employs eight managerial accountants. Your desk is one of several managerial accountant desks near the lift door of the open plan office on Level 3. When you arrive at work, you find on your desk an envelope without any addressee name. You open it and find it contains a letter naming another managerial accountant who sits at the desk that backs on to yours and is your best friend. The letter states, "Here is this month's retainer. Sorry for the delay I have been on leave". It is signed by a competitor. It contains $5,000 cash. You conclude the envelope has been left on the wrong desk.

Recognize this ethical dilemma is a conflict between two ethical principles. As shown in Figure 10–1, it involves

- The ethical principle of *honesty* (you should tell your supervisor what your best friend is doing)
- The ethical principle of *objectivity* (you should not be influenced by personal feelings or opinions about your best friend when considering and representing facts)

Figure 10–1 Ethical dilemma after accidental discovery of unethical behavior by one of your peers.

Plan the responses by considering the consequences for you and your friend. The fact that competitors have access to the office and presumably to organization information is a concern. Use the ethical principle of objectivity to plan a discussion with your immediate manager.

Resolve the ethical dilemma by communicating immediately, but retain the envelope.

This ethical dilemma has physical evidence to corroborate the assertion, does not involve bypassing the immediate manager, and does not require external assistance. Nonetheless, it is a difficult decision that will have consequences for the friendship.

Scenario 10–2: Subtle Invitation With an Incentive to Behave Unethically

Scenario: You have been in discussion with three suppliers for a $2.5 million contract for a new enterprise resource planning system. During small-talk during those discussions you advised your sporting interests, forthcoming marriage and house purchase. As a flagship organization, you know that this choice will be copied by at least seven other organizations. Supplier C phones you to check if you received their answers to the supplementary questions that you sent to all suppliers. Supplier C then tells you their finance division will approve a loan of $750,000 for your house mortgage at 2 percent less than the market rate, if they are successful. They do not know they are already the lowest and most favorably considered of the three tenders in the preliminary evaluation.

Recognize this ethical dilemma involves a conflict between two ethical standards. As shown in Figure 10–2, it involves

* The ethical standard of *competence* (in this case, expertise in running a tender and negotiating a favorable contract)
* The ethical standard of *credibility* (disclose all information that affects a decision even though their quote is already the lowest)

Plan the responses by asking the caller whether this is an official Supplier C proposal or initiated by them as the sales manager at Supplier C. It is desirable to know the genesis of the unethical action because it may exclude Supplier C entirely from further negotiations. Explain the ethical

Figure 10–2 Ethical dilemma from a subtle invitation to behave unethically with an incentive.

position of the buying organization. Use the ethical standard of credibility. A contract should be awarded on the grounds of meeting the selection criteria, not for offering unrelated incentives to the deal.

Resolve the ethical dilemma by refusing the unethical offer and leave it at that. Again, inform the manager, but in light of the answers given by Supplier C, consider whether the supplier may try to influence other higher managers in the organization. There is also the issue of their existing favorable rating. It will be necessary to widen the contract selection committee to ensure objectivity. Since it was a phone call, there is no supporting documentary evidence (e.g., tape recording, video surveillance). This lack of clarity and strength in the evidence may work against informing any third parties (e.g., CEO of Supplier C; industry regulator) though. Depending upon discussions with senior management, the managerial accountant may arrange for Supplier C to reiterate their ethical lapse in a way that provides the acceptable evidence.

Scenario 10–3: Request to Conceal Unethical Behavior

Scenario: At the sales manager's request, you have been working with the sales department to improve their budgeting and recording of expenses which uncovered a mix of high unfavorable and favorable variances across a range of accounts. You have just told the Sales Manager that you are now satisfied they are accurately recording expenses. The sales manager asks you to write a report confirming motor vehicle, and entertainment expenses are low. You found controls over them have been lax, and some expenses were recorded as part of the new sales showroom and offices. You also know the previous managerial accountant left after refusing to accept these costs should be classified as selling overhead and building fitout.

Recognize the ethical dilemma involves a conflict between two ethical standards. As shown in Figure 10–3, it involves

- The ethical principle of responsibility (managers and employees should be held accountable for their actions)
- The ethical standard of competence (this concerns expertise in budgeting and variance analysis)

Figure 10–3 Ethical dilemma recognized from being asked to conceal unethical behavior.

Plan the responses by clarifying with the Sales Manager whether they realize that these expenses are not low. Follow this up by explaining the misclassifications arise from sales administration staff incorrectly code expenditure on the payment approval vouchers. If the Sales Manager concedes there are coding errors and that motor vehicle and entertainment expenses should be made visible whether or not they were incurred to benefit of the organization, then the Sales Manager should cancel the unethical request. If the Sales Manager perseveres, then the managerial accountant will need to negotiate further so terminate the conversation. Then discuss with the senior managerial accountant and CFO. It will be difficult for a lower-level managerial accountant to negotiate with a highly placed Sales Manager. Since the coding of expense vouchers occurs in the Sales department, any change will have to be made by the financial account and so it is appropriate for the CFO to become involved. This may result in the collegiate relationship between the managerial accountant and the Sales Manager being disrupted, but it would be difficult for the managerial accountant to resist future pressures from the Sales Manager that may be even more corrupting.

10.5 Consequences of Public Expectations for High Standards of Ethical Behavior of Accountants and Auditors

The high public expectations for accountants have consequences for their selection to enter the profession, and prosecution for wrongdoing. Schmidt and Hunter (1998) confirmed the importance of ethics in selection. Their study examined the relative predictive power of 19 different ways of selecting people for jobs. They found that an integrity test was the fourth (after a work sample test, intelligence test and structured interview). This ranking that uses almost a century of studies suggests that ethical employees benefit the organization in ways not always appreciated. The history of corporate behavior worldwide reveals numerous deficiencies which were associated with personal ethics that showed willingness for self-deception (Josephson, 1992). The beneficial legislative[6] protection[7] of afforded companies imposed on them controls over their activities and reporting standards, but no ethical obligations.

Accountants have been held by the community and government[8] to the highest ethical standards because they are responsible for producing information that can affect everyone. Their standards are higher than ordinary individuals, and beyond those of many other professions owing to the important stewardship role they fulfill in producing information used in reporting.[9] Recent public pronouncements by regulatory and prosecutorial authorities that appeared in news media illustrate that white-collar crime is no longer treated leniently:

- In USA, "a certified public accountant who was the business manager for singer-songwriter Alanis Morissette, as well as other well-known entertainment and sports figures, was sentenced today to six years in federal prison for stealing approximately $7.2 million from his clients" (USA Attorney General's office Central District of California, May 3, 2017).

- In EU, "a disgraced former judge already in jail for deception has had another two years added to her sentence for false accounting" (Irish Independent, July 29, 2018).

- In Australia, "Justice Haesler said Accountants 'hold important positions of trust and [they] needed to be aware [I will send you to] jail if [you] breach that trust and act dishonestly'". (*The Weekend Australian Business Review*, July 18–19, 2015)

- Governments and regulators are aware that ethical obligations are at a higher standard than mere compliance with the law. This arises because the law lags behind many common social phenomena, and only sets minimum standards, which often have loopholes or defenses. In the past, unethical individuals have been able to rely on the fact that only after a major financial catastrophe is new or amended legislation introduced. In any case, enforcement depends upon the regulator having actionable legislation, funding to investigate and willingness to prosecute rather than settle with the organization. This becomes difficult as organizations enlarge their economic boundaries beyond nations to minimize tax obligations. Thus, very large organizations have been moving assets and liabilities around interlinked corporations, but also transactions and supply relationships in ways that may be ultimately legal but with outcomes of little value to society. The ethics of these supra-organizations remain to be investigated, but it appears that global agreement on transparency and taxation is a major step.

10.6 Exemplars of and Coaching in Ethical Behavior During Coursework

Managerial accountants need to have exemplars of ethical behavior and coaching during coursework to practice behaving ethically. Exemplars are the teaching staff that can show they apply the ethical code to themselves. Examples include discussing the ethical dilemmas they face in administering the course, setting and marking assessment, as well as course syllabus and content. The value of these ethical exemplars is that students see that ethical dilemmas are commonplace. They are not reserved for occasions when there are weighty matters. These can provide the students with sufficient examples to allow them to identify exemplar managers in their organization. If approached, most managers will gladly accept a mentor role for ethical behavior.

Coaching comes from the psychological theory of conditioning. As with any new behavior, there is the requirement to make it a habit (Hull, 1943). Psychology suggests that habit formation requires cues, repetition of the behavior and a reward (Lally, van Jaarsveld, Potts & Wardle, 2010). Both the employee who is acting unethically and the employee who knows it is occurring can be the focus of coaching. The employee who is behaving unethically receives single-stage coaching. They are asked to reconsider their own behavior by reflecting on past ethical lapses to understand why they occurred and what should be done about them. That is, to allow them to plan the response as though it was happening now in real time and decide the action they should take. It also ensures they attend to the future, so they do not keep repeating ethical lapses. Those who know another employee is acting unethically, have two-stage coaching. The first stage is to discourage the employee from behaving unethically. The second stage is to monitor and report any likelihood the employee will continue to act unethically. The reward in this form of practical coaching is students understand that others will be looking at their behavior and judging whether what they do is ethical.

10.7   Self-Care Obligation Under the Ethical Standard of Competence

In an ordinary day, a managerial accountant has to meet with many different personality types, prepare information and take part in discussions that can affect the future career and earnings of managers and employees. Based on allied health professional reports, symptoms managerial accountants can report include:

- Distress, shock and guilt when employees are affected
- Shame and self-blame concerning the information they provided
- Feelings of incompetency and responsibility for adverse outcomes
- Expectations of blame from managers and family members
- Negative perceptions of colleagues
- Fear of litigation over employment related matters

Self-care is a poorly recognized obligation of managerial accountants under the competency standard. It is an important component of competency because professional competency may be affected by physical and mental and issues. Physical issues include tiredness, unhealthy sleeping patterns, injuries, weight, lack of appetite, substance abuse and mobility. Mental concerns include feeling anxious or worried, emotional outbursts, quiet or withdrawn from life, and feeling guilty or worthless. Some of these symptoms are best assessed as changes in behavior. Some others, such as death or incapacitation of a colleague, friend or family member need also to be considered. The consequences of lack of self-care can be unethical behavior, dishonesty, pathological behavior and substance abuse. It may be possible to conceal or compensate for incompetence in the short term but that is not viable for the long-term. The accounting profession is currently silent on self-care. University studies do not train managerial accountants about self-care. Nor is it part of admission to the accounting profession. So, it is important that managerial accountants develop their own culture of self-care.

10.8   Self-Care Assessment and Formulation of Action Plan

A self-care plan should be oriented to the person. Together the biopsychosocial model of health (Engel, 1977) and the ecological systems theory (Bronfenbrenner, 1979) propose a broad view that attributes health outcomes to the intricate and variable dynamic interactions of factors that are biological (e.g., genetic, biochemical), psychological (mood, personality, behavior, etc.) and social (cultural, familial, socioeconomic, medical, etc.). These can be translated to six domains that consider the person as a whole (Saakvitne, Pearlman & Staff, 1996):

- Mind self-care (mental health)
- Body self-care (physical health)
- Emotional self-care (emotional health)
- Social relationship self-care (social needs and networks)
- Spiritual self-care (sources of comfort and guidance)
- Work self-care (working in a safe and protective manner)

For each of the six domains specific factors are identified. The self-care plan consists of an assessment which uses separate columns to self-report on

- Current position or the current state for each factor
- Barriers to maintaining self-care for the domain
- How to overcome the barriers
- Currently practiced strategies to avoid or reduce negative effects
- Proposed specific and time-bounded actions that will address barriers and negative effects

Table 10–2 reformulates these domains and specific factors as a plan to remedy omissions and overcome barriers.

The self-care plan is a snapshot. The managerial accountant should regularly review and update it, but what could have been done differently should not be interpreted as what ought to have been done. While it can be kept private, informal discussion with confidants may lead to additional avenues of support being identified and alternate means found to overcome barriers. This may result in complete reformulation of the

Table 10–2 Self-care template for current assessment, identifying impediments, and plan to remedy omissions and overcome barriers.

Current Position		Impediments			Plan	
Domain	*Factor*	*Current Status*	*Barriers to Maintaining Self-Care*	*Current Strategies That Reduce or Avoid Negative Effects*	*How Barriers Will Be Overcome*	*Proposed Actions*
Mind	Attitudes Attention & awareness Beliefs Cause & effect Comprehension Consciousness Creativity Discourse Habits Imagination Memory Perception Problem solving Reasoning					
Welfare of the body[10]	Breathing Exercise Nutrition Posture Sleep Self-soothing system Water intake					
Emotions	Awareness of thoughts, feelings and sensations Beliefs Boundary setting Garden Journal/Diary of thoughts Self-talk					

Current Position		Impediments			Plan	
Domain	Factor	Current Status	Barriers to Maintaining Self-Care	Current Strategies That Reduce or Avoid Negative Effects	How Barriers Will Be Overcome	Proposed Actions
Spirituality	Birds & animals appreciation Contemplation Flowers & trees observation Ground/land sensing Mediation Purpose and meaning Quiet surroundings Reading Solitude Sea/lake Sky & stars					
Social relationships	Assistance Collegiate support Concern Co-operation Encouragement Support Trust					
Work	Absences Finance Innovation Mentoring Morale Supervision Time management Travel					

self-care plan or change in emphasis. The template assumes that individual differences require different specific factors for self-care. The managerial accountant can judge which actions (from the plan or unplanned) have the most benefit. Assessment can highlight deficiencies in self-care, but prevention is assisted by understanding happiness as a self-care behavior.

10.9   Preventive Mental Self-Care Using Understanding and Avoidance

Happiness is an important contributor to mental self-care (Vaillant, 2003). Gilbert (2006) makes three points about happiness that impact self-care. First imagination is unreliable but usually accepted uncritically. This means that predictions about self-care in the future are likely to be erroneous. Second, the present is frequently misperceived. So, conclusions about self-care are likely to ignore apparently obvious shortcomings and contain some self-delusional aspects. Third, unhappy outcomes are exaggerated or rationalized. So, this can lead to repeating the same unsatisfactory events and outcomes that impede self-care and overlooking opportunities that may facilitate self-care. Thus, self-care without any assessment as already proposed may lead to incorrect judgments about what will bring happiness. That is, self-care behavior that seeks happiness may be misdirected. Resilience studies make the point that a major negative experience can produce a positive perception of their life (Windle, 2011). This suggests that separate self-care assessments should occur for negative experiences. In summary, as the managerial accountant reflects, they should separate pre-feeling (imagination) from feeling (experience) to reduce mis-estimation of current self-care status, barriers to self-care and proposed actions.

Another area of self-care prevention occurs where the managerial accountant deals with people likely to exhibit pathological behaviors. Since there are clinical definitions for diagnosis, this discussion of self-care is only to identify some symptoms and suggests safe responses. Behaviors are pathological when there is a continued and pervasive pattern of extreme, unacceptable behavior accompanied by powerful feelings. Symptoms include attempting to humiliate other people, taking credit for someone else's work, sabotage and an unreasonable focus on mistakes. Some pathological behavior occurs with sociopaths. They are charmers and manipulators without a conscience, without the ability to measure, or willingness to measure, the morality of their decisions and actions (Hare, 1993). A sociopath[11] has a narcissistic personality (Stout, 2005): an inflated sense of their own importance, a deep need for excessive attention and admiration, troubled relationships, and a lack of empathy for others. The managerial accountant will be aware of 'flare-ups' and recognize that their own sense of antagonism and frustration is due to experiencing this behavior (Egan, Chan & Shorter, 2014). Generally, avoidance is a prudent tactic by minimizing interaction.

The final aspect of prevention is taking a holistic approach to work–life and attempting to maintain a balance between the two. This approach has been proven to help psychologists proactively managing stress, prevent burnout and promote well-being has three aspects (Bamonti et al., 2014; Norcross & Guy, 2007). The managerial accountant therefore needs to establish work–life balance as a habit early in their career. This is only successful if is integrated with daily routines that undertake frequent and regular monitoring by ensuring adequate time is allowed for self-care activities (e.g., healthy sleep pattern, emotional and cognitive reapprais- als). This may require planning to ensure there are adequate financial resources to support self-care. To overcome the self-delusion tendency discussed earlier, the managerial accountant also needs to make arrange- ments to obtain independent advice from supportive colleagues who have time to observe and discuss well-being (physical, emotional and mental). They should be briefed to watch for indicators such as imbalance in work–life, fatigue, impaired concentration and attention (as forgetfulness), illness, loss of appetite, anxiety, distress, anger and loss of enjoyment (Carter, 2011). However, these can be due to other causes so their ability to per- ceive new changes is also important (Kushner, Kessler & McGaghie, 2011). As a policy matter, accounting professional bodies should as a priority mandate preventive and responsive interventions as a continuous development responsibility and budget to ensure self-care is discussed at conferences and is promoted in its programs so that processes are imple- mented before distress becomes evident or competencies are impaired.

10.10 Conclusion on a Commitment to Ethical Behavior and Self-Care

The role and responsibilities of the managerial accountant include ethical behavior and self-care. Placed at the center, ethics and self-care connects all the other principles in the managerial accountant's compass. The ethi- cal code comprising principles and standards is simple compared to some other professions (e.g., psychologists). Inside the organization, because the managerial accountant has contact with many others in the organization they soon become a model for ethical (or unethical) behavior and may be indirectly responsible for the ethical lapses committed by others. Large-scale ethical lapses can be responsible for organization failure. Arthur Andersen[12] was closed when they were found guilty of shredding Enron documenta- tion. As noted earlier, the repercussions of an ethical lapse go beyond the individual employees who were involved and affect innocent parties. For this reason, ethical emphasis was placed equally on those who know about unethical behavior coming forward, so it is addressed while it is developing.

However, some management accountants still have difficulty comply- ing owing a lack of commitment for the reasons discussed earlier. By aligning ethical behavior to self-care, the apparent short term, usually financial gains, are balanced against health and well-being. The longitudinal study by Vaillant (2003) offers conclusive evidence that early to mid-life attention to self-care repays itself in health and satisfaction. The continuing media exposure of accountants in financial manipulation, sporting scandals and administrative malfeasance confirms that the eventually the ethical lapse becomes widely known. Some ethical lapses are due to lack of self-care. A managerial accountant will create a culture of self-care around them. They will be alert to situations where their own professional competence is affected by emotional[13] distress, burnout, or even secondary traumatic stress. They will provide leadership where they notice others suffering. As discussed earlier, this can be as simple as suggesting a colleague privately completes a self-care assessment to become aware of their current situation.

With the discussion of all five cardinal points of the managerial accountant's compass and context complete, the next part is the evaluation. Chapter 11 provides an evaluation, summarizes conclusions on using it and considers directions for its further development.

Notes

1. There are even higher standards of ethics than the level discussed in this section. The Bhagavad Gita (Chapple, 2009) and the yoga sutras of Pantanjali (Bryant, 2009) contrast dhama with kama. The concepts of 'dharma' means right or selfless action taken without attachment to the outcome, while 'karma' is self-serving action taken for its transient pleasures with attachment to the outcome. Being selfless is a most difficult practice. Contentment, joy or bliss requires selfless devotion to actions.

2. Some other theories also are relevant. Stoic theory encourages forbearance (Aurelius, 1964), appreciating change (Heraclitus, 2015) and emotionally resilience to misfortune (Cicero, 1991; Epictetus, 2014). Care ethics seeks to incorporate feminized virtues and values such as compassion and empathy (Noddings, 1984). Anarchist ethics advocates solidarity, equality and justice-serving behavior that will enhance human's preference and capacity for freedom and well-being (Kropotkin, 1902). The ethics of nonviolent resistance is proposed by La Boétie (2007) who uses the concept of voluntary servitude to refer to habitual behavior. Individual agency and the concept of individual are challenged by state Mohist consequentialism, which considers the contributes to the basic goods of a state (Mo, 2014). Postmodernism argues there is an ethical remainder in particular lived experience that ethical principles cannot reclaim humanity (Bauman, 1993). Finally, Baudrillard (1994) claims that in the consumer society, the hedonistic morality is being legitimized.

3. Other principles and standards could be added or substituted, but this would extend and complicate the ethical code giving opportunities for interpretation and thus creating loopholes and excuses for non-observance.

4. The public may expect the management accountant to uphold additional ethical principles or standards. The code is not exhaustive, and many more instances of morality—for example social or business principles—could be considered for inclusion in ethical standards, such as (a) public interest, (b) collegiality or friendship, (c) following the normal lines of reporting, (d) loyalty to the company, and (e) respect for one's manager. Although a

project is underway by the International Federation of Accountants International Ethics Standards Board to consider the ethical principle of public interest, the above principles and standards are the only ones currently active in the ethical code.

5. The managerial accountant does not delay action hoping that the situation will change, the parties involved will confess or an obligation of confidentiality is released. The managerial accountant should not accept information on the condition of confidentiality unless they also obtain agreement that if there is any later downside to the inappropriately shared information, they are released from the agreement; the managerial accountant may need to work with the parties to ensure prompt sharing of the information, or transition to action.

6. In the United Kingdom: UK Companies Act of 1844 and the related UK Limited Liability Act (1855). In United States, controls rested in the states (e.g., 1811 for New York), but the prevalence of big business trusts resulted in the Sherman Antitrust Act, 1890. In the aftermath of depression, federal legislation created the Securities Act of 1933 and Securities and Exchange Act of 1934 to obligate businesses to disclose material information to public investors.

7. The primary benefits are separation of the assets of the shareholders from those of the corporation; the ability to be sued and to sue; and perpetual succession. Since these benefits were originally ill-defined, it is logical that acquiring shares in other organizations should open up complex financing options only apparent much later. Although some early commentators recognized the growing importance of trusts and leveraged borrowings (e.g., Veblen, 1978) the focus remained gains and losses rather than the continued social benefit of the corporation.

8. Some accountants think that they are immune from this obligation because they are more insulated from ordinary society and tend to think the rules don't apply to them. In some cases, they have the resources to make problems 'go away', so they are less exposed to the adverse consequences of their unethical behavior. A third area is that they may care less about what other people think. These factors may have greater influence if the accountant is wealthy although this is not to suggest that all upper-class people are cheats. That is far from the truth.

9. Accountants have a responsibility to provide independent advice that is not affected by monetary or personal considerations.

10. The expression 'welfare of the body' comes from the discussion in Wood (1962). Arguably, yoga is attentive to these matters more than most health disciplines and gives a comprehensive set of recommended behaviors.

11. Checklists are readily available. Examples are provided in Stout (2005), and Hare (1993).

12. In 2002, Arthur Andersen name voluntarily surrendered its licenses to practice as a public accountant in the United States of America. In 2005, the US Supreme Court overturned an obstruction of justice conviction; there may have been prosecutorial overzealousness (Powell, 2014). Rights to the name were acquired in 2014 from Arthur Andersen LLC, and it now trades as Andersen Tax and does not have an audit practice.

13. In achievement-related contexts there are dominant causes of failure (as well as success). These are associated with human negative emotions such as anger, guilt, hopelessness, and shame (Weiner, 1985). Since expectancy governs behavior, attention to these is an important part of self-care.

Part V

Perspective on the Managerial Accountant's Compass

11 Evaluation of the Managerial Accountant's Compass and Conclusion

The managerial accountant's compass supports the managerial accountant moving fluidly between a range of roles and responsibilities, so evaluation should consider its applications, limitations, anticipated criticisms, benefits, and implications for policy planning and directions for future development. The broad question is one of effectiveness not efficiency or economy (Rossi, Lipsey & Freeman, 2004). This evaluation therefore considers conditions and predictable outcomes. It does not measure knowledge of managerial accounting or management, or the application of managerial accounting methods and models. It begins by reconsidering the scenarios presented in Chapter 1.

11.1 Applications: Reconsidering the Vignettes From Chapter 1

The managerial accountant's compass can be applied to each of the six vignettes from Chapter 1 by considering the role and responsibilities of the managerial accountant. Each vignette is introduced by specifying the parent organization and the evident issues. The assumed goal is supporting a management decision. The major uses of the managerial accountant's compass are then shown. As discussed in Chapter 8, the entire managerial accounting compass is reviewed but the starting point depends on the case. Where there is potential for different implementations or outcomes they are suggested.

- Mercedes Benz is proposing to abandon robotic production of their premier sedan. The managerial accountant would begin with context and then the cardinal points. Trends to individualization allow customers to customize their order for high value luxury goods so motor vehicle industry manufacturing is responding by becoming small-batch oriented. The managerial accountant would make the new costs visible to ensure revenue was adequate and contribute a strategic assessment to understand whether these new sources of value creation and capture were sustainable.

- Deutsche Bank, in crisis, is proposing to change the scale of their operations as an urgent cost reduction strategy. The managerial accountant will begin with a horizontal view (selecting methods and models, recognizing their boundaries and constraints and ethical overlay). It is essential to plan the financial and non-financial consequences of the program and establish indicators to track progress and reveal emerging concerns.
- Austrade offered very large performance incentives to staff. The managerial accountant will immediately consider the horizontal view (methods, models, ethical conduct, boundaries, constraints). They will reimagine the system with preventive and corrective controls. It also needs contextualizing so a comparison of the organization with not-for-profit practices will begin a contextual evaluation. After completion, the managerial accountant will work with others to evaluate whether changes to conduct have occurred and the likelihood of similar revelations.
- The Organization of the Petroleum Exporting Countries (OPEC) has an inelastic product, so it uses pricing to control supply and demand. A managerial accountant in an organization dependent upon oil from OPEC will begin with the context in the managerial accountant's compass. They need to consider the factors that cause price changes. Historic industry and trend information are available, but also geographical socio-economic factors are influential. They can determine options. For example, whether a model is feasible or whether it is better to build closer relationships with supplier or their intermediaries (e.g., improving the supply chain to reduce total cost).
- Australia Post delivers letters unprofitably and parcels very profitably. A managerial accountant attached to the minister's office receiving a request for a government subsidy can begin with all the contextual factors to understand why costs in the same network are different. It will be important to create a model, independent of Australia Post, for different sets of common costs and cost allocations. Performance evaluation can also explore what incentives are in place to increase letter volumes and breakeven.
- Optus is an oligopoly telco that offers both pre-paid and post-paid plans. The retrenchment of customer service and network employees to fund sports stars to promote it in the media changes its cost structure. The managerial accountant is often a pawn in management strategy[1] but can begin with context to explore whether this is characteristic of the industry sector or previewing a new trend. Allied to this, the managerial accountant can model the immediate and medium-term consequences for customer service and network support. The boundary of this re-usable model can extend to the financial statements.

These vignettes mixed planned and crisis decisions. Many organizations do not continuously monitor their competitive position and proactively adjust in small increments. The vignettes showed organizations dealing with major strategic and operational changes which require the managerial accountant to concern themselves with the details of implementation and its success. Many industries and organizations face challenges because there is greater government scrutiny, new forms of commercial disruption or from antagonizing their stakeholders. Using the managerial accountant's compass can discover emerging and latent issues as well as suggest different implementation options. Nonetheless, the managerial accountant's compass has some limitations.

11.2   Limitations of the Managerial Accountant's Compass

The limitations of the managerial compass concern its use as a metaphor; its separation of ethics from its other compass points; its exclusion of knowledge, skills and abilities; and its admixture of normative rules and guidelines. In part, these limitations arise from focusing the role and responsibilities of the managerial account on information required for analysis, making judgements, and providing support for decision making. As noted in Chapters 3 and 7 potentially there can be many acceptable responses to a problem or opportunity.

Although the managerial compass uses a metaphor consisting of five points, its weakness is that three of the compass points comprise pairs of categories (north: goals and principles; east: boundaries and constraints; west: methods and models). This was done deliberately to avoid masking them with a unifying label, which concealed they were split into a pair. It may be that emerging issues in managerial accounting in the twenty-first century will lead to these groupings being revised or entirely superseded. However, the metaphor of the compass may remain. As there is no mandatory sequence between them, they can be considered either horizontally or vertically, so any regrouping is unlikely to require the compass points to be arranged hierarchically instead of peers.

By making ethics the central compass point, it may give the impression that ethics is considered separately to the other points, or it is outnumbered by them. It is deliberately placed centrally for two reasons: first, because ethical conduct must always be considered; second, because the consequences of behaving ethically may result in unpleasant or unfair consequences for the managerial accountant. The discussion in Chapter 10 emphasized that the managerial accountant must maintain up-to-date understanding of what this eventuality may mean for them. Anthony, Hawkins and Merchant (2011: 418) put this clearly:

> The problem is the accountant may not believe [they will receive]. . . protection [from retribution]. Also, publicly challenging a superior's decision is, at a minimum, unsettling. Moreover, the accountant may

fear being informally blacklisted. . . . Each individual needs to be sensitive to these issues, so that, to the extent possible, such problems can be avoided and unpleasant personal dilemmas minimized.

History shows whistle-blowers receive a variety of unsupportive reactions: outright disbelief, questioning their own motives, ostracism, and even challenges over their mental health. Serious difficulties, such as complicity, arise because earlier ethical transgressions are overlooked. Chapter 10 highlighted the importance of reporting to minor matters in case they are symptoms of larger concerns.

The managerial accountant's compass does not demand specific knowledge, skills and abilities, although Chapter 5 suggests some of them. No knowledge is specified. No minimum skill set is identified. No generic or specific abilities are required. This is deliberate. Knowledge changes, and there are many sources of reliable information. Skills and abilities are distributed so there are individual differences and managerial accountants can compensate in one area for deficiencies in another. In many cases, the double-bind of resource pressures and constraints will hamper the managerial accountant from properly understanding the information. By working through all five points of the managerial accountant's compass, the managerial accountant can systematically identify the knowledge, skills and abilities needed task-by-task. Gaps may be filled by consulting others in the organizational or professional colleagues.

Finally, the managerial accountant's compass deliberately provides a mix of normatively described rules and advisory guidelines. Generally, their description has been framed to draw attention to issues rather than mandate specific action. This applies the Wittgensteinian view of discourse discussed in Chapter 2 that actions can always be justified as conforming to the rule. So previous chapters have provided information about the kinds of issues and concerns that the managerial accountant may encounter. The managerial accountant must use judgment to select and apply them but their relationships with others can be used to seek guidance on analysis, judgments and presenting recommendations. Where the normative rules and guidelines appear to be unsuitable, the managerial accountant can simply return to the processes identified by the compass points and factors identified by context and begin their analysis there as it should assist decision making and implementation. Nevertheless, some residual criticisms are likely to remain.

11.3   Anticipated Criticisms of the Managerial Accountant's Compass

Notwithstanding the previous limitations, two main criticisms are anticipated. The first is the deployment of the managerial accountant's compass in the service of social control and discipline (Foucault, 1977).

Inevitably, some of the performance information produced by the managerial accountant will be used by senior managers and functional managers to enact oppressive behaviors. The history of organizations is replete with examples of top-down attempts to control and improve outputs as well as examples of resistance by managers and employees. The most noteworthy example is the British motor industry of the 1960s–1980s period. A wider criticism of managerial accounting sees it as the handmaiden of capitalism (e.g., Braverman, 1998: 39). The difficulty with this view is that there were parallel actions under communism reported by Trotsky (Deutscher, 1980) and socialist and Marxist traditions that have constituted capitalism according to the feminist critique (Gibson-Graham, 2006). It seems invidious to single out the managerial accountant as making the major contribution to social control and discipline since as Gay (1995) points out, this overlooks the contingent factors, complexity, anxiety and stupidity, of holders of power. Moreover, it overlooks the powerful role of the board in setting performance objectives that are cascaded throughout the organization and enforced by and managerial committees who usually receive as well as offer incentives for accomplishing the desired outcomes. The ethical value of the managerial accountant's code discussed earlier may lead the managerial accountant to either refuse oppressive tasks or rationalize them. As was noted in Chapter 10, this is personal. The consequences for the ethical managerial accountant can be financial, physiological and psychological.

The second anticipated criticism concerns the lack of instruction in applying the managerial accountant's compass. No processes are provided to define goals, methods, models, boundaries, constraints, or collegiate relationships with others. This is mainly due to the impossibility of encompassing every managerial accounting task and its relevant inputs. In any case, there are many satisfactory descriptions available for reference either as documents or as advice from colleagues and professionals. Equally, the managerial accountant's compass avoids discussion of traps and pitfalls that the managerial accountant may encounter. One reason is the influence of individual beliefs, attitudes and preference for risk that cannot be predicted. Another is the possible influence of heuristics and biases discussed in Chapter 7. Of course, a managerial accountant who improperly uses a technique incorrectly calculates or estimates carelessly cannot avoid errors of commission. The managerial accountant's compass can reduce the likelihood of a black swan event (Taleb, 2010) by encouraging a systematic approach that integrates different approaches. However, the description already provided uses the assumption that the managerial accountant is interested in continuous learning. Even if the managerial accountant does not work in a learning organization where knowledge sharing, and tolerance of dissent occur, the self-care discussed earlier suggests they can build a learning and reflective environment around themselves. The managerial accounting compass does encourage a broader view of an issue together with concretization of an answer or conclusion using the points of the compass in context. When combined with benefit of reflection, the managerial accountant's compass offers the best mitigation against being 'caught out' by an omission or pursuing a misdirection.

11.4   Benefits of the Managerial Accountant's Compass

The major benefit of the managerial accountant's compass is its unique orienting and integrating function. Specifically, it provides three benefits. First, it systematizes thinking and reflection. Second, it brings together matters that are normally disparate. Third, it ensures that ethics is considered across all matters for which it is used. Finally but equally importantly, it facilitates communication with non-accountants. Each is now reviewed.

The managerial accountant's compass systematizes reflection and thinking by organizing knowledge into categories, and establishing relationships among them. It fosters inquiry to explore, refute and modify thinking to avoid habitual thinking (Dewey, 1986) without making bets (Duke, 2018). It allows reflection, that is, a conscious response to both a situation and the experience of it (Boud, 1985). Using the managerial accountant's compass can replace existing pre-conceived ideas, provide a new means to observe, facilitate absorption of new information, and change existing frameworks of perceiving the world. This is consistent with the approach taken by gestalt psychologists (e.g., O'Leary, 1992) and learning psychologists (e.g., Piaget, 2001). More recently, it re-emerged in discussion of heuristics and cognitive biases (Kahneman, 2012) discussed in Chapter 7. Frequent use of the managerial accountant's compass can condition memory (Mace, 1968) and can displace stereotyped schemas and inferior heuristics. For example, a narrow analytical focus which creates misdirection can be shifted to goals and constraints. The managerial accountant's compass does not go as far as specifying generic sequences of actions, often called scripts (Schank & Abelson, 1977). This is because the aim is to recall and marshal as many items as possible so that they are available to all the compass points and context factors. They constitute a multi-dimensional cube of information that can be applied to organizational opportunities and problems. The managerial accountant's compass leaves open the recognition of new content, problem solving, creativity and the incorporation of new learning. Unlike other tools (e.g., industrial economics, big-data analytics) which will overlook, reject, restrict, misinterpret or reshape alternative views, the managerial accountant's compass will accommodate and assimilate (Piaget, 2001) changes to personal knowledge with their connections to it. This adaptive capability can help managers do their job better by integrating and customizing the information (both financial and non-financial) for the specific goal.

Examples include the profitability of new and existing products, product groups, brand categories, customers, distribution channels, regions and the assessment of investment opportunities with new equipment. Unlike financial accountants who are constrained by mandatory accounting standards, corporate legislation and stock exchange listing rules (if a public company), managerial accountants have a wide remit to guide their information compilation and frame it into reports, recommendations and informed decisions.

Another benefit is the managerial accountant's compass brings together matters that are normally treated as disparate. This occurs at two levels. First, the individual elements are now assembled around the compass points. Establishing goals for managerial accounting is never given much thought yet is responsible for many of the apparent failures in managerial accounting (Johnson & Kaplan, 1987; Johnson, 2002). Some come from placing undue emphasis on the financial side. Managerial accountants have rarely been able to point to any driving principles or guidelines when compiling and presenting information, but this is now addressed. Twelve primarily tacit principles have been identified. Second, relationships can be established between information prompted by the context and the compass points. The most basic relationships between the cardinal points are horizontal and vertical. There are also adjacent relationships. For example, goals and principles apply to both methods and models, and boundaries and constraints. This assembly of elements and the relationships between them juxtaposes them so the managerial accountant can discover both similar and contrasting aspects. However, the cardinal points can also be viewed against the context factors. As suggested in Chapter 8, it is possible to begin anywhere and move in any direction. This gives the model a dynamic capability.

The third benefit is its attention to ethics. Recent publicity has shown that some accountants and auditors have forgotten their responsibility to provide independent advice, that is not affected by monetary or personal considerations when advising or recommending decisions. By placing ethical conduct and self-care at the center of the compass, it accepts that behaving ethically is difficult, and there are many occasions when an ethical lapse is possible. By being in the center, ethical conduct and self-care are shown to have more than a single point of failure. An ethical lapse may be associated with the compass points (goals and principles, boundaries and constraints, relationships with others, or methods and models), or with the context (geographical socioeconomic factors, industry sector, organization characteristics or trends and particular characteristics). Therefore, an ethical dilemma can arise in conjunction with any of these elements. The managerial accountant's compass encourages applying the ethical code to each element, rather than applying it generally or in the background.

Finally it facilitates communication with non-accountants. This occurs in several ways. It suggests topics for discussion. It helps to make for collegiate relationships by giving an open yet flexible agenda by showing that the managerial accountant welcomes information and does not use stereotyped solutions or preconceived answers. The elements of the managerial accountant's compass give some independence, showing managers and employees that what concerns the managerial accountant is what will be to the advantage of the organization. This should foster trust and establish a network of employees and managers who can be approached for reciprocal assistance.

The managerial accountant has been an essential part of the organization for over 100 years and has a continuing place in managing the organization. The managerial accountant's compass provides a framework for the foreseeable future allowing managerial accountants to apply their critical and reflective mind toward sustainable views of costs, performance and strategy providing imaginative, creative, and insightful recommendations and decisions. Having reviewed benefits, its scope is confirmed.

11.5 Scope of the Managerial Accountant's Compass

The previous discussion of the benefits of the managerial accountant's compass lacked a description of its scope or subject matter. There are five areas where the managerial accountant's compass is applied. First, it also applies equally to operations and strategy, so it is not aligned to only the short term or the long-term. Second, it supports continuity of the business by incorporating longitudinal characteristics. Third, it applies equally to projects as well as routine operations, so it does not require exceptions to be made. Fourth, it allows investigation of management fads. Finally, it can contribute to policy. Thus, the managerial accountant's compass is not restricted in its application to particular industries or organizations.

The basic level of scope of the managerial accountant's compass is operations and strategy. At the operational level it is concerned with the short-term and medium-term profitability and performance of the organization. At the strategic level it helps understanding the competitive context of the organization. Both operational and strategic levels involve understanding how resources are augmented, allocated, deployed, leveraged, developed, performed, and how value is created and captured for the organization. The favorable and selective view given in financial statements can misdirect attention. The routine matters for examination suggested by the entire managerial accountant's compass ensure these are examined each time it is used, warranting the consistency of focus.

Timewise, the managerial accountant's compass provides a longitudinal view. It places the organization in the business life cycle stages and economic life cycle of boom and bust. This is useful for understanding cost structure and an antidote for a short-term focus on the 'bottom line' that can be detrimental to building long-term relationships with customers and suppliers. It also can mitigate against developing strategic positions in markets and channels that can reveal opportunities for innovation. It allows the managerial accountant to explain the trade-offs between short- and long-term encouraging the sensitive use of budgets and controls (Hope & Fraser, 2003), always bearing in mind the potential for producing dysfunctional behavioral consequences.

Thirdly, the managerial accountant's compass is applicable to projects. A project brings into close focus the relationship between expenses and the general ledger.[2] In a project the managerial accountant will consider whether project expenses should be capitalized or expensed in the period, whether there are unfavorable variances and the progress toward implementation. Once it commences the project is less susceptible to contextual factors. Iterative and incremental project practices can mean that financial and non-financial information does not show progress accurately (Oliver & Walker, 2006). A review each month of the compass points is likely to suggest reporting questions irrespective which project method[3] is used. It can also act as a barometer on social relations and help troubleshoot report unreliability and reconsider scoping decisions.

Fourth is its handling of fads. The diffusion of innovation theory (Rogers, 2003) suggests that there will always be fads in business. Fads are both a vocabulary and a related tool or technique claimed to engender success, often but not always requiring specialized consulting assistance (Brindle & Stearns, 2001; Collins, 2000). The managerial accountant will be faced with numerous fads. Some will be suggested by managers; others will be highlighted by media. In the past it has been difficult to critically evaluate them or even determine to what sound theory or method they depend upon. The managerial accountant's compass offers an evaluation method because it requires a multidimensional assessment specific to an organization challenge or opportunity. This rests on the premise that understanding a problem before trying to solve it ensures the right problem is then addressed (Deming, 2000).

Finally, it can propose and evaluate public policy. Public policy addresses social values and perceived problems by proposing rectification action or anticipating public behavior. A policy contribution can occur in a variety of areas: market failure, distributional goal fulfillment, efficiency at the lowest cost, service delivery reach, correcting previous government policy failures, addressing limitations of the competition framework (Dye, 2007). The managerial accountant's compass can assist with analysis, evaluating options and implementation. This can occur as a by-product of analyzing information from the organization for a separate issue, or, be a dedicated analysis with the sole intention of evaluating the impact of a policy. Of course, the issue of political will and political choice fall outside the managerial accountant's compass because there are other non-rational factors involved (e.g., election pork-barrelling). The managerial accountant's compass will also not assist write public policy statements. Given this scope, the managerial accountant can therefore feel confident the managerial accountant's compass has wide application. Research directions tend to follow from the review of scope.

11.6   Directions for Future Development of the Managerial Accountant's Compass

Three research directions are proposed using three methods: experiment, self-report and ethnographic field studies. First, the experimental method can control the conditions of use of the managerial accountant's compass. The objective is to determine the effect of the curse of knowledge (Fischhoff, 1975; Camerer, Loewenstein & Weber, 1989). It occurs where the better-informed party is unable to ignore their better information and optimally exploit their information asymmetry. In other words, the better-informed agent misjudges what the lesser-informed party intends. When applied to the managerial accountant's compass, this is an experimental research question involving treatments between two groups. A further condition may use the effects of bias discussed in Chapter 7. The objective is to consider whether the lack of the managerial accountant's compass would make any difference to experienced and inexperienced managerial accountants. The outcome would be refinement of the managerial accountant's compass. Second, to conduct field studies of decisions made by managerial accountants with and without the managerial accountant's compass. The objective would be to produce individual case studies of both success and failure. For example, across operational and strategy situations, whether communication was facilitated using the managerial accountant's compass, with cross sectional and longitudinal decision making, and with routine operations and projects. The outcome would be to discover redundancy, omissions or weaknesses in the model. However, the effects of redundancy would have to be explored as redundancy may enhance validity through triangulation. Third, to use ethnographic shadowing of individual managerial accountants in a range of organizations. The objective is to see how they use the managerial accountant's compass either by itself or in conjunction with other methods and knowledge. The potential areas of study would include desk work alone in the office, and for on-the-spot decision making at meetings. The outcome would be to simplify the model. The use in classrooms has not been proposed as that has already been completed over an extended period and resulted in the penultimate model. However, if research in the classroom is conducted, it is recommended that it be aligned with an examination question to separate shared work from individual use.

11.7   Final Summary and Conclusion

The managerial accountant's compass is directed at managerial accountants at all levels. It will appeal to the conscientious managerial accountant who wishes to improve the information they provide and their decision support and is aware that a structured systematic approach is more consistent than shortcuts and intuition. It will not be adopted by a managerial accountant who wants to exercise power, is predisposed to favor particular individuals, or has already made up their mind, because they cannot dress up their decision as the managerial accountant's compass opens up too many areas to questions that may reveal their motivation. There is also an opportunity to use the managerial accountant's compass in training and coursework where scenarios can be used, and model answers can be provided. If this is done, it is recommended that worked examples be provided as they are proven to increase learning (Sweller, Ayres & Kalyuga, 2011).

In summary, the design of the managerial compass consists of inner processes and outer states. The inner processes consist of four cardinal points together with the center. The four cardinal points comprise goals and principles; boundaries and constraints; methods and models; and collegiate relationships with others. The fifth point located at the center is a high standard of ethical conduct and self-care. The outer states frame the processes and is called context. It comprises: geographical socioeconomic factors, industry sector characteristics, organizational characteristics, and trends and particular events. The cardinal points are arranged as a compass and give the analytical framework its name: the managerial accountant's compass.

The managerial accountant's compass can be used to both assess what exists as well as what is missing. It is not biased toward complex models or advanced statistical analysis. Since managerial accounting knowledge has become management knowledge, the managerial accountant can use the managerial accountant's compass to explore for gaps and misunderstandings held by non-accounting managers, which may result in poor decisions. Conversely, they can encourage the non-accounting manager to use them as a sounding board to explore the foundations for their decisions building a collegiate relationship. Of course, using the managerial accountant's compass benefits the organization, but it can also be transferred to a future employer benefiting the managerial accountant. The managerial accountant's compass provides a guide to how a managerial accountant can plan and undertake their role and responsibilities for career success without stumbling or setbacks.

Notes

1. The managerial accountant may know there are better options or believe there are flaws in the implementation plan. Levitt (1960) called for a comprehensive imagination to reformulate strategy and policies by expanding the market to return the industry to growth. For example, the Hollywood studios defined themselves as being in the movie business, not the entertainment business. Narrow definition of purpose overlooks opportunities and allows customers to be lost.

2. For example, Callahan, Stetz and Brooks (2011) suggest that decisions can have both intended and unintended consequences, so it is necessary to consider more than just how project income and expense impact the general ledger. So managerial accounting in a project will simultaneously consider the greatest tax and cost savings, assessing risks to the project, reputational and personal capital, and relation to a company's mission, objectives and strategy to continually determine whether to continue as planned, find a different solution or scrap the project altogether.

3. The three common project management methodologies are PMBOK, PRINCE2 and Agile. PMBOK (Project Management Body of Knowledge) provides a substantial framework for contract management and scope management but emphasizes the role of the project manager in decision making. PRINCE2 (Projects in a Controlled Environment) is the second version of a project management program that focuses on aiding the project manager to oversee projects on behalf of an organization's senior management. It requires a single standard approach to the management projects. The agile methodology is more flexible, making it better able to produce deliverables without the need for substantial changes and reworking. Tasks can be broken down into smaller stages, and this allows for substantial risk reduction through earlier assessment, testing and analysis. It is suited where the project is small and needs to be adaptable.

Appendix
Research Positioning

Most discussions of research encourage the author to make clear their research perspective. There are many approaches with varying subsidiaries. The one I use draws on the relationships suggested by Crotty (1998) which are expressed as a research planning database (Oliver, 2018). It is by no means perfect. His death shortly after publication deprives us of any expansion and revision he may have contemplated to overcome its ambiguities and omissions. The dual status of phenomenology and feminist research shown in his chapter 1 table is left unexplained. The place of specific theories in empirical work is unremarked despite using the label theoretical perspective for what are philosophical assumptions. His collapsing of ontology and epistemology overlooks their need for independent assessment. For example, critical realism uses a realist ontology with a constructivist epistemology (Maxwell, 2012).

This research takes a realist, post-positivist, normative approach as its objective is to improve the information and decision support roles and responsibilities of managerial accountants. Several research perspectives were used over a period of more than 10 years. The controversial Delphi structured communication technique was used to gather information from respondents within their domain of expertise (Fischer, 1978; Sackman, 1975). Delphi differs from surveys and interviews which try to identify 'what is', by attempting to address 'what could/should be' (Miller, 2006). More recently, discourse analysis was used to understand the use of spoken and written language in context with attention to its structure, form, organization, order, or patterns (Antaki, Billig, Edwards & Potter, 2003). This research, which I call discursive accounting, continues. Narrative (Oliver & Snowden, 2005) was used to place anecdotes and tales in organizational context. Social complexity theory (Byrne, 2013) was used to recognize chaotic and fractal aspects of information. The original impetus for the investigation came from my time at Metal Manufactures Limited. I particularly acknowledge the support from John A. Allen, its Finance Director, but all the staff at Corporate Head Office contributed, and divisional staff were also involved.

The broad approach used (a) a central topic with initial guiding questions to elicit answers, (b) a panel of independent experts (c) seeking reasons and conclusions, (d) repeated individual questioning with their prior answer used if they were absent in a later round (Ludlow, 1975), (e) controlled feedback, (f) aggregation of issues that emerged (Mitroff & Turoff, 1975), (g) treating residuals as perimeter issues until they could be unified by further research and (h) applying justifiable corrections (Dalkey & Helmer, 1963) with non-numeric information (Strauss & Zeigler, 1975). The basic guiding questions used to elicit accounting practices for problems and functions were: (1) What information do you seek and use? (2) What assisted or influenced your analysis, interpretation and decision? (3) What structure, framework or perspective did you follow? Guiding questions for the functions and personal qualities of the managerial accountant used the framework presented in Chapter 5 supplemented with inquiries about performance and decision making.

Selection of informants was targeted. To encourage candor, all participants were guaranteed absolute confidentiality of themselves and their responses (Linstone, 1975). Participants were considered expert end users of accounting information by their role and responsibilities. These methods have some limitations. Since responses were self-reported, they lack the standards of evidence or objectivity (Hill & Fowles, 1975). While there was overlap, there was also disagreement. In those cases, the research attended to maverick views (Linstone, 1975). In hindsight, with some reworking, the theoretical perspective of ethnomethodology (Bittner, 1973; Mehan & Wood, 1975; Sharrock & Anderson, 1991) which avoids Cartesian dualism (Coulter, 1991) may have been better as it is concerned "to discover the things that persons in particular situations do, the methods they use, to create the patterned orderliness of social life" (Garfinkel, 2002: 6) which occurs in real time (Sharrock & Button, 1991) and which can offer insight into the "daily routines of business life in the modern world" (Anderson, Hughes & Sharrock, 1989: 7). After the development of the managerial accountant's compass, it was tested in the classroom and examinations with cases and scenarios. It showed that it discerns organization concerns and stimulates practical reasoning.

References

A large number of references are provided as the topic is broad. The criterion for selecting references is threefold. First those who initiated debates are recognized, although where there was a later edition it is used. Many of these early debates predate the routine computerization of publications that began 1994–1995. This citation watershed has two consequences (a) those difficult-to-find earlier publications are cited less frequently and probably are not examined, (b) the google-based bias for post-1995 references which it indexes have greater influence. As a result, these references span the nineteenth and twentieth century. This ensures the context and subtleties of the earlier debate are acknowledged avoiding later simplification, characterization and omissions. It also allows comparison with later findings. Second more recent publications that extend the debate or reach a different conclusion, are also identified. Third publications which show practitioner viewpoints are included to show the interplay between them and academic research. This also shows where common knowledge to practitioners is addressed by academics and less rarely, vice versa. URL's are correct as at the time the manuscript is finalized.

A certified public accountant who was the business manager for singer-songwriter Alanis Morissette (2017, May 3). USA Attorney General's Office Central District of California. Retrieved https://www.justice.gov/usao-cdca/pr/cpa-sentenced-6-years-federal-prison-embezzling-72-million-alanis-morissette-and-other

A disgraced former judge already in jail (2017, January 3) https://www.independent.ie/irish-news/jailed-exjudge-gets-two-more-years-29128399.html

Ackoff, R. L. A. (1967). Management misinformation systems. *Management Sciences*, 14(4), B147–B156.

Ackoff, R. L. A. (1969). *Concept of corporate planning*. New York: Wiley.

Ackoff, R. L. A. (1989). From data to wisdom: Presidential address to ISGSR, June 1988. *Journal of Applied Systems Analysis*, 16, 3–9.

Ackoff, R. L. A., & Churchman, C. W. (1955). Operational accounting and operations research. *Journal of Accounting*, 99(2), 53–59.

Adizes, I. (1988). *Corporate lifecycles: How and why corporations grow and die and what to do about it*. Paramus, NJ: Prentice-Hall.

Aerts, W. (1994). On the use of accounting logic as an explanatory category in narrative accounting disclosures. *Accounting, Organizations and Society*, 19(4–5), 337–353.

Ahrens, T., & Chapman, C. S. (2007). Management accounting as practice. *Accounting, Organizations and Society*, 32(1), 1–27.

Akerlof, G. A. (1970). The market for "lemons": Quality uncertainty and the market mechanism. *The Quarterly Journal of Economics*, 84(3), 488–500.

Alexander, C. S., & Becker, H. J. (1978). The use of vignettes in survey research. *Public Opinion Quarterly*, 42(1), 93–104.

Amenta, E. (2005). State-centered and political institutionalist theory: Retrospect and prospect. In T. Janoski, R. Alford, A. Hicks, & M. A. Schwartz (Eds.), *Handbook of political sociology: States, civil societies, and globalization* (pp. 96–114). New York: Cambridge University Press.

Anderson, M., Banker, R., & Janakiraman, S. (2003). Are selling, general and administrative costs 'sticky'? *Journal of Accounting Research*, 41(1), 47–63.

Anderson, R. J., Hughes, J. A., & Sharrock, W. W. (1989). *Working for profit: The social organization of calculation in an entrepreneurial firm*. Aldershot, UK: Avebury/Gower.

Anderson, S. M., & Chen, S. (2002). The relational self: An interpersonal socio-cognitive theory. *Psychological Review*, 109(4), 619–645.

Anderson, S. W. (2007). Managing costs and cost structure throughout the value chain: Research on strategic cost management. In C. S. Chapman, A. G. Hopwood, & M. D. Shields (Eds.), *Handbook of management accounting research* (Vol. 2, pp. 451–506). Oxford: Elsevier.

Anscombe, G. E. M. (1958). Modern moral philosophy. *Philosophy*, 33(124), 1–19.

Anon. (2015). *How professional services can disrupt its way out of automation*. Knowledge@Wharton. Retrieved from http://knowledge.wharton.upenn.edu/article/how-professional-services-can-disrupt-its-way-out-of-automation/

Antaki, C., Billig, M., Edwards, D., & Potter, J. (2003). Discourse analysis means doing analysis: A critique of six analytic shortcomings. *Discourse Analysis Online*, 1(1). Retrieved from www.shu.ac.uk/daol/previous/v1/n1/index.htm

Anthony, R. N., Hawkins, D. F., & Merchant, K. A. (2011). *Accounting: Text and cases* (13th ed.). New York: McGraw-Hill. (Originally published 1959).

Aristotle. (1996). *Physics* (R. Waterfield, Trans.). Oxford: Oxford University Press.

Aristotle. (2002). *The Nicomachean ethics of Aristotle* (S. Broadie, & C. Rowe, Trans. & Eds.). Oxford: Oxford University Press.

Aristotle. (2004). *The art of rhetoric* (H. C. Lawson-Tancred, Trans.). London: Penguin Books. (Originally published 1991).

Armstrong, J. S. (2001). *Principles of forecasting: A handbook for researchers and practitioners*. New York: Springer.

Ashton, T. S. (1925). The records of a pin manufactory, 1814–1821. *Economica*, 15, 281–292.

Atkinson, A. A. (1998). Strategic performance measurement and incentive compensation. *European Management Journal*, 16(5), 552–561.

Aurelius, M. (1964). *Meditations* (M. Staniforth, Trans.). Harmondsworth, UK: Penguin Classics.

Avon, J. (2013). *The handbook of financial modeling: A practical approach to creating and implementing valuation projection models*. New York: Apress.

Baiman, S. (1982). Agency research in managerial accounting: A survey. *Journal of Accounting Literature*, 1(1), 154–213.

Baiman, S. (1990). Agency research in managerial accounting: A second look. *Accounting, Organizations and Society*, 15(4), 341–371.

Bain, J. S. (1944–1947). *The economics of the pacific coast petroleum industry* (3 vols.). Berkeley, CA: University of California Press.

Bain, J. S. (1951). Relation of profit rate to industry concentration. *Quarterly Journal of Economics*, 65(3), 293–324.

Bain, J. S. (1954). Economies of scale, concentration and the condition of entry in twenty manufacturing industries. *American Economic Review*, 44(1), 15–39.

Bain, J. S. (1956). *Barriers to new competition: Their character and consequences in manufacturing*. Boston, MA: Harvard University Press.

Balakrishnan, R. M., & Soderstrom, N. (2009). *Cross sectional variation cost stickiness* (Working Paper). Iowa City, IA: University of Iowa.

Ball, R. (2009). The global financial crisis and the efficient market hypothesis: What have we learned? *Journal of Applied Corporate Finance*, 21(4), 8–16.

Bamonti, P. M., Keelan, C. M., Larson, N., Mentrikoski, J. M., Randall, C. L., Sly, S. K., Travers, R. M., & McNeil, D. W. (2014). Promoting ethical behavior by cultivating a culture of self-care during graduate training: A call to action. *Training and Education in Professional Psychology*, 8(4), 253–260.

Bandler, R., & Grinder, J. (1989). *The structure of magic: A book about language and therapy*. Palo Alto, CA: Science & Behavior Books. (Originally published 1975).

Banker, R. D., Datar, S. M., & Kaplan, R. S. (1987). Productivity measurement and management accounting. *Journal of Accounting, Auditing & Finance*, 4(4), 528–554.

Barker, C., & Galasinski, D. (2001). *Cultural studies and discourse analysis: A dialogue on language and identity*. London: Sage.

Barnard, C. (1938). *The functions of the executive*. Cambridge, MA: Harvard University Press.

Barnard, C., & Simon, H. A. (1947). *Administrative behavior: A study of decision-making processes in administrative organization*. New York: Macmillan.

Barnes, J. (1993). *Aristotle's posterior analytics*. Oxford: Clarendon Press.

Barney, J. B. (1986). Strategic factor markets: Expectations, luck, and business strategy. *Management Science*, 32(10), 1231–1241.

Barney, J. B. (1991). Firm resources and sustained competitive advantage. *Journal of Management*, 17(1), 99–120.

Barney, J. B., Wright, M., & Ketchen, D. J. (2001). The resource-based view of the firm: Ten years after 1991. *Journal of Management*, 27(6), 625–641.

Baron, J. (2008). *Thinking and deciding* (4th ed.). Cambridge: Cambridge University Press. (Originally published 1988).

Basseches, M., & Mascolo, M. F. (2009). *Psychotherapy as a developmental process*. New York: Routledge/Taylor & Francis Group.

Baucus, M. S., & Near, J. P. (1991). Can illegal corporate behavior be predicted? An event history analysis. *Academy of Management Journal*, 34(1), 9–36.

Baudrillard, J. (1994). *Simulacra and simulation*. Ann Arbor, MI: The University of Michigan Press.

Baudrillard, J. (1998). *The consumer society*. Paris: Gallimard.

Bazerman, M. H., & Neale, M. A. (1992). *Negotiating rationally*. New York: Free Press.

Behrmann, E., & Rauwald, C. (2016). Mercedes boots robots from the production Line. *Bloomberg*, 26 February. Retrieved from www.bloomberg.com/

news/articles/2016-02-25/why-mercedes-is-halting-robots-reign-on-the-production-line

Bentham, J. (1996). *The collected works of Jeremy Bentham: An introduction to the principles of morals and legislation* (J. H. Burns, & H. L. A. Hart, Eds.). Oxford: Clarendon Press. (Originally published 1789).

Berle, A. A., & Means, G. C. (1968). *The modern corporation and private property* (2nd ed.). New York: Harcourt, Brace and World. (Originally published 1932).

Berliner, C., & Brimson, J. A. (Eds.). (1988). *Cost management for today's advanced manufacturing: The CAM-I conceptual design.* Boston, MA: Harvard Business School Press.

Birnberg, J. G., Luft, J., & Shields, M. D. (2007). Psychology theory in management accounting research: Review article. In C. S. Chapman, A. G. Hopwood, & M. D. Shields (Eds.), *Handbook of management accounting research* (Vol. 1, pp. 113–135). Oxford: Elsevier.

Bittner, E. (1973). Objectivity and realism in sociology. In G. Psathas (Ed.), *Phenomenological sociology* (pp. 109–125). New York: Wiley.

Blackwood, N. (2014). *Advanced Excel reporting for management accountants.* New York: Wiley.

Blake, R. R., & Mouton, J. (1964). *The managerial grid: The key to leadership excellence.* Houston, TX: Gulf Publishing.

Blattberg, C. (2004). *Welfare: Towards the patriotic Corporation: From pluralist to patriotic politics: Putting practice first.* New York: Oxford University Press. (Originally published 2000).

Blenko, M. W., Mankins, M. C., & Rogers, P. (2010). *Decide and deliver: 5 Steps to breakthrough performance in your organization.* Boston, MA: Harvard Business Review Press.

Bodmer, E. (2014). *Corporate and project finance modeling: Theory and practice.* New York: Wiley.

Bonczek, R. H., Holsapple, C. W., & Whinston, A. B. (1980). Future directions for developing a decision support system. *Decision Sciences*, 11(4), 616–631.

Bordin, E. S. (1976). The generalizability of the psychoanalytic concept of the working alliance. *Psychotherapy: Theory, Research and Practice*, 16(3), 252–260.

Boud, D. (1985). Promoting reflection in learning: A model. In D. Boud, R. Keogh & D. Walker (Eds.), *Reflection, turning experience into learning*. London: Kogan Page.

Bourdieu, P. (1998). *Practical reason: On the theory of action.* Stanford, CA: Stanford University Press.

Bower, J. L., & Christensen, C. M. (1995). Disruptive technologies: Catching the wave. *Harvard Business Review*, 73(1), 43–53.

Bowman, K. (2010). *Background paper for the AQF Council on generic skills.* Adelaide, South Australia: South Australian Department of Further Education Employment Science and Technology on behalf of the Australian Qualifications Framework Council. Retrieved from www.aqf.edu.au/wp-content/uploads/2013/06/Generic-skills-background-paper-FINAL.pdf

Boyns, T., & Edwards, J. R. (2013). *A history of management accounting: The British experience.* London: Routledge.

Brausch, J. M., & Taylor, T. C. (1997). Who is accounting for the cost of capacity? *Management Accounting*, (February), 44–46, 48–50.

Braverman, H. (1998). *Labor and monopoly capital: The degradation of work in the Twentieth Century* (anniversary ed.). New York: Monthly Review Press. (Originally published 1974).

Breadmore, R. G. (1971). *O & M: Organization and methods: An introductory guide.* London: Teach Yourself Books.

Brindle, M. C., & Stearns, P. N. (2001). *Facing up to management faddism: A new look at an old force.* New York: Praeger.

Broadbent, J. (2011). Discourses of control, managing the boundaries. *The British Accounting Review,* 43(4), 264–277.

Bromwich, M. (1990). The case for strategic management accounting: The role of accounting information for strategy in competitive markets. *Accounting, Organizations and Society,* 15(1–2), 27–46.

Bronfenbrenner, U. (1979). *The ecology of human development: Experiments by nature and design.* Cambridge, MA: Harvard University Press.

Bryant, E. F. (2009). *The yoga sutras of Pantanjali with insights from the traditional commentators.* New York: North Point Press Division of Farrar, Straus and Giroux.

Bullen, C., & Rockart, J. F. (1981). A primer on critical success factors. *Center for information systems research, 69. Working paper: 1220–81 Report.* Cambridge, MA: Massachusetts Institute of Technology. Retrieved from http://hdl.handle.net/1721.1/1988

Burke, L. (2016). Optus to axe more than 1000 jobs, report. *The Australian,* 1 March. Retrieved from www.news.com.au/finance/work/careers/optus-to-axe-more-than-1000-jobs-report/news-story/9a1f037dd9d1c9c1a35fac0f8cbfed9a

Burns, J., & Baldvinsdottir, G. (2005). An institutional perspective of accountants' new roles: The interplay of contradictions and praxis. *European Accounting Review,* 14(4), 725–757.

Burns, J., & Scapens, R. (2000). Conceptualizing management accounting change: An institutional framework. *Management Accounting Research,* 11(1), 3–25.

Buzan, T. (2005). *Mind maps at work: How to be the best at your job and still have time to play.* New York: New American Library.

Byrne, D. (2013). *Complexity theory and the social sciences: The state of the art.* Abington, UK, Oxford: Routledge.

Callahan, K. R., Stetz, G. S., & Brooks, L. M. (2011). *Project management accounting: Budgeting, tracking, and reporting costs and profitability* (2nd ed.). New York: Wiley. (Originally published 2007).

Callon, M. (1998). *The laws of the markets* (Sociological Review Monograph). Oxford, UK: Blackwell.

Camerer, C., Loewenstein, G., & Weber, M. (1989). The curse of knowledge in economic settings: An experimental analysis. *Journal of Political Economy,* 97(5), 1232–1254.

Campbell, A., Whitehead, J., & Finkelstein, S. (2009). *Think again: Why good leaders make bad decisions and how to keep it from happening to you.* Boston, MA: Harvard Business School Press.

Caplan, E. H. (1971). *Management accounting and behavioural science.* Reading, MA: Addison-Wesley.

Capon, N., Farley, J. U., & Hoenig, S. (1996). *Toward an integrative explanation of corporate financial performance.* New York: Kluwer.

Carrol, R. (2018). *Bullet journal*. Downloaded from www.bulletjournal.com.

Carter, S. B. (2011). *High octane women: How superachievers can avoid burnout*. New York: Prometheus Books.

Cataldo, J. M., & McInnes, J. M. (2011). The accounting identity and the identity of accountants: Accounting's competing paradigms through the prism of professional practice. *Accounting and the Public Interest*, 11(1), 116–129.

Chamberlin, E. H. (1933). *The theory of monopolistic competition: A re-orientation of the theory of value*. Cambridge, MA: Harvard University Press.

Chambers, R. J. (1965). Financial information and the securities market. *Abacus*, 1(1), 3–30.

Chambers, R.J. (1986). *Financial management: A study of the bases of financial decisions in business* (4th ed.). Sydney: Law Book Company. (Originally published 1947).

Chambers, R. J. (2006). *Accounting, evaluation and economic behavior*. Darlington, Australia: Sydney University Press. (Originally published 1966).

Chandler, A. D. (1977). *The visible hand: The managerial revolution in American business*. Cambridge, MA: Harvard University Press.

Chapple, C. K. (2009). *The Bhagavad Gita: Twenty-fifth-anniversary edition* (W. Sargeant (Trans.). Albany, NY: Excelsior Press.

Chatfield, M. (1971). The origins of cost accounting. *Management Accounting (USA)*, 52(12), 11–14.

Checkland, P. (1999). *Systems thinking, systems practice: Includes a 30-year retrospective*. New York: Wiley. (Originally published 1981).

Cheung, S. N. S. (1987). Economic organization and Transaction-Costs. In *The New Palgrave: A Dictionary of economics* (Vol. 2, pp. 55–58). London: Palgrave.

Christensen, C. M. (1997). *The innovator's dilemma: When new technologies cause great firms to fail*. Boston, MA: Harvard Business School Press.

Christensen, C. M. (2006). The ongoing process of building a theory of disruption. *Journal of Product Innovation Management*, 23(1), 39–55.

Christensen, C. M., Raynor, M. E., & McDonald, R. (2015). What is disruption? *Harvard Business Review*, 93(12), 44–53.

Church, A. H. (1995). Overhead: The cost of production preparedness. *Journal of Cost Management*, (Summer), 66–71. Reprint of Church, A. H. (1931). Overhead: The cost of production preparedness. *Factory and Industrial Management*, (January), 38–41.

Churchman, C. W. (1961). *Prediction and optimal decision: Philosophical issues of a science of values*. Englewood Cliffs, NJ: Prentice-Hall.

Cialdini, R. B. (2006). *Influence: The psychology of persuasion* (Rev. ed.). New York: Collins. (Originally published 1984).

Ciborra, C. U., Braa, K., Cordella, A., Dahlbom, B., Failla, A., Hanseth, O., Hepsø, V., Ljungberg, J., & Monteiro, E. (2001). *From control to drift: The dynamics of corporate information infrastructures* (Rev. ed.). Oxford: Oxford University Press. (Originally published 2000).

Cicero. (1948). *On the orator, Books I-II* (Loeb classical library No. 348) (E. W. Sutton & H. W Rackham, Eds.). Boston, MA: Harvard University Press.

Cicero. (1991). *On duties* (M. T. Griffith, & E. M. Atkins, Eds.). Cambridge: Cambridge University Press.

Clark, C. (1940). *The conditions of economic progress*. London: Macmillan.

Clarke, F. L., & Dean, G. W. (2007). *Indecent disclosure: Gilding the corporate lily*. Port Melbourne, Australia: Cambridge University Press.

Clower, R. W. (1959). Stock and flow quantities: A common fallacy. *Economica*, 26(103), 251–252.

Coase, R. (1937). The nature of the firm. *Economica*, 4(16), 386–405.

Coase, R. (1960). The problem of social cost. *Journal of Law and Economics*, 3(1), 1–44.

Coff, R. W. (1999). When competitive advantage doesn't lead to performance: The resource-based view and stakeholder bargaining power. *Organization Science*, 10(2), 119–133.

Collins, D. J. (2000). *Management fads and buzzwords: Critical-practical perspectives*. Abingdon, UK: Routledge.

Collis, D. J., & Montgomery, C. A. (1995). Competing on resources: Strategy in the 1990s. *Harvard Business Review*, 73(4), 118–129.

Conner, K. R. (1991). A historical comparison of resource-based theory and five schools of thought within industrial organization economics: Do we have a new theory of the firm? *Journal of Management*, 17(1), 121–154.

Constantine, L. L., & Lockwood, L. A. D. (1999). *Software for use: A practical guide to the models and methods of usage-centered design*. New York: ACM Press/Addison-Wesley.

Cooper, C. (2008). *Extraordinary circumstances: The journey of a corporate whistleblower*. New York: Wiley.

Cooper, R. (1988a). The rise of activity-based costing part one: What is an ABC system? *Journal of Cost Management*, 2(2), 45–54.

Cooper, R. (1988b). The rise of activity-based costing part two: When do I need an ABC system? *Journal of Cost Management*, 2(3), 41–48.

Cooper, R. (1989a). The rise of activity-based costing part three: How many cost drivers do you need and how do you select them? *Journal of Cost Management*, 2(4), 34–46.

Cooper, R. (1989b). The rise of activity-based costing part four: What does a activity-based system look like? *Journal of Cost Management*, 3(1), 38–49.

Cooper, R., & Kaplan, R. S. (1991). Profit priorities from activity-based costing. *Harvard Business Review*, 69(3), 130–135.

Cooper, R., & Kaplan, R. S. (1992). Activity-based systems: Measuring the cost of resource usage. *Accounting Horizons*, 6(3), 1–13.

COSO (Committee of Sponsoring Organization of the Treadway Commission). (2013). *Internal control integrated framework* (Updated). New York: Author. (Original framework published 1992).

Coulter, J. (1991). Cognition: 'Cognition' in an ethnomethodological mode. In G. Button (Ed.), *Ethnomethodology and the human sciences* (pp. 176–195). Cambridge: Cambridge University Press.

Council of Supply Chain Management Professionals. (2013). *Supply chain management terms and glossary*. Retrieved from https://cscmp.org/sites/default/files/user_uploads/resources/downloads/glossary-2013.pdf?utm_source=cscmpsite&utm_medium=clicklinks&utm_content=glossary&utm_campaign=GlossaryPDF

Covaleski, M. A., Dirsmith, M. W., Heian, J. B., & Samuel, S. (1998). The calculated and the avowed: Techniques of discipline and struggles over identity in big six public accounting firms. *Administrative Science Quarterly*, 43(2), 293–327.

Coyne, K. P. (1986). Sustainable competitive advantage: What it is, what it is not. *Business Horizons*, 29(1), 54–61.

Coyne, K. P., Coyne, S. T., & Coyne, E. J., Sr. (2010). When you've got to cut costs: A practical guide to reducing overhead by 10%, 20%, or (wince) 30%. *Harvard Business Review*, 88(5), 74–82.

Crawford, C. C., & Demodovich, J. W. (1983). *Crawford slip method: How to mobilize brainpower by think tank technology*. Los Angeles, CA: School of Public Administration/University of Southern California.

Crawford, C. C., & Krone, R. M. (1984). *Productivity improvement by the Crawford slip method: How to write, publish, instruct, supervise, and manage for better job performance*. Los Angeles, CA: School of Public Administration/ University of Southern California.

Crossman, P. (1953). The genesis of cost control. *The Accounting Review*, 28(4), 522–527.

Crotty, M. (1998). *The foundations of social research: Meaning and perspective in the research process*. Thousand Oaks, CA: Sage.

Cyert, R. M., & March, J. G. (1963). *A behavioral theory of the firm*. Englewood Cliffs, NJ: Prentice-Hall.

Czarniawska, B. (1997). *Narrating the organization: Dramas of institutional identity*. Chicago, IL: University of Chicago Press.

Daft, R. (1983). *Organization theory and design*. New York: West.

Dalkey, N., & Helmer, O. (1963). An experimental application of the Delphi method to the use of experts. *Management Science*, 9(3), 458–467.

Damien, T., & James, C. (Eds.). (2016). *Towns under siege: Developments in Australian takeovers and schemes*. Sydney: Herbert Smith Freehills.

Daniel, D. R. (1961). Management information crisis. *Harvard Business Review*, 39(5), 111–116.

Danielian, N. R. (1939). *A. T. & T.: The story of industrial conquest*. New York: The Vanguard Press.

De Bono, E. (1992). *Serious creativity: Using the power of lateral thinking to create new ideas*. New York: Harper Business.

Debruine, M., & Sopariwala, P. R. (1994). The use of practical capacity for better management decisions. *Journal of Cost Management*, (Spring), 25–31.

Deming, W. E. (2000). *Out of the crisis*. Cambridge, MA: MIT Press. (Originally published 1986).

Demski, J. S. (2010). *Managerial uses of accounting information*. New York: Springer-Verlag.

Demski, J. S., Gerald, A., & Feltham, G. A. (1976). *Cost determination: A conceptual approach*. Ames, IA: Iowa State University Press.

Dervin, B. (1998). Sense-making theory and practice: An overview of user interests in knowledge seeking and use. *Journal of Knowledge Management*, 2(2), 36–46.

Deutscher, I. (1980). *The prophet unarmed: Trotsky 1921–1929*. Oxford: Oxford University Press.

Dewey, J. (1986). How we think (Rev. ed.). In J. Dewey (Ed.), *The later works* (Vol. 8) (J. A. Boyston, Ed.). Carbondale, IL: Southern Illinois University Press. (Originally published 1933).

Dickey, R. (Ed.). (1960). *Accountants' cost handbook* (2nd ed.). New York: Ronald Press. (Originally published 1944).

DiMaggio, P. J., & Powell, W. W. (1983). The iron-cage revisited: Institutional isomorphism and collective rationality in organizational field. *American Sociological Review*, 48(4), 147–160.

Dionysiou, D. D., & Tsoukas, H. (2013). Understanding the (re)creation of routines from within: A symbolic interactionist perspective. *Academy of Management Review*, 38(2), 181–205.

Ditillo, A. (2004). Dealing with uncertainty in knowledge-intensive firms: The role of management control systems as knowledge integration mechanisms. *Accounting ,Organizations and Society*, 29(3–4), 401–421.

Donaldson, T., & Preston, L. E. (1995). The stakeholder theory of the corporation: Concepts, evidence, and implications. *Academy of Management Review*, 20(1), 65–91.

Douglas, M. T. (1990). Converging on autonomy: Anthropology and institutional economics. In O. E. Williamson (Ed.), *Organization theory: From Chester Barnard to the present and beyond* (pp. 98–115). Oxford: Oxford University Press.

Dowling, J., & Pfeffer, J. (1975). Organizational legitimacy: Social values and organizational behavior. *The Pacific Sociological Review*, 18(1), 122–136.

Drexler, K. E. (2007). *Engines of creation: The coming era of nanotechnology.* New York: Doubleday. (Originally published 1986).

Drucker, P. F. (1954). *The practice of management.* London: Heinemann.

Drucker, P. F. (1974). *Management: Tasks, responsibilities, practices.* New York: Harper & Row.

Drucker, P. F. (1964). *Managing for results: Economic tasks and risk-taking decisions.* London: Heinemann.

Drucker, P. F. (1980). *Managing in turbulent times.* London: Butterworth-Heinemann.

Drury, C., & Tayles, M. (1995). Issues arising from surveys of management accounting practice. *Management Accounting Research*, 6(3), 267–280.

Duke, A. (2018). *Thinking in bets: Making smarter decisions when you don't have all the facts.* New York: Portfolio/Penguin Books.

Duncan, J. C. (1909). A definition of accounting. *American Economic Association Quarterly*, 3rd Series, 10(1), 75–84.

Duncker, K. (1945). On problem solving (S. Lynne, Trans.). *Psychological Monographs*, 58(5), i-113.

Dunmire, P. (2008). The rhetoric of temporality: The future as linguistic construct and rhetorical resource. In B. Johnstone & C. Eisenhart (Eds.), *Rhetoric in detail: Discourse analyses of rhetorical talk and text* (pp. 81–111). Amsterdam: John Benjamins.

Durkin, P., & Lynch, J. (2016). Dead letter day looms for Aussie Post. *The Australian Financial Review*, 27 February, p. 8.

Dye, T. R. (2007). *Understanding public policy* (12th ed.). Upper Saddle River, NJ: Prentice-Hall. (Originally published 1972).

Earl, M., & Hopwood, A. G. (1980). From management information to information management. In H. C. Lucas, F. F. Land, T. J. Lincoln, & K. Supper (Eds.), *The information systems environment: Proceedings of the IFIP TC8.2 Working conference on the information systems environment. Bonn, West Germany, 11–13 June 1979* (pp. 3–13). Amsterdam: North-Holland.

Easterby-Smith, M., & Araujo, L. (1999). Current debates and opportunities. In M. Easterby-Smith, L. Araujo, & J. Burgoyne (Eds.), *Organizational learning and the learning organization* (pp. 1–21). London: Sage.

Eccles, T. (1993). Implementing strategy: Two revisionist perspectives. In J. Henry, G. Johnson, & J. Newton (Eds.), *Strategic thinking: Leadership and the management of change* (pp. 311–323). New York: Wiley.

Eccles, R. G., Newquist, S. C., & Schatz, R. (2007). Reputation and its risks. *Harvard Business Review*, 85(2), 104–114.

Edwards, J. D. (1958). This new costing concept: Direct costing? *The Accounting Review*, 33(4), 561–567.

Edwards, J. D., & Potter, J. (1993). Language and causation: A discursive model of description and attribution. *Psychological Review*, 100(1), 23–41.

Egan, V., Chan, S., & Shorter, G. W. (2014). The dark triad, happiness and subjective well-being. *Personality and Individual Differences*, 67, 17–22.

Eisenberg, M. (1984). Ambiguity as strategy in organizational communication. *Communication Monographs*, 51(3), 227–242.

Eisenhardt, K. (1989). Agency theory: An assessment and review. *Academy of Management Review*, 14(1), 57–74.

Engel, G. L. (1977). The need for a new medical model: A challenge for biomedicine. *Science*, 196, 129–136.

English, L. P. (1999). *Improving data warehouse and business information quality: Methods for reducing costs and increasing profits*. New York: Wiley.

Epicetus. (2014). *Discourses, fragments, handbook* (C. Hill, Ed. & R. Hard, Trans.). Oxford: Oxford World's Classics.

Ernest & Young. (2015). *Megatrends: Making sense of a world in motion*. New York: Ernest & Young.

Esfandiary, F. M. [FM2030] (1977). *Telespheres*. New York: Popular Library CBS Publications.

Evans-Pritchard, E. E. (1937). *Witchcraft, oracles and magic among the Azande*. Oxford: Oxford University Press.

Fama, E. F. (1970). Efficient capital markets: A review of theory and empirical work. *Journal of Finance*, 25(2), 383–417.

Fama, E. F., & Jensen, M. C. (1983). Agency problems and residual claims. *Journal of Law & Economics*, 26(2), 327–349.

Fasarany, M. G., Aslan, A., & Barandagh, M. I. (2015). Sticky cost behavior and accounting conservatism: Evidence from Tehran stock exchange. *International Journal of Accounting Research*, 2(3), 38–44.

Feldman, M. S., & March, J. G. (1981). Information in organizations as signal and symbol. *Administrative Science Quarterly*, 26(2), 171–186.

Feldman, M. S., & Pentland, B. T. (2003). Reconceptualizing organizational routines as a source of flexibility and change. *Administrative Science Quarterly*, 48(1), 94–118.

Felin, T., & Foss, N. J. (2009). Organizational routines and capabilities: Historical drift and a course-correction toward microfoundations. *Scandinavian Journal of Management*, 25(2), 157–167.

Fess, P. E. (1961). The theory of manufacturing costs. *The Accounting Review*, 36(3), 446–453.

Fiedler, F. E. (1964). A theory of leadership effectiveness. In L. Berkowitz (Ed.), *Advances in experimental social psychology* (Vol. 1, pp. 149–190). New York: Academic Press.

Firth, A. (1995). 'Accounts' in negotiation discourse: A single-case analysis. *Journal of Pragmatics*, 23(2), 199–226.

Fischer, R. G. (1978). The Delphi method: A description, review, and criticism. *Journal of Academic Librarianship*, 4(2), 64–70.

Fischhoff, B. (1975). Hindsight is not equal to foresight: The effect of outcome knowledge on judgment under uncertainty. *Journal of Experimental Psychology: Human Perception and Performance*, 1(3), 288–299.

Fisher, I. (1896). What is capital? *Economic Journal*, 6(24), 509–534.

Fisher, R., & Ury, W. (2012). *Getting to yes: Negotiating agreement without giving in* (3rd ed.). New York: Random House Business Books. (Originally published 1981).

Flamholtz, E. (1996). *Effective management control: Theory and practice*. New York: Springer.

Flesher, D. L., & Flesher, T. K. (1996). McKinsey, James O. (1889–1937). In M. Chatfield & R. Vangermeersch (Eds.), *History of accounting: An international encyclopaedia* (pp. 410–411). New York: Garland Publishing.

Flesher, D. L., & Previts, G. J. (2013). Donaldson Brown (1885–1965): The power of an individual and his ideas over time. *The Accounting Historians Journal*, 40(1), 79–101.

Fligstein, N. (1985). The spread of the multidivisional form among large firms, 1919–1979. *American Sociological Review*, 50(3), 377–391.

Fombrun, C., & Shanley, M. (1990). What's in a name? Reputation building and corporate strategy. *Academy of Management Journal*, 33(2), 233–258.

Forrester, J. W. (1968). Industrial dynamics: A response to Ansoff and Slevin. *Management Science*, 14(9), 601–618.

Foster, G., & Gupta, M. (1994). Marketing, cost management and management accounting. *Journal of Management Accounting Research*, 6(3), 43–77.

Foucault, M. (1977). *Discipline and punish: The birth of the prison* (A. Sheridan, Trans.). London: Allen Lane. (Originally published 1975).

Francis, J., Philbrick, D., & Schippe, K. (1994). Shareholder litigation and corporate disclosures. *Journal of Accounting Research*, 32(2), 137–164.

Freeman, R. E. (1984). *Strategic management: A stakeholder approach*. Boston, MA: Pitman.

Freeman, R. E., & Reed, D. E. (1983). Stockholders and stakeholders: A new perspective on corporate governance. In C. J. Huizinga (Ed.), *Corporate governance: A definitive exploration of the issues* (pp. 169–205). Los Angeles, CA: UCLA Extension Press. Reprinted in *California Management Review*, 25(3), 88–106.

Gabriel, Y. (1995). The unmanaged organization: Stories, fantasies and subjectivity. *Organization Studies*, 16(3), 477–501.

Gagné, R. M. (1984). Learning outcomes and their effects: Useful categories of human performance. *American Psychologist*, 39(4), 377–385.

Galinsky, A., & Schweitzer, M. (2015). *Friend & foe: When to cooperate, when to compete, and how to succeed at both*. New York: Crown Business.

Gantt, H. L. (1994). The relation between production and costs. *Journal of Cost Management*, (Spring), 4–11. (Originally published 1915 by the American Society of Engineers in their Proceedings, pp. 109–128).

Garfinkel, H. (2002). *Ethnomethodology's program: Working out Durkheim's aphorism* (A. W. Rawls, Ed.). Lanham, MD: Rowman & Littlefield.

Garner, S. P. (1947). Historical development of cost accounting. *The Accounting Review*, 22(4), 385–389.

Garner, S. P. (1954). *Evolution of cost accounting to 1925*. Tuscaloosa, AL: University of Alabama Press.

Gay, P. (1995). *The bourgeois experience Victoria to Freud: The cultivation of hatred*. London: Fontana.

George, A. (1972). The case for multiple advocacy in making foreign policy. *The American Political Science Review*, 66(3), 751–785.

Germany, R., & Muralidharan, R. (2001). The three phases of value capture: Finding competitive advantage in the information age. *Strategy + Business*, 22, 1–2.

Gibbs, G. (1958). New cost accounting concepts. *The Accounting Review*, 33(1), 96–101.

Gibson-Graham, J. K. (2006). *The end of capitalism (as we knew it): A feminist critique of political economy* (Rev. ed.). Minneapolis, MN: University of Minnesota Press. (Originally published 1996).

Gigerenzer, G. (1996). On narrow norms and vague heuristics: A reply to Kahneman and Tversky. *Psychological Review*, 103(3), 592–596.

Gigerenzer, G., & Selten, R. (2002). *Bounded rationality: The adaptive toolbox*. Cambridge, MA: MIT Press.

Gigerenza, G., Todd, P. M., & ABC Research Group (Eds.). (1999). *Simple heuristics that make us smart*. New York: Oxford University Press.

Gilbert, D. (2006). *Stumbling on happiness*. New York: Knopf.

Goffman, E. (1959). *The presentation of self in everyday life*. New York: Doubleday.

Goffman, E. (1974). *Frame analysis: An easy on the organization of experience*. Cambridge, MA: Harvard University Press.

Goldratt, E. (1990). *Theory of constraints*. Croton-on-Hudson, NY: North River Press.

Goldstein, D. G., & Gigerenzer, G. (1999). The recognition heuristic: How ignorance makes us smart. In G. Gigerenzer, P. M. Todd, and ABC Research Group, *Simple heuristics that make us smart* (pp. 37–58). New York: Oxford University Press.

Gordon, M. J. (1964). Postulates, principles and research in accounting. *The Accounting Review*, 39(2), 251–263.

Gorz, A. (1989). *Critique of economic reason*. London: Verso.

Gourvish, T. (1972). *Mark Huish and the London and North-Western railway*. London: Newton Abbott.

Govindarajan, V., & Trimble, C. (2010). *The other side of innovation: Solving the execution challenge*. Boston, MA: Harvard Business Review Press.

Gox, R. (2000). Strategic transfer pricing, absorption costing, and observability. *Management Accounting Research*, 11(3), 327–348.

Grandjean, P., & Landrigan, P. J. (2014). Neurobehavioral effects of developmental toxicity. *The Lancet Neurology*, 13(3), 330–338.

Grant, A. (2013). *Give and take: Why helping others drives our success*. New York: Viking.

Grant, R. M. (1991). The resource-based theory of competitive advantage. *California Management Review*, 33(3), 114–135.

Griffiths, I. (1987). *Creative accounting: How to make your profits what you want them to be*. London: Sidgwick Jackson. (Originally published 1986).

Hajkowicz, S. (2015). *Global megatrends: Seven patterns of change shaping our future*. Clayton South, Australia: CSIRO Publishing.

Hall, M. (2010). Accounting information and managerial work. *Accounting, Organizations and Society*, 35(5), 301–315.

Hall, P. A., & Taylor, R. C. R. (1996). Political science and the three institutionalisms. *Political Studies*, 44(5), 936–957.

Hall, R. L. (1992). The strategic analysis of intangible resources. *Strategic Management Journal*, 13(2), 135–144.

Hall, R. L., & Hitch, C. J. (1939). Price theory and business behavior. *Oxford Economic Papers*, 2(1), 12–45.

Hall, S. (1996). Who needs identity? In S. Hall & P. Du Gay (Eds.), *Questions of cultural identity* (pp. 1–17). London: Sage.

Hamel, G., & Prahalad, C. K. (1993). Strategy as stretch and leverage. *Harvard Business Review*, 71(2), 75–84.

Hammer, M., & Champy, J. (2006). *Reengineering the corporation: A manifesto for business revolution* (Rev. and updated ed.). New York: HarperCollins Business. (Originally published 1993).

Hanks, K., & Belliston, L. (1990). *Rapid viz: A new method for the rapid visualization of ideas* (2nd ed.). Menlo Park, CA: Crisp. (Originally published 1980).

Hansen, M. T., Nohria, N., & Tierney, T. J. (1999). What's your strategy for managing knowledge? *Harvard Business Review*, 77(2), 106–116.

Hardy, C. (1996). Understanding power: Bringing about strategic change. *British Journal of Management*, 7(Special Issue), S3–S16.

Hare, R. D. (1993). *Without conscience: The disturbing world of the psychopaths among us*. New York: Guilford Press.

Harré, H. R. (1970). *The principles of scientific thinking*. London: Macmillan.

Harris, M., Kriebel, C., & Raviv, A. (1982). Asymmetric information, incentives, and intrafirm resource allocation. *Management Science*, 28(6), 604–620.

Harrison, D., & Yu, J. W. (1990). *The spreadsheet style manual*. Homewood, IL: Dow Jones-Irwin.

Harrison, G. (1980). The stock-flow distinction: A suggested interpretation. *Journal of Macroeconomics*, 2(2), 111–128.

Hastie, R., & Dawes, R. M. (2001). *Rational choice in an uncertain world: The psychology of judgement and decision making*. Thousand Oaks, CA: Sage.

Haunschild, P. R., & Miner, A. S. (1997). Modes of interorganizational imitation: The effects of outcome salience and uncertainty. *Administrative Science Quarterly*, 42(3), 472–500.

Hayzen, A., & Reeve, J. (2000). Examining the relationships in productivity accounting. *Management Accounting Quarterly*, 1(4), 32–39.

Heider, F. (1958). *The psychology of interpersonal relations*. New York: Wiley.

Heinrichs, J. (2017). *Thank you for arguing: What Aristotle, Lincoln, and Homer Simpson can teach us about the art of persuasion* (3rd ed.). New York: Penguin Books. (Originally published 2007).

Henri, J.-F. (2006). Management control systems and strategy: A resource- based perspective. *Accounting, Organizations and Society*, 31(6), 529–558.

Heraclitus. (2015). *Fragments: A text and translation with a commentary* (T. M. Robinson, Trans. & Ed.). Toronto, Canada: University of Toronto.

Hergert, M., & Morris, D. (1989). Accounting data for value chain analysis. *Strategic Management Journal*, 10(5), 175–188.

Herling, J. (1962). *The great price conspiracy: The story of ant-trust violations in the electrical industry*. Washington, DC: Robert B. Luce.

Hersey, P., & Blanchard, K. H. (1969). *Management of organizational behavior: Utilizing human resources*. NJ: Prentice-Hall.

Herzberg, F. (1964). The motivation-hygiene concept and problems of manpower [sic]. *Personnel Administrator*, 27(1), 3–7.

Hill, K. Q., & Fowles, J. (1975). The methodological worth of the Delphi forecasting technique. *Technological Forecasting and Social Change*, 7(1), 119–192.

Hilton, R. W., & Platt, D. E. (2014). *Managerial accounting: Creating value in a dynamic business environment* (10th ed.). New York: McGraw-Hill. (Originally published 1991).

Hirshleifer, J., Glazer, A., & Hirshleifer, D. (2005). *Price theory and applications: Decisions, markets and information* (7th ed.). Cambridge: Cambridge University Press. (Originally published 1976).

Hofer, C. W. (1975). Toward a contingency theory of business strategy. *Academy of Management Journal*, 18(4), 784–810.

Ho, T. S., & Lee, S. B. (2004). *The Oxford guide to financial modeling: Applications for capital markets, corporate finance, risk management and financial institutions*. New York: Oxford University Press.

Hogg, N. (1994). *Business forecasting using financial models: How to use the key techniques of financial modelling to interpret business proposals*. London: Financial Times Management.

Hoopes, D. G., Madsen, T. L., & Walker, G. (2003). Guest editors' introduction to the special issue: Why is there a resource-based view? Toward a theory of competitive heterogeneity. *Strategic Management Journal*, 24(10), 889–902.

Hoorens, V. (1993). Self-enhancement and superiority biases in social comparison. *European Review of Social Psychology*, 4(1), 113–139.

Hope, J., & Fraser, R. (2003). *Beyond budgeting*. Boston, MA: Harvard Business School Press.

Hopper, T., & Macintosh, N. (1993). Management accounting as a disciplinary practice: The case of ITT under Harold Geneen. *Accounting, Organizations and Society*, 4(2), 181–216.

Hopwood, A. G. (1984). Accounting and the pursuit of efficiency. In A. G. Hopwood & C. R. Tomkins (Eds.), *Issues in public sector accounting* (pp. 167–187). London: Phillip Allen.

Hopwood, A. G. (1987). The archeology of accounting systems. *Accounting, Organizations and Society*, 12(3), 207–234.

Horngren, C. T., Datar, S. M., Foster, G., Rajan, M. V., & Ittner, C. (2015). *Cost accounting: A managerial emphasis* (15th ed.). Upper Saddle River, NJ: Pearson. (Originally published 1962).

Horngren, C. T., & Sorter, G. H. (1961). Direct costing for external reporting. *The Accounting Review*, 36(1), 84–93.

Horvath, A. O., & Luborsky, L. (1993). The role of the therapeutic alliance in psychotherapy. *Journal of Consulting Clinical Psychology*, 61(4), 561–573.

Huff, D. (1954). *How to lie with statistics*. New York: Norton.

Hull, C. L. (1943). *Principles of behavior: An introduction to behavior theory*. New York: Appleton-Century-Crofts.

Huntington, S. P. (2006). *Political order in changing societies*. New Haven, CT: Yale University Press. (Originally published 1968).

Huntington, S. P. (1996). *The clash of civilizations and the remaking of world order*. New York: Simon & Schuster.

Institute of Management Accountants. (2017). *The statement of ethical professional practice*. Montvale, NJ: Institute of Management Accountants, 28 July 2005. Retrieved from www.imanet.org/PDFs/Public/Press_Releases/STATEMENT%20 OF%20ETHICAL%20PROFESSIONAL%20PRACTICE_2.2.12.pdf

International Accounting Standards Board. (2018).*Conceptual framework for financial reporting*. London: IFRS Foundation.

International Federation of Accountants. (1998). *Management accounting concepts*. New York: IFAC.

Irwin, T. H. (1990). *Aristotle's first principles* (Rev. ed). Oxford: Clarendon Press. (Originally published 1988).

Ittner, C., & Larcker, D. (2006). *Non-financial performance measures: What works and what doesn't*. Retrieved from http://knowledge.wharton.upenn.edu/ article/non-financial-performance-measures-what-works-and-what-doesnt/

Jameson, M. (1988). *A practical guide to creative accounting*. London: Kogan Page.

Janis, I. L. (1959). Decisional analysis: A theoretical analysis. *Journal of Conflict Resolution*, 3(1), 6–27.

Jensen, M., & Meckling, W. H. (1976). Theory of the firm: Managerial behavior, agency costs and ownership structure. *Journal of Financial Economics*, 3(4), 305–360.

Johnson, G., Scholes, K., & Whittington, R. (2008). *Exploring corporate strategy: Text and cases* (8th ed.). London: Financial Times/Prentice-Hall. (Originally published 1983).

Johnson, H. T. (1975). Management accounting in an early integrated industrial: E. I. DuPont de Nemours Powder Company 1903–1912. *Business History Review*, 49(2), 184–204.

Johnson, H. T. (1981). Toward a new understanding of nineteenth-century cost accounting. *The Accounting Review*, 56(3), 510–518.

Johnson, H. T. (2002). *Relevance regained: From to-down control to bottom-up empowerment*. New York: Free Press.

Johnson, H. T., & Kaplan, R. S. (1987). *Relevance lost: The rise and fall of management accounting*. Boston, MA: Harvard Business Review Press.

Johnson, M., & Johnson, T. (2000). *How to solve word problems in algebra: A solved problem approach* (2nd ed.). New York: McGraw-Hill. (Originally published 1976).

Johnston, A., Lefort, F., & Tesvic, J. (2017). *Secrets of successful change implementation*. Sydney: McKinsey. Retrieved from www.mckinsey.com/business-functions/operations/our-insights/secrets-of-successful-change-implementation

Joos, M. (1968). *The English verb: Form and meanings* (2nd ed.). Madison, WI: University of Wisconsin Press. (Originally published 1964).

Josephson, M. S. (1992). The need for ethics education in accounting. In W. S. Albrecht (Ed.), *Ethical issues in the practice of accounting* (pp. 1–20). Cincinnati, OH: South-Western Publishers.

Juran, J. M. (1995). *Managerial breakthrough* (Rev. ed.). New York: McGraw-Hill. (Originally published 1965).

Justice Haesler said Accountants 'hold important positions of trust and [they] needed to be aware [I will send you to] jail if [you] breach that trust and act dishonestly' (2015, July 18–19). *The Weekend Australian Financial Review*, p. 10.

Kahn, A. E. (1966). The tyranny of small decisions: Market failures, imperfections, and the limits of economics. *Kyklos*, 19(1), 23–47.

Kahneman, D. (2012). *Thinking fast and slow*. New York: Farrar, Strauss & Giroux.

Kahneman, D., Lovallo, D., & Sibony, O. (2011). The big idea: Before you make that big decision . . . *Harvard Business Review*, 89(6), 50–60.

Kahneman, D., & Tversky, A. (1984). Choices, values, and frames. *American Psychologist*, 39(4), 341–350.

Kant, I. (1999). *Critique of pure reason* (P. Guyer, & A. W. Wood, Trans. & Eds.). Cambridge: Cambridge University Press. (Originally published 1781).

Kaplan, R. S. (1984). The evolution of management accounting. *The Accounting Review*, 65(3), 390–418.

Kaplan, R. S., & Anderson, S. R. (2004). Time driven activity-based costing. *Harvard Business Review*, 82(11), 131–138.

Kaplan, R. S., & Anderson, S. R. (2007). *Time-driven activity-based costing: A simpler and more powerful path to higher profits*. Boston, MA: Harvard Business School Press.

Kaplan, R. S., & Bruns, W. (1987). *Accounting and management: Field study perspectives*. Boston, MA: Harvard Business School Press.

Kaplan, R. S., & Cooper, R. (1998). *Cost and effect: Using integrated cost systems to drive profitability and performance*. Boston, MA: Harvard Business School Press.

Kaplan, R. S., & Norton, D. P. (2001). Transforming the balanced scorecard from performance measurement to strategic management: Part I. *Accounting Horizons*, 15(1), 87–104.

Karaian, J. (2014). *The chief financial officer: What CFOs do, the influence they have, and why it matters* (Economist Books). London: Profile Books.

Kauhanen, A., & Napari, S. (2010). *Performance measurement and incentive plans*. Lönnrotinkatu, Finland: The Research Institute of the Finnish Economy.

Keil, M., Cule, P. E., Lyytinen, K., & Schmidt, R. C. (1998). A framework for identifying software project risks. *Communications of the ACM*, 41(11), 76–83.

Kelemen, M. (2003). *Managing quality: Managerial and critical perspectives*. Thousand Oaks, CA: Sage.

Kendall, G., & Wickham, G. (1999). *Using Foucault's methods*. Thousand Oaks, CA: Sage.

Kennedy, G. (2012). *Everything is negotiable: How to get the best deal everytime* (4th ed.). London: Random House Business Books. (Originally published 1982).

Kenny, A. J. P. (2003). *Action, emotion and will* (2nd ed.). London: Routledge. (Originally published 1963).

Kepner, C. H., & Tregoe, B. B. (2013). *The new rational manager: An updated edition for the new world*. Princeton, NJ: Princeton Research Press.

Ketchen, Jr., D. J., Thomas, J. B., &. Snow, C. C. (1993). Organizational configurations and performance: A comparison of theoretical approaches. *The Academy of Management Journal*, 36(6), 1278–1313.

Keynes, M. (1939). Relative movements of real wages and output. *The Economic Journal*, 49(193), 34–51.

Klan, A., & Bearup, G. (2016). Austrade staff paid $12M in bonuses. *The Australian*, 1 March, p. 3.

Klemstine, C. F., & Maher, M. W. (2013). *Management accounting research: A review and annotated bibliography*. New York: Routledge Library Edition Accounting. (Originally published 1984).

Koch, R. (2017) *The 80/20 principle: The secret to achieving more with less*. Updated 20th anniversary edition of the productivity and business classic (3rd ed.) London: Nicholas Brealey Publishing (Originally published 1998).

Kolakowski, L. (1989). *The presence of myth*. Chicago, IL: University of Chicago Press. (Originally published in French 1972).

Koller, T., Dobbs, R., & Huyett, B. (2010). *Value: The four cornerstones of corporate finance*. New York: Wiley.

Kotter, J. (1978). *Organizational dynamics, diagnosis and intervention*. Reading, MA: Addison-Wesley.

Kotter, J. P., & Heskett, J. L. (1992). *Corporate culture and performance*. New York: The Free Press.

Kozbelt, A., Beghetto, R. A., & Runco, M. A. (2010). Theories of creativity. In J. Kaufman & R. C. Sternberg (Eds.), *The Cambridge handbook of creativity* (pp. 20–47). Cambridge: Cambridge University Press.

Kropotkin, P. (1972). *Mutual aid: A factor in evolution*. London: Alan Lane. (Originally published 1902).

Kushner, R. F., Kessler, S., & McGaghie, W. C. (2011). Using behavior change plans to improve medical student care. *Academic Medicine*, 86(7), 901–906.

La Boétie, E. de. (2007). *The politics of obedience*. Montreal, Canada: Black Rose Books. (Originally published in English as Anti-dictator 1942).

Lally, P., van Jaarsveld, C. H. M., Potts, H. W. W., & Wardle, J. (2010). How are habits formed: Modeling habit formation in the real world. *European Journal of Social Psychology*, 40(6), 998–1009.

Lander, J. P. (2013). *R for everyone: Advanced analytics and graphics* (Addison-Wesley Data & Analytics Series). Boston, MA: Addison-Wesley Professional.

Lang, T. (1958). *Cost accountant's handbook*. New York: Ronald Press. (Originally published 1944).

Langfield-Smith, K. (2008). Strategic management accounting: How far have we come in 25 years? *Accounting, Auditing and Accountability Journal*, 21(2), 204–228.

Laranjeiro, N., Soydemir, S. N., & Bernardino, J. (2015). *A survey on data quality: classifying poor data*. IEEE 21st Pacific Rim International Symposium on Dependable Computing (PRDC), 8–20 November 2015, Zhangjiajie, China, 179–188. New York: IEEE.

Larsen, J. G. (1952). Utilizing past, present and future costs. *N.A.C.A. Bulletin*, February, p. 695.

Lawrence, P. R., & Lorsch, J. W. (1967). Differentiation and integration in complex organizations. *Administrative Science Quarterly*, 12(1), 1–47.

Lazonick, W. (1983). Industrial organization and technological change: The decline of the British cotton industry. *The Business History Review*, 57(2), 195–236.

Lehto, S. (2010). *Chrysler's turbine car: The rise and fall of Detroit's coolest creation*. Chicago, IL: Chicago Review Press.

Leicht, K. T., & Fennell, M. L. (2001). *Professional at work: A sociological approach*. New York: Wiley-Blackwell.

Leonard-Barton, D. (1992). Core capabilities and core rigidities: A paradox in managing new product development. *Strategic Management Journal*, 13(S1, Special Issue: Strategy process: Managing corporate self-renewal), 111–125.

Lepper, G. (2000). *Categories in text and talk*. London: Sage.

Levitt, T. (1960). Marketing myopia. *Harvard Business Review*, 38(4), 45–56.

Lin, Y., & Wu, L. (2014). Exploring the role of dynamic capabilities in firm performance under the resource-based view framework. *Journal of Business Research*, 67(3), 407–413.

Linstone, H. A. (1975). Eight basic pitfalls: A checklist. In H. A. Linstone & M. Turoff (Eds.), *The Delphi method: Techniques and applications* (pp. 571–586). Boston, MA: Addison-Wesley Publishing Company, Advanced Book Program.

Locke, E. A. (1968). Toward a theory of task motivation and incentives. *Organizational Behavior and Human Performance*, 3(2), 157–189.

Locke, E. A., & Latham, G. P. (1990). *A theory of goal setting and task performance*. Englewood Cliffs, NJ: Prentice-Hall.

Louis, M. R. (1980). Surprise and sense-making: What newcomers experience in entering unfamiliar organizational settings. *Administrative Science Quarterly*, 25(2), 226–251.

Lucas, R. E. (1972). Expectations and the neutrality of money. *Journal of Economic Theory*, 4(2), 103–124.

Ludlow, J. (1975). Delphi inquiries and knowledge utilization. In H. A. Linstone & M. Turoff (Eds.), *The Delphi method: Techniques and applications* (pp. 102–123). Reading, MA: Addison-Wesley Publishing Company, Advanced Book Program.

Macdonell, D. (1986). *Theories of discourse: An introduction*. Oxford, UK: Blackwell.

Mace, C. A. (1968). *The psychology of study* (Rev. ed.). Harmondsworth, UK: Pelican. (Originally published 1932).

Macher, J. T., & Richman, B. D. (2008). Transaction-cost economics: An assessment of empirical research in the social sciences. *Business and Politics*, 10(1), Article 1.

Machlup, F. (1979). Uses, value, and benefits of information. *Knowledge: Creation, Diffusion, Utilization*, 1, 62–81.

Macintosh, N. B., Shearer, T., Thornton, D. B., & Welker, M. (2000). Accounting as simulacrum and hyperreality: Perspectives on income and capital. *Accounting, Organizations and Society*, 25(1), 13–50.

MacIntyre, A. S. (2007). *After virtue: A study in moral theory* (3rd ed.). Notre Dame, IN: University of Notre Dame. (Originally published 1981).

Maister, D., Green, C. H., & Galford, R. (2001). *The trusted advisor* (New ed.). New York: Simon & Schuster. (Originally published 2000).

Makadok, R. (2001). Toward a synthesis of the resource-based view and dynamic-capability views of rent creation. *Strategic Management Journal*, 22(5), 387–401.

March, J., & Simon, H. (1958). *Organizations*. New York: Wiley.

Marshall, A. (1890). *Principles of economics* (Vol. 1). London: Macmillan.

Marx, K. (1990). *Capital* (Vol. 1) (B. Fowkes, Trans.). London: Penguin Books. (Originally published 1867).

Mason, E. S. (1939). Price and production policies of large-scale enterprise. *American Economic Review*, 29(1), 61–74.

Massini, S., Lewin, A. Y., Numagami, T., & Pettigrew, A. M. (2002). The evolution of organizational routines among large western and Japanese firms. *Research Policy*, 31(8–9), 1333–1348.

Maxwell, J. A. (2012). *A realist approach for qualitative research*. Thousand Oaks, CA: Sage.

Maynard, D. W. (2003). *Bad news, good news: Conversational order in everyday talk and clinical settings*. Chicago, IL: University of Chicago Press.

McKelvey, W. (1982). *Organizational systematics: Taxonomy, evolution, and classification*. Los Angeles, CA: University of California Press.

McKinsey, J. O. (1920). *Bookkeeping and accounting*. Cincinnati, OH: South-Western Publishers.

McKinsey Consulting Organization (1971). The 1968 McKinsey report on computer utilization. In T. W. McRae (Ed.), *Management information systems: Selected readings* (pp. 94–122).

McNair, C. J. (1994). The hidden costs of capacity. *Journal of Cost Management*, (Spring), 12–24.

Mead, G. H. (1934). *Mind, self and society from the standpoint of social behavior*. Chicago, IL: University of Chicago Press.

Meehl, P. E. (1992). Needs (Murray, 1938) and state variables (Skinner, 1938). *Psychological Reports*, 70(2), 407–450.

Mehan, H., & Wood, H. (1975). *The reality of ethnomethodology*. New York: Wiley.

Meyer, J. W., (1986). Social environments and organizational accounting. *Accounting, Organizations and Society*, 11(4–5), 345–356.

Meyer, J. W., & Rowan, B. (1977). Institutionalized organizations: Formal structure as myth and ceremony. *American Journal of Sociology*, 83(2), 340–363.

Miles, R., & Snow, C. (1978). *Organization strategy, structure and process*. New York: McGraw-Hill.

Mill, J. S. (1871). *Utilitarianism* (4th ed.). London: Longmans, Green, Reader, & Dyer. (Originally published 1861).

Miller, E. J., & Rice, A. K. (1967). *Systems of organization: The control of task and sentient boundaries*. London: Tavistock Publications.

Miller, H. (1996). The multiple dimensions of information quality. *Information Systems Management*, 13(2), 79–82.

Miller, J. A. (1996). *Implementing activity based management in daily operations*. New York: Wiley.

Miller, L. E. (2006). Determining what could/should be: The Delphi technique and its application. *Paper presented at the Meeting of the 2006 Annual Meeting of the Mid-Western Educational Research Association*, October, 2006. Columbus, Ohio.

Miller, P., & O'Leary, T. (1987). Accounting expertise and the politics of the product: Economic citizenship and modes of corporate governance. *Accounting, Organizations and Society*, 18(2–3), 187–206.

Minto, B. (2010). *The Minto pyramid principle: Logic in writing, thinking, & problem solving* (3rd ed.). London: Financial Times/Prentice-Hall. (Originally published 1987).

Mintzberg, H. (1979). *The structuring of organizations: A synthesis of the research*. Englewood Cliffs, NJ: Prentice-Hall.

Mintzberg, H. (1987). The strategy concept: Five P's for strategy. *California Management Review*, 30(1), 11–24.

Mintzberg, H. (2009). *Managing*. Harlow, UK: Financial Times/Prentice-Hall.

Mintzberg, H., Raisinghani, D., & Theoret, A. (1976). The structure of 'unstructured' decision processes. *Administrative Science Quarterly*, 21(2), 246–275.

Mitnick, B. M. (1974). *The theory of agency: The concept of fiduciary rationality and some consequences*. Unpublished Ph.D. dissertation, Department of Political Science, University of Pennsylvania. University Microfilms No. 74–22, 881.

Mitnick, B. M. (1975). The theory of agency: The policing 'paradox' and regulatory behavior. *Public Choice*, 24, 27–42.

Mitroff, I. I. (1983). *Stakeholders of the organizational mind*. San Francisco, CA: Jossey-Bass.

Mitroff, I. I., & Turoff, M. (1975). Philosophical and methodological foundations of Delpi. In H. A. Linstone & M. Turoff (Eds.), *The Delphi method: Techniques and applications* (pp. 17–36). Boston, MA: Addison-Wesley Publishing Company, Advanced Book Program.

Mo, Z. (2014). *The book of Master Mo* (I. Johnston, Trans.). London: Penguin Classics.

Montgomery, R. (2018). New ideas offer new ways to lose cash. *The Weekend Australian Business Review*, 7–8 April, p. 33.

Moore, G. A. (2014). *Crossing the chasm: Marketing and selling disruptive products to mainstream customers* (3rd ed.). New York: HarperCollins Business. (Originally published 1991).

Moran, E. (2018). Don't just go along for the ride with Tesla: There's a rocky road ahead. *The Weekend Australian Business Review*, 7–8 April, p. 33.

Moravec, H. (1998). *Robot: Mere machine to transcendent mind*. New York: Oxford University Press.

Morgan, M. (1993). *Creating workforce innovation: Turning individual creativity into organizational innovation*. Sydney, Australia: Allen & Unwin.

Morris, E., Fitzpatrick, M. R., & Renaud, J. (2016). A pan-theoretical conceptualization of client involvement in psychotherapy. *Psychotherapy Research*, 26(1), 70–84.

Morris, J. R. (1987). *Dow Jones-Irwin guide to financial modelling*. Homewood, IL: Dow Jones-Irwin.

Moss, M. F., & Haseman, W. C. (1957). Some comments on the applicability of direct costing to decision making. *The Accounting Review*, 32(2),184–193.

Mourelatos, A. P. D. (1978). Events, processes, and states. *Linguistics and Philosophy*, 2(3), 415–434.

Musson, A. E. (1957). James Nasmyth and the early growth of mechanical engineering. *Economic History Review, Second Series*, 10(1), 121–127.

Nagle, T., & Müller, G. (2018). *The strategy and tactics of pricing: A guide to growing more profitably* (6th ed.). London: Routledge. (Originally published 1987).

Naisbitt, J. (1984). *Megatrends: Ten new directions transforming our lives*. New York: Warner Books. (Originally published 1982).

Nelms, H. (1981). *Thinking with a pencil*. Berkeley, CA: Ten Speed Press. (Originally published 1957).

Nelson, R. R., & Winter, S. G. (1982). *An evolutionary theory of economic change*. Boston, MA: Belknap Press of Harvard University Press.

New Uber COO wants more strategy and less controversy (2017). *Financial Times*, 21 December. Retrieved from https://www.ft.com/content/46f68336-e5f3-11e7-8b99-0191e45377ec

Newell, B. R., Lagnado, D. A., & Shanks, D. R. (2007). *Straight choices: The psychology of decision making*. New York: Psychology Press.

Nixon, B. (2006). Strategic choice and management control systems: A review of theories and challenges for development. In Z. Hoque (Ed.), *Methodological issues in accounting research: Theories, methods and issues* (pp. 105–127). London: Spiramus Press.

Nixon, B., & Burns, J. (2012). The paradox of strategic management accounting. *Management Accounting Research*, 23(4), 229–244.

Noddings, N. (1984). *Caring: A feminine approach to ethics & moral education*. Berkeley, CA: University of California Press.

Norcross, J. C., & Guy, J. D., Jr. (2007). *Leaving it at the office: A guide to psychotherapist self-care*. New York: Guilford Press.

OECD. (2004). *Principles of organizational governance*. Paris: Author. (Originally published 1999).

Ohmae, K. (1982). *The mind of the strategist: The art of Japanese business*. New York: McGraw-Hill. (Originally published 1975).

Ohno, T. (1988). *Toyota production system: Beyond large-scale production*. Portland, OR: Productivity Press.

O'Leary, E. (1992). *Gestalt therapy: Theory, practice and research*. London: Chapman & Hall.

Oliver, G. R. (2012). *Foundations of the assumed business operations and strategy body of knowledge (BOSBOK)*. Darlington, Australia: Darlington Press.

Oliver, G. R. (2018). *Research foundry* [A Research Planning Runtime Database in Filemaker, Vol. 17]. Woolloomooloo, Australia: Author (Softcopy available on request from the author).

Oliver, G. R., & Snowden, D. J. (2005). Patterns of narrative in organizational knowledge sharing: Refolding the envelope of art-luddism and techno-fabulism. In G. Schreyögg & E. Schmidt (Eds.), *Knowledge management and narratives: Organizational effectiveness through storytelling*. Berlin: Verlag.

Oliver, G. R., & Walker, R. G. (2006). Reporting on software development projects to senior managers and the board. *Abacus*, 42(1), 43–65.

Otley, D. (2016). The contingency theory of management accounting and control: 1980–2014. *Management Accounting Research*, 31, 45–62.

Packer, G. (2014). Cheap words: Amazon is good for customers: But is it good for books? *New Yorker*, 17 February, 90(1), 66–73. Retrieved from www.newyorker.com/magazine/2014/02/17/cheap-words

Panko, R. R. (1998). What do we know about spreadsheet errors? *Journal of End User Computing*, 10(2), 15–21.

Parker, M. B., Moleshe, V., De la Harpe, R., & Wills, G. B. (2006). An evaluation of Information quality frameworks for the World Wide Web. *Paper presented at the 8th Annual Conference on WWW Applications*, Bloemfontein, Free State Province, South Africa.

Parmenter, D. (2015). *Key performance indicators (KPI): Developing, implementing and using winning KPIs* (3rd ed.). New York: Wiley. (Originally published 2007).

Paynter, J. W. (1947). The department store controller's part in business policy. *The Accounting Review*, 22(4), 390–393.

Pennings, J. M. (1964). The relevance of the structural-contingency model for organizational effectiveness. *Administrative Science Quarterly*, 20(3), 393–410.

Penrose, T. E. (1959). *The theory of the growth of the firm*. Oxford, UK: Blackwell.

Pfister, J. (2009). *Managing organizational culture for effective internal control: From practice to theory*. Dordrecht: Springer.

Piaget, J. (2001). *The language and thought of the child* (3rd ed.) (M. R. Gabain, Trans.). London: Routledge. (Originally published in French in 1923).

Pickerd, J. S., Summers, S., & Wood, D. A. (2015). An examination of how entry-level staff auditors respond to tone at the top vis-à-vis tone at the bottom. *Behavioral Research in Accounting*, 27(1), 79–98.

Pierson, P., & Skocpol, T. (2002). Historical institutionalism in contemporary political science. In I. Katznelson & H. V. Milner (Eds.), *Political science: The state of the discipline* (pp. 693–721). New York: Norton.

Polanyi, M. (1966). *The tacit dimension*. New York: Doubleday.

Porter, M. (1990). *Competitive strategy: Techniques for analyzing industries and competitors with a new introduction*. New York: Free Press. (Originally published 1980).

Porter, M. (1998). *Competitive advantage: Creating and sustaining superior performance with a new introduction*. New York: Free Press. (Originally published 1985).

Post, J. E., Lee, E., Preston, L. E., & Sachs, S. (2002). *Redefining the corporation: Stakeholder management and organizational wealth*. Stanford, CA: Stanford University Press.

Potter, J. (1996). *Representing reality: Discourse, rhetoric and social construction*. London: Sage.

Powell, S. (2014). *Licensed to lie: Exposing corruption in the Department of Justice*. Dallas, TX: Brown Books Publishing Group.

Power, M., & Laughlin, R. (1992). Critical theory and accounting. In M. Alvesson & H. Willmott (Eds.), *Critical management studies* (pp. 113–135). London: Sage.

Prahalad, C. K., & Hamel, G. (1990). The core competence of the corporation. *Harvard Business Review*, 68(3), 79–91.

Previts, G., & Samson, W. (1999–2000). Reporting for success: The Baltimore and Ohio railroad and management information. *Business and Economic History*, 28(2), 235–254.

Prusak, L., & Davenport, T. H. (2001). *Working knowledge: How organizations manage what they know*. Boston, MA: Harvard Business School Press.

Quinn, R. E., & Cameron, K. (1983). Organizational life cycles and shifting criteria of effectiveness: Some preliminary evidence. *Management Science*, 29(1), 33–51.

Reddin, W. J. (1970). *Managerial effectiveness*. New York: McGraw-Hill.

Reed, R., & DeFillippi, R. (1990). Causal ambiguity, barriers to imitation, and sustainable competitive advantage. *Academy of Management Review*, 15(1), 88–102.

Reichers, A. E. (1987). An interactionist perspective on newcomer socialization rates. *Academy of Management Review*, 12(2), 278–287.

Reisman, G. (1996). *Capitalism: A treatise on economics*. Ottawa, IL: Jefferson Books.

Remus, D., & Levy, F. S. (2016). *Can robots be lawyers? Computers, lawyers and the practice of law.* (Originally published 2015). Retrieved from https://papers.ssrn.com/sol3/papers.cfm?abstract_id=2701092

Ribeiro, J. A., & Scapens, R. W. (2006). Institutional theories in management accounting change: Contributions, issues and paths for development. *Qualitative Research in Accounting & Management*, 3(2), 94–111.

Ricardo, D. (2005). *The works and correspondence of David Ricardo* (Principles of Political Economy and Taxation, Vol. 1) (P. Sraffa, & M. H. Dobb, Eds.). Indianapolis, IN: Liberty Fund. (Originally published 1817).

Rich, P. (2011). *Understanding, assessing, and rehabilitating juvenile sexual offenders* (2nd ed.). New York: Wiley. (Originally published 2005).

Richard, P. J., Devinney, T. M., Yip, G. S., & Johnson, G. (2009). Measuring organizational performance: Towards methodological best practice. *Journal of Management*, 35(3), 718–804.

Richardson, R. (1996). *Professional's guide to robust spreadsheets: Using examples in Lotus 1–2–3 and Microsoft Excel.* Greenwich, CT: Manning.

Ridgeway, V. F. (1956). Dysfunctional consequences of performance measurements. *Administrative Science Quarterly*, 1(2), 240–247.

Rivett, B. H. P. (1962). Effecting change in stable industrial situations. *Operational Research Quarterly*, 13(2), 133–144.

Rivett, B. H. P. (1980). *Model building for decision analysis.* New York: Wiley.

Robbins. L. (1935). *An essay on the nature and significance of economic science* (2nd ed.). London: Macmillan. (Originally published 1932).

Robbins, L. (1938). Interpersonal comparisons of utility: A comment. *Economic Journal*, 48(192), 635–641.

Robert Walters (2015). *The Robert Walters global salary survey* (16th ed). London: Author. Retrieved from https://www.robertwalters.com.au/content/dam/robert-walters/global/files/salary-survey/complete-salary-survey-2015.pdf

Roberts, J. (2009). Faith in numbers. *Ephemera*, 9(4), 335–343.

Robertson, S. I. (2017). *Problem solving: Perspectives from cognition and neuroscience* (2nd. ed.). London: Routledge. (Originally published 2001). Hove, UK: Psychology Press.

Robinson, J. (1933). *The economics of imperfect competition.* London: Macmillan.

Roeder, M. (2011). The diminishing returns of the information age. In D. Hale & L. H. Hale (Eds.), *What's next: Unconventional wisdom on the future of the economy* (pp. 292–302). New Haven, CT: Yale University Press.

Rogers, E. M. (2003). *Diffusion of innovations* (5th ed.). New York: Free Press. (Originally published 1962).

Rogers, J. L., & Stocken, P. C. (2005). Credibility of management forecasts. *The Accounting Review*, 80(4), 1233–1260.

Rohlfs, J. H. (2003). *Bandwagon effects in high technology industries.* Cambridge, MA: MIT Press.

Rosenberg, M. B. (2015). *Nonviolent communication: A language of life* (3rd ed.). Encinitas, CA: PuddleDancer [sic] Press. (Originally published 1999).

Rosenzweig, P. (2014). *The halo effect: . . . And the eight other business delusions that deceive managers* (Rev. ed.). New York: Free Press. (Originally published 2007).

Ross, S. A. (1973). The economic theory of agency: The principal's problem. *American Economic Review*, 62(2), 134–139.

Rossi, P. H., Lipsey, M. W., & Freeman, H. E. (2004). *Evaluation: A systematic approach* (7th ed.). Thousand Oaks, CA: Sage. (Originally published 1985).

Rothery, A. (1990). *Modeling with spreadsheets*. Lund, Sweden: Chartwell-Bratt.

Rowe, C., Birnberg, J. G., & Shields, M. D. (2008). Effects of organizational process change on responsibility accounting and managers' revelations of private knowledge. *Accounting, Organizations and Society*, 33(4), 164–198.

Rubenstein, A. H., & Geisler, E. (2003). *Installing and managing workable knowledge management systems*. Westport, CT: Praeger.

Rubin, K. (2007). Accounting as myth maker. *Australian Accounting, Business and Finance Journal*, 1(2), Article 2. Retrieved from http://ro.uow.edu.au/cgi/viewcontent.cgi?article=1006&context=aabfj

Rugman, A., & D'Cruz, J. (1997). The theory of the flagship firm. *European Management Journal*, 15(4), 403–412.

Rumelt, R. P. (1984). Towards a strategic theory of the firm. In R. B. Lamb (Ed.), *Competitive strategic management* (pp. 556–571). Englewood Cliffs, NJ: Prentice-Hall.

Rumelt, R. P. (1991). How much does industry matter? *Strategic Management Journal*, 12(3), 167–185.

Rutherford, M. (1994). *Institutions in economics: The old and the new institutionalism*. Cambridge: Cambridge University Press.

Saakvitne, K. W., Pearlman, L. A., The Staff of the Traumatic Stress Institute, & Center for Adult & Adolescent Psychotherapy. (1996). *Transforming the pain: A workbook on vicarious traumatization*. New York: Norton.

Sackman, H. (1975). *Delphi critique: Expert opinion, forecasting, and group process*. Santa Monica, Lexington, MA: Lexington Books. (Originally published 1974 by Rand Corporation as Delphi assessment).

Sacks, H. (1984). On doing 'being ordinary'. In J. M. Atkinson & J. Heritage (Eds.), *Structures of social action: Studies in conversation analysis* (pp. 413–429). Cambridge: Cambridge University Press.

Sacks, H. (1992). In G. Jefferson (Ed.). *Lectures on conversation* (2 vols.). Oxford: Blackwell.

Salter, M. (2008). *Innovation corrupted: The origins and legacies of Enron's collapse*. Boston, MA: Harvard Business School Press.

Schank, R. C., & Abelson, R. P. (1977). *Scripts, plans, goals and understanding: An inquiry into human knowledge structures*. Hillsdale, NJ: Erlbaum.

Schaubroeck, J. M., Avolio, B. J., Lord, R. G., Dimotakis, N., Hannah, S. T., Kozlowski, S. W. J., Trevino, L. K., & Peng, A. C. (2012). Embedding ethical leadership within and across organization levels. *Academy of Management Journal*, 55(5), 1053–1078.

Schein, E. (1992). *Organizational culture and leadership: A dynamic view*. San Francisco, CA: Jossey-Bass.

Schilbach, T. (1997). Cost accounting in Germany. *Management Accounting Research*, 8(3), 261–276.

Schmidt, F. L., & Hunter, J. E. (1998). The validity and utility of selection methods in personnel psychology: Practical and theoretical implications of 85 years of research findings. *Psychological Bulletin*, 124(2), 262–274.

Schön, D. A. (1973). *Beyond the stable state: Public and private learning in a changing society*. Harmondsworth, UK: Penguin Classics.

Schumpeter, J. A. (1947). The creative response in economic history. *Journal of Economic History*, 7(2), 149–159.

Schumpeter, J. A. (1954). *History of economic analysis*. London: Allen & Unwin.

Schwartz, B. (2004). *The paradox of choice: Why more is less*. New York: HarperCollins Business.

Scott, M. B., & Lyman, S. M. (1968). Accounts. *American Sociological Review*, 33(1), 46–62.

Seidman, S. (1992). Postmodern social theory as narrative with a moral intent. In S. Seidman & D. G. Wagner (Eds.), *Postmodernism and social theory: The debate over general theory*. Cambridge, MA: Blackwell.

Shank, J., & Govindrajan, V. (1991). Strategic cost management and the value chain. *Journal of Cost Management*, 5(4), 5–21.

Shank, J., & Govindrajan, V. (1992). Strategic cost management: The value chain perspective. *Journal of Cost Management*, 6(3), 179–197.

Sharrock, W., & Anderson, B. (1991). Epistemology: Professional skepticism. In G. Button (Ed.), *Ethnomethodology and the human sciences* (pp. 51–76). Cambridge: Cambridge University Press.

Sharrock, W., & Button, G. (1991). The social actor: Social action in real time. In G. Button (Ed.), *Ethnomethodology and the human sciences* (pp. 137–175). Cambridge: Cambridge University Press.

Shea, D. (2016). *Behavioral approaches for counsellors*. Thousand Oaks, CA: Sage.

Shell, G. R. (2006). *Bargaining for advantage: Negotiation strategies for reasonable people* (2nd ed.). New York: Penguin Books. (Originally published 2001).

Shiller, R. (2003). From efficient markets theory to behavioral finance. *Journal of Economic Perspectives*, 17(1), 83–104.

Shim, J. (2008). *Management accountant's standard desk reference* (Various Publishers). London: Global Professional Publishing.

Siguenza-Guzman, L., Van den Abbeele, A., Vandewalle, J., Verhaaren, H., & Cattrysse, D. (2013). Recent evolutions in costing systems: A literature review of time-driven activity-based costing. *Review of Business and Economic Literature*, 58(1), 34–65.

Simon, H. (2015). *Confessions of the pricing man: How price affects everything*. New York: Springer.

Simon, H. A. (1956). Rational choice and the structure of the environment. *Psychological Review*, 63(2), 129–138.

Simon, H. A. (1979). Rational decision making in business organizations. *American Economic Review*, 69(4), 493–513.

Simon, H. A., Dantzig, G. B., Hogarth, R., Piott, C. R., Raiffa, H., Schelling, T. C., Shepsle, K. A., Thaier, R., Tversky, A., & Winter, S. (1987). Decision making and problem solving. *Interfaces*, 17(5), 11–31.

Simon, H. A., Guetzkow, H., Kozmetsky, G., & Tyndall, G. (1954). *Centralization versus decentralization in organizations*. New York: Controllership Foundation.

Simons, R. (1994). *Levers of control: How managers use innovative control systems to drive strategic renewal*. Boston, MA: Harvard Business Review Press.

Skinner, D. J. (1994). Why firms voluntarily disclose bad news. *Journal of Accounting Research*, 32(1), 1, 38–60.

Smith, A. (1976). *An inquiry into the nature and causes of the wealth of nations* (Glasgow ed., 2 vols) (R. H. Campbell, & W. B. Todd, Eds.). Oxford: Oxford University Press. (Originally published 1776).

Soliman, M. T. (2008). The use of DuPont analyses by market participants. *The Accounting Review*, 83(3), 823–853.

Speckbacher, G. (2017). Creativity research in management accounting: A commentary. *Journal of Management Accounting Research*, 29(3), 49–54.

Spraakman, G. P. (1999). Management accounting at the historical Hudson's Bay Company: A comparison to 20th century practices. *Accounting Historians Journal*, 26(2), 35–63.

Stirling, W. (2003). *Satisficing games and decision making: With applications to engineering and computer science*. Cambridge: Cambridge University Press.

Stout, M. (2005). *The sociopath next door: The ruthless versus the rest of us*. New York: Broadway Books.

Strauss, H. J., & Zeigler, L. H. (1975). The Delphi technique and its uses in social science research. *Journal of Creative Behavior*, 9(4), 253–259.

Strong, D., Lee, Y., & Wang, R. (1997). Data quality in context. *Communications of the ACM*, 40(5), 103–110.

Subramaniam, C., & Watson, M. W. (2016). Additional evidence on the sticky behavior of costs. In M. J. Epstein & M. A. Malina. *Advances in Accounting*, 26, 275–305.

Suchman, L. A. (1987). *Plans and situated actions: The problem of human-machine communication* (Learning in Doing: Social, Cognitive and Computational Perspectives). Cambridge: Cambridge University Press.

Sultan, R. G. M. (1974). *Pricing in the electrical oligopoly: Vol. 1, Competition or collusion*. Cambridge: MA: Harvard University Press.

Susskind, R., & Susskind, D. (2015). *The future of the professions: How technology will transform the work of human experts*. New York: Oxford University Press.

Sweller, J., Ayres, P., & Kalyuga, S. (2011). *Cognitive load theory*. New York: Elsevier.

Takatera, S., & Sawabe, N. (2000). Time and space in income accounting. *Accounting, Organizations and Society*, 25(8), 787–798.

Taleb, N. N. (2010). *The black swan: The impact of the highly improbable* (2nd ed.). New York: Random House Business Books. (Originally published 2007).

Taylor, F. W. (1911). *The principles of scientific management*. New York: Harper Brothers.

Taylor, R. S. (1986). *Value-added processes in information systems*. Norwood, NJ: Ablex.

Teece, D. J. (1990). Contributions and impediments of economic analysis to the study of strategic management. In J. W. Frederickson (Ed.), *Perspectives on strategic management* (pp. 39–80). New York: Harper Business.

Teece, D. J., Pisano, G., & Shuen, A. (1997). Dynamic capabilities and strategic management. *Strategic Management Journal*, 18(7), 509–533.Thommes, M. C. (1992). *Proper spreadsheet design*. Boston, MA: Boyd & Fraser.

Thorndyke, E. L. (1920). A constant error in psychological ratings. *Journal of Applied Psychology*, 41(1), 25–29.

Tiessen, P., & Waterhouse, J. H. (1983). Towards a descriptive theory of management accounting. *Accounting, Organizations and Society*, 8(2–3), 251–267.

Tofler, A. (1965). The future as a way of life. *Horizon*, 7(3), 108–115.

Tsang, E. (1997). Organizational learning and the learning organization: A dichotomy between descriptive and prescriptive research. *Human Relations*, 50(1), 57–70.

Tufte, E. (2001). *The visual display of quantitative information* (2nd ed.). Cheshire, CT: Graphics Press. (Originally published 1992).

Tyson, T. N. (1992). The nature and environment of cost management among early 19th century U.S. textile manufacturers. *Accounting Historians Journal*, 19(1), 1–24.

Vaillant, G. (2003). *Aging well: Surprising guideposts to a happier life from the landmark Harvard study of adult development.* New York: Little Brown.

Vatter, W. J. (1950). *Managerial accounting* (Preliminary ed.). Englewood Cliffs, NJ: Prentice-Hall.

Veblen, T. (1978). *The theory of the business enterprise.* New York: Transaction Publishers. (Originally published 1904).

Verrecchia, R. E. (1983). Discretionary disclosure. *Journal of Accounting and Economics*, 5(1), 179–194.

Vroom, V. H., & Yetton, P. W. (1973). *Leadership and decision-making.* Pittsburgh, IL: University of Pittsburgh Press.

Wacht, R. F. (1984). A financial management theory of the nonprofit organization. *The Journal of Financial Research*, 7(1), 37–45.

Waldrop, M. (1992). *Complexity: The emerging science at the edge of order and chaos.* New York: Simon & Schuster.

Wang, R. Y., & Strong, D. M. (1996). Beyond accuracy: What data quality means to data consumers. *Journal of Management Information Systems*, 12(4), 5–33.

Weick, K. E. (1979). *The social psychology of organizing.* Reading, MA: Addison-Wesley Publishing Company.

Weick, K. E. (1995). *Sensemaking in organizations.* Thousand Oaks, CA: Sage.

Weil, R. L. (2005). Accounting magic. In R. L. Weil & M. W. Maher (Eds.), *Handbook of cost management* (2nd ed., pp. 187–196). New York: Wiley. (Originally published 1978).

Weiner, B. (1985). An attributional theory of achievement motivation and emotion. *Psychological Review*, 92(4), 548–573.

Wells, M. (2006). *Accounting for common costs.* Sydney, Australia: Darlington Press. (Originally published 1978).

Wernerfelt, B. (1984). The resource-based view of the firm. *Strategic Management Journal*, 5(2), 171–180.

Wieder, D. L. (1974). *Language and social reality: Telling the code of the street: An ethnomethodological ethnography.* The Hague: Mouton.

Williamson, O. E. (1975). *Markets and hierarchies: Analysis and antitrust implications: A study in the economics of internal organization.* New York: Free Press.

Williamson, O. E. (1981). The economics of organization: The transaction-cost approach. *American Journal of Sociology*, 87(3), 548–577.

Wilson, P. F., Dell, L. D., & Anderson, G. F. (1993). *Root cause analysis: A tool for total quality management.* Milwaukee, WI: ASQ Quality Press.

Winch, P. (1990). *The idea of a social science* (2nd ed.) London: Routledge. (Originally published 1958).

Windle, G. (2011). What is resilience? A review and concept analysis. *Reviews in Clinical Gerontology*, 21(2), 152–169.

Wittgenstein, L. (2009). *Philosophical investigations* (4th ed.) (P. M. S. Hacker, & J. Schulte, Trans.). Chichester, UK: Wiley-Blackwell. (Originally published 1953).

Wolfe, M. (1955). The concept of economic sectors. *The Quarterly Journal of Economics*, 69(3), 402–420.

Wood, E. (1962). *Yoga* (Rev. ed.). Harmondsworth, UK: Pelican. (Originally published 1959).

Zeff, S. A. (1978). The rise of 'economic consequences'. *Journal of Accountancy,* 146(6), 56–63.

Zins, C. (2007). Conceptual approaches for defining data, information, and knowledge. *Journal of the American Society for Information Science and Technology,* 58(4), 479–493.

Index of Industries, Organizations, and Products

Index of Topics

Note: Suffix *d* denotes definitions. Page numbers in bold indicate tables. Page numbers in italic indicate figures.